Jesus, the untold story

Gerjo van der Horst

Fiola Publishers
www.fiola.nl

© 2018 Fiola Publishers
Benedendijk 14a
8121 AD Olst, the Netherlands

www.fiola.nl

ISBN 978-90-819910-3-2

Original title:
Jezus, het onbekende verhaal,
2018 Uitgeverij Fiola, Olst - the Netherlands

Translated by Tessera Translations BV, the Netherlands,
www.tessera-trans.com

With very special thanks to Steve Balsamo.
Without his tremendous emotions while singing 'Gethsemane'
this book probably would never have been written.

Bethlehem

She was buried on a beautiful spring day. The sun's magic had covered the trees in blossom and birds were busy building nests. The burgeoning springtime contrasted starkly with Joseph's sorrow. The long nights that he had spent by her sickbed had taken their toll and pale he was standing by her grave. He had torn his clothing as a sign of mourning. He watched his fellow villagers carrying the coffin to the grave, listening as they recited the familiar psalms although he himself could scarcely utter a word. The emotions of the last few days had been suffocating. Missing her was an intolerable burden. He loved her so dearly - how could he carry on without her? The ritual of washing and then dressing her in a simple white funeral cloth had been too much for him. He had hardly been able to do anything - putting stockings on her lovely slender feet had been all he could do. And now she was lying there in that coffin and the very idea that he would shortly have to throw three shovelfuls of earth on it made a shiver of horror run down his spine.

The cortège had now reached the grave. Joseph watched them lowering the coffin respectfully into the Earth. Now he had to say Kaddish, the traditional prayer for the dead. But he was still not able to speak properly. Then someone put an arm around his shoulders. He looked up and saw the encouragement in his father's face and heard him say the first words:

"May His great Name be exalted and sanctified in the world that He created as He willed..."

His father gave an encouraging squeeze of his arm and Joseph's voice sounded husky as he took over: "...and may His reign last through your life and throughout the lives of all of the house of Israel, swiftly and soon. Now say Amen."

His fellow villagers answered with a respectful "Amen." With the help of his father, who stayed loyally at his side, Joseph continued the long prayer until it ended with them all saying "Amen". Joseph was relieved to put that part behind him. He picked up the shovel that was waiting for him by the grave. It had to be done, so best get it over with quickly. He shovelled three spadefuls of earth onto the coffin and then forced himself to watch as first his father and then his friends followed his example. The coffin disappeared slowly under the sand. Then the group left the cemetery. In the hall adjoining the synagogue, the villagers filed past to offer him their condolences. It was a long line: her cheerful nature had made her popular. Joseph had no idea how many hands he had shaken. When everyone had finally said farewell and he was alone again with his parents and Rabbi Barachi who had led the service, he sank down onto a chair, overcome by all the emotions. His mother came to sit next to him and caressed his hand.

"Are you sure you don't want us to come with you?" she asked sympathetically. "I think it would be better for you not to be alone right now. Or you could come with us - Nazareth isn't all that far."

But Joseph shook his head decisively.

"Being alone is just what I want," he said firmly. "All those people today! They all meant well, but right now I don't want to see anybody. Let me be - I'll be fine."

He held her hand for a moment, then thanked the rabbi and went home. And there in his own home, in the privacy of his own room, he let his tears flow, crying passionately until he had no more tears to give.

Joseph mourned for a week. Then he resumed his work as a carpenter. The physical exertion did him good and ensured that he could not wallow in his suffering for too long. His best friends Reuben and Gideon came by regularly to see how he was getting on. They often talked about religious matters and the state of their country. The Roman occupation was the main topic of conversation. The longer it lasted, the more they yearned to be able to live in peace again and work in accordance with God's will, as they had done in the time of the great King David. Their King Herod was not making things easier. He had been ruling with a tight rein for forty years and he did not hesitate to show his admiration for the Roman emperor

Augustus. He had ordered a palace to be built in Jerusalem that was every bit as splendid as Augustus' residence in Rome. He had not been able to achieve the same status as that great emperor, though, a fact that gnawed at him more and more, rankling increasingly the older he became. He did admittedly have a group of admirers, the Herodians, but most Jews only tolerated him because they were convinced that the Messiah, the true heir to the throne, would be born soon. Everything was going to change when this descendant of David would make his appearance. The Roman occupation would come to an end and Herod would have to renounce his throne. That idea was making the ruler paranoid: he suspected everyone of being an enemy and even his own family were scared of him.

"Have you heard about Herod's wife?" asked Reuben when they were together one evening. "They say she's fled to her homeland and taken her sons with her. Herod must've been livid when he found out!"

"Why'd she do that?" said Joseph in surprise. "I thought Herod was supposed to be a good match for her."

"He is," nodded Reuben, "but she didn't feel safe anymore. There are rumours that their oldest son Archelaus wanted to murder his father and take the throne for himself. Herod probably reckoned she knew about the plot and was supporting her son."

"Well, I'd say that's just what she should have done," spoke Gideon sharply. "I'd be happy to see the back of Herod!"

"As if we'd be any better off with Archelaus," remarked Joseph. "I wouldn't say that someone who's killed their own father is going to make a good king!"

"True enough," agreed Reuben. "But the way I heard it, Archelaus was only making his move before his father did. It seems as if Herod himself had plans to kill not only Archelaus but also his other son, the younger Herod!"

"Why would a father do that?" was Joseph's shocked response. "Isn't having children the most wonderful thing that can happen to anyone? Murdering your own children is just mocking God's plan!"

"It shows you what a sick mind he's got," said Gideon, worried. "He simply won't tolerate any threats to his power, even if they come from his own son, who would be entitled to the throne in the end anyway."

Joseph shook his head.

"I wonder if things will ever be right again in our country," he sighed. "God certainly is testing us. We've been waiting for so long now that I sometimes lose faith that our heir to the throne will ever come, even though I'm from the house of David."

Reuben and Gideon too felt that they were living in dark and unpromising times and for a moment they were all quiet. Then Reuben burst out,

"But I still don't intend to lose heart. Hasn't God always reached out a helping hand to us in the past? And didn't He always do that in our darkest moments? Maybe these are exactly the times that we can expect something!"

Joseph and Gideon nodded. Reuben was right: they should keep hoping, otherwise all was lost. When they said their farewells at the end of the evening, they embraced each other heartily, grateful that their friendship at least was still strong.

One day, after Joseph had been to the service at the synagogue, Rabbi Barachi came to him.

"Would you stay a moment, Joseph?" he said in a friendly tone. "I haven't talked with you for quite a while and I'm interested in how you're coping."

Joseph nodded in agreement. At Barachi's house, the rabbi poured them both something to drink. But the conversation remained stilted. Joseph was not really in the mood for superficial pleasantries. Barachi thought he looked dejected. It was no fun being a widower at thirty-two, with no wife or children. He genuinely felt for the other man and asked in concern,

"And so Joseph, are you able to manage on your own like that?"

Joseph shrugged.

"I don't reckon I've got much choice," was his cynical response. "After all, I've got to get on with my life."

"You shouldn't really stay alone," said Barachi sympathetically. "Why don't you marry again? The mourning period is over now and you're perfectly allowed to look for another wife."

Joseph turned his head away because he did not want Barachi to notice his grief. But the rabbi had seen it nonetheless and he put a hand on Joseph's shoulder.

"Don't get me wrong," he said gently. "I'm not saying that someone else can replace her. But seeing you so lonely makes me unhappy. And on top of that, it would be good if you became a father. After all, you belong to the house of David and that line mustn't die out!"

Joseph laughed mockingly.

"What woman would want an old widower like me?" he asked bitterly. "What's more, I haven't had any children yet, so whether I'll ever be a father is very much open to question."

"I can imagine that's the way you think about it," nodded Barachi. "But maybe we should give Fate a helping hand. Here, read this. It's a message that a courier brought me this morning. I don't think it's mere coincidence."

He handed him a sheet of parchment. Joseph saw that it came from the Saducees, the priestly order of the temple in Jerusalem. He started reading and soon realised why Barachi wanted to show it to him. The priests mentioned a girl, Mary, whom they had brought up lovingly for many years after her own parents had died. She had received the best possible education in the temple. She was beautiful, they said, but the most unusual thing about her was that she was wise beyond her years, more so than anyone of that age that they had ever seen before. They were so surprised at this that they had become convinced that she was predestined to continue the family tree of King David. That was why they were looking for descendants in that line, to create the ideal circumstances for the birth of the Messiah, the one true king of Israel.

Joseph became increasingly irritated as he read the words. Why was Barachi meddling in his business? He was perfectly capable of deciding for himself whether he wanted to remarry and with whom. Annoyed, he threw the letter aside.

"I'm sure you mean it well," he spoke sullenly, "but what's a girl like that going to want from an old carpenter like me?"

Barachi picked up the paper.

"You shouldn't do yourself down like that!" he answered sharply. "Being a carpenter is an excellent trade. And you've had a proper apprenticeship too. We Essenes are known for that, aren't we?"

Joseph stood up. His whole being was rebelling against this impertinent interference in his personal life.

"That may well be so," he said testily, "but I'm perfectly happy being alone. I've already got used to it."

"Sure, sure!" Barachi saw straight through him, though. "And I suppose you want to deny you're from the house of David too! For that reason alone, you ought to respond to the priests' invitation!"

But Joseph had no intention of letting anyone lay down the law to him. He picked up his coat and said bluntly,

"I'm very sorry, but the priests will have to look for someone else. I don't like the idea at all. And it would be better if you didn't meddle with my life so much!"

He left the astonished Barachi standing there and went home. When he got there, he was still angry. He went straight to his workshop and threw his coat aside. He grabbed some tools and was about to start work when he suddenly saw the small figurine that he had made some time earlier. It was only little, but he had put a lot of time and care into making it. It was of a pregnant woman, and the rounded shapes were just right. He picked it up and thought about his conversation with Reuben and Gideon a while earlier, and the priests' anticipation that he might possibly be able to play a part in the arrival of the Messiah. The pain of his involuntary childlessness suddenly pierced deep into his heart. How would he ever be able to tell anyone just how much this pained him and that he would far rather avoid any new disappointments. An intense feeling of powerlessness came over him and he threw the figurine away wildly in a fit of pique. It came down hard on the floor, rolled underneath his workbench and lay there, lost.

A couple of weeks later, Joseph was outside sanding down a table, he saw a rider in the distance coming towards him. The man rode up to his holding and dismounted in front of the house. Joseph could tell from his clothing that he was one of the Saducees, the priests of the temple in Jerusalem. The priest turned to him and said politely,

"Shalom, my good man. You're Joseph the carpenter, aren't you? Son of Jacob, born of the house of David?"

"Yes, that's me," nodded Joseph. "But what brings you here? We don't often have the honour of receiving such exalted guests here."

His words were friendly enough, but tinged with an edge of mistrust nevertheless.

"I was wondering how you are doing," answered the man with a concerned expression. "We heard that your wife passed away some time ago and that you've been alone since then. We hope that you have been able to come to terms with your loss."

Joseph said nothing for a moment, but recovered quickly and replied,

"I'm fine, thank you. My parents are still alive, thankfully, and they come and visit me regularly. And I've got plenty of friends who keep an eye on me, so I mustn't complain. But, to be honest, I can't imagine that you came here just to find out how I'm coping."

He looked suspiciously at the man, who was taken aback by the direct remark and his eyes avoided Joseph's questioning stare.

"You're right," he admitted reluctantly. "I'd like to talk to you, if I may. Now, if that's convenient?"

Joseph looked at the table he was making, but decided that the job could well be finished later.

"Yes, that's fine," he nodded.

He picked up a rag and wiped the sand off his hands.

"You can put your horse in the stable, just round the corner there. Meanwhile I'll get something to eat."

The priest thanked him. While he was sorting out his horse, Joseph fetched a pitcher of cool water and some bread. When they had sat down a little later to eat, the priest asked,

"I came past the South Mountain on my way here. What's being built on top of the hill? And why is so much water being taken up there?"

Joseph burst into a laugh. With a touch of sarcasm in his voice, he replied,

"Oh, so you've seen that monstrosity, have you? Another of Herod's mad schemes. The water is for a so-called paradise garden that he's had built on the top of the hill. His cronies are already calling it the Paradise Mountain. And we have to keep going back and forth to the well to get our water! And those towers - they're the corners of the palace that is going to be built. I suppose he reckons that people will finally accept him as the Messiah if he comes to live in Bethlehem. As if the Messiah would come as an old and bitter man who has nothing better to do than chase after an impossible dream!"

"The Herodians do think he's the Messiah, though," said the

priest, contradicting him. "But I agree with you. Our order believes that the Messiah will be born from the line of David, and in the town of Bethlehem. That's why we sent a letter to your rabbi a little while ago. Didn't he give it to you? I'm only asking, because we haven't received an answer yet."

Annoyed, Joseph looked up. His intuition had been correct: this visit was not nearly so innocent as the man had wanted it to look. He answered gruffly,

"Yes, I did read that letter, but I didn't feel like answering it."

He hesitated for a moment and then continued,

"I was married for fourteen years, but my wife and I never had any children. So why should I have written back? I'm afraid I'm not the one you should be speaking to."

But the priest was not going to give up so easily.

"Maybe you're mistaken," was his friendly rejoinder. "After all, didn't Abraham and Sarah have their first child when they were much older? And surely a good Essene like yourself must be eager to see the coming of the Messiah? Or would you rather accept yet more of Herod's idiocies?"

Joseph hesitated again. He had actually been thinking about the matter quite a bit lately. Was it fair to let his own uncertainties outweigh the much greater interests that might be involved? The priest continued,

"We've already visited a number of men from the house of David, but none of them were nearly as suitable a husband for Mary as you are. The portents really do point towards you. Would you perhaps consider travelling to Jerusalem with me and at least making Mary's acquaintance?"

Joseph did not know how to respond. Life as a widower certainly was a lonely existence, but equally he was not really ready for another wife. And this Mary was still young, more a girl rather than a partner who was his equal, which was what he was used to. He shrugged and sighed,

"I don't know. Is this really God's will? I mean, I'm not a good match for a youngster like her. She would be better off with someone of her own age."

"Easy to say that before you've even met her!" said the priest with a smile, and with conviction he added, "I've never seen anyone before of her age who is so mature. You won't believe it! Anyway - you'll only be able to decide for yourself if you come with me, of course."

He had put Joseph neatly back on the spot, and made him hesitate once again. He looked away, with Herod's huge hilltop home on the South Mountain in his mind's eye, another folly spawned by the king giving free rein to his megalomania. He pictured how Herod might be standing there, gazing out over the land below. And how that unloving, power-hungry gaze could taint Joseph's beloved Bethlehem. He stood up and paced back and forth, lost in his thoughts. When Barachi had given him the letter to read, he had been as stubborn as a mule: he was not going to let others dictate his life. But the priest had made the effort to come all the way from Jerusalem to see him, and that put things in a different perspective. And suddenly he knew what he had to do. He turned to the man and said,

"I shall come with you. I don't know whether it's the right thing to do and I've no idea at all what will come of it, but I do trust in the fact that God sent you here."

The priest breathed a sigh of relief. He had not really expected any more that Joseph would agree to accompany him.

"Then I suggest I should come and pick you up tomorrow," he said with a smile.

Jerusalem was only a couple of hours' journey from Bethlehem. Joseph had harnessed his donkey to pull the cart and the priest was on horseback next to him. It was still morning when they reached the city. As always, it was bustling with activity. The temple drew people from all over the Jewish provinces, as well as many people from other countries who came to see the city. Herod's colossal palace, built up against the city wall was a sight worth seeing. And you could buy just about anything you could imagine at the exotic stalls and shops in the narrow alleyways of the Lower Town. The priest led Joseph through the maze of streets to the temple. The outer courtyard was seething with people. Sacrificial animals could be bought, the temple tax could be paid and money could be exchanged for the special temple coins. Although Joseph had been there often enough in the past, he always found it a wonderful sight. For a moment he wondered whether King Solomon had envisaged all this when he built this splendid temple in God's honour. The colonnade with its tall, slender pillars had become the place where the sick and beggars gathered, hoping to scrape a few coins together. It had once been a calm and restful spot, but the quiet was now broken by bleating sheep, cooing doves and the strident voices of merchants, haggling vehemently as they tried to get the best possible price for their goods. Joseph was amazed to see that the priest clearly thought this was all perfectly normal, given that he paid it no attention as he led Joseph to an annexe where the seventy strong High Council had his seat.

The most important grouping in the High Council were the Saducees, who took care of the services in the temple and made sure that all the religious rules were strictly observed. The Pharisees were well represented too, though. The two leading figures in the Council's activities were undoubtedly Hillel and Shammai. These two priests were each other's opposites in many ways. Shammai had a heavy-handed approach, insisting that the rules of the Torah should be respected, and people often asked him for advice about the instructions given in those holy writings. Hillel, on the other hand, felt that these rules were often too restrictive and he attempted to update them to fit the times they were living in and give people a little more scope. This often annoyed Shammai, who would have preferred his colleague to toe the line more strictly. All in all, they complemented each other well and the Council functioned as well as could be expected under the Roman occupation. In particular, the Council was united by the common desire to see the arrival of the Messiah. Joseph knew the leading members.

"Who do you think will speak to us?" he asked.

"Our appointment is with Hillel," answered his companion. "He has spoken to Mary. She knows that I went to Bethlehem to talk to you, so she won't be surprised to hear that you have arrived."

He opened the annexe door and led the way to Hillel's chamber. Joseph had to admit that he was feeling somewhat tense. But Hillel greeted him amicably and offered him a seat. When Joseph had sat down, the priest asked him interested,

"How are you coping, Joseph? Are you managing to earn a living, as a carpenter?"

Joseph nodded in relief, because this question was easy to

answer. Proudly, he answered,

"Certainly! I'm nowhere near able to take on all the jobs that people are offering me, and everyone is always happy with my work."

"That's good to hear," said Hillel with a smile. "And how is the Essene community in Bethlehem getting on? I understand you're in the minority there. Are you managing to stick to your own customs and traditions?"

Joseph nodded again.

"We're a minority, that's true enough, but that actually brings our community together, as I discovered after my wife died. I've had so much help from my friends then! What bothers us most at the moment, though, is that Herod is throwing his weight around more and more in Bethlehem. His plans for the South Mountain are a real pain in the neck. On top of that, there are some persistent rumours flying around about occult rituals that he is involved with in the caves around Bethlehem."

Hillel shook his head.

"Those have reached us as well," he spoke worriedly. "Apparently he worships Adonis there. That's why we make such efforts to keep our religion pure, and we do everything we can for the promised Messiah. That's also why you're here now, of course. I understand you've agreed to meet Mary."

Joseph laughed uncertainly and fiddled with his coat.

"I can't say I'm terribly enthusiastic about the whole idea," he said honestly, "but meeting her seemed like the least I could do."

Hillel gave him an encouraging nod.

"Which we do appreciate a lot," was his friendly reply. "I agreed with Mary that I'd fetch her once you had arrived. So I'll go and get her now, if that's all right with you."

"Yes, that's fine," nodded Joseph with a brief sigh, because he realised that there was no way back any longer.

Hillel had to smile at this shyness, which did not really suit someone of that age. He stood up and left the room. Joseph was glad of a moment to pull himself together. He paced around a little, nervously, wondering what on earth he ought to say to the girl when she appeared. Might he not simply seem terribly old and insignificant in her eyes? He sat down again and checked his clothing. Maybe he would have been better off wearing something else. But it was too late for that now. He heard footsteps in the corridor and the door opened. He looked up and saw Hillel walking in with the prettiest girl he had ever seen.

She was still young, no more than fourteen perhaps, and she had wonderful black hair that she had plaited and pinned up around her head. She was wearing simple clothing, which if anything accentuated her slender figure. She looked at him frankly. Joseph was immediately enchanted by her and his nervousness melted away, although it was difficult not to be aware of the feeling that he could have been her father. Hillel gave them an encouraging nod and then discreetly left the room. Mary knelt down and stayed there with her head bowed, waiting politely until he spoke to her. Her subservience embarrassed him. He reached out a friendly hand towards her and said,

"Do please stand up. Treating women as inferior isn't a habit of mine - as I see it, God created men and women equal."

Mary looked up in surprise, with a grateful smile that warmed his heart.

"Thank you for your kind words, sir," she said.

Her voice was clear and pleasant.

"I ought to tell you that I have so far mostly lived in the women's house and I haven't been in the company of men very often. Perhaps that's why I don't know the best way to behave."

She stood up and sat down next to him. Once again, she waited until Joseph took the lead and spoke to her first.

"Do you like living here, Mary?" he asked. "Do the priests look after you well?"

"Oh yes, of course," she replied, "although it wasn't easy for me at first because I missed my parents so much. I was only eight when they died and I was terribly sad."

"Yes, that must have been a difficult time for you," nodded Joseph understandingly. "I know all too well what it's like when God suddenly takes away someone you love so dearly."

Mary looked at him sympathetically and said softly,

"I've been told that your wife passed away recently and that the mourning period is only just over. I'm very sorry for your loss. But I'm sad to hear that you blame God for her death - as if He would take pleasure in making you feel lonely. I'd rather see it as the soul being accepted lovingly by Him into His kingdom, after the body has done its duty here. So I'm certain your wife is in good hands."

Joseph felt a lump in his throat at her touching words and the kindly way in which she had reprimanded him made him ashamed of his unthinking remark.

"You're right, of course," he apologised, "but it really is difficult for me to see it that way sometimes. Some days are better than others, but there are times when I'm still rather gloomy and I find it difficult to find my way. I hope you won't mind."

Mary gave him an encouraging nod.

"Of course not, sir," she said gently. "I think I'd find it harder to understand if you didn't show any grief. At any rate, now I know that you aren't afraid to show your feelings. And who knows - maybe I can bring a little light into your life again."

Her smile touched his heart once again. Joseph smiled back at her cautiously and asked,

"So they've told you what the plan is? That you will be leaving with me and coming to live with me?"

"Yes, they've told me," she replied honestly. "And it would seem that they've made a good choice for me. You seem very friendly and I will be happy to look after you, sir, if you will let me."

Her open face, her honesty and her friendly voice soothed Joseph's wounded heart and the one thing he had never expected happened after all: he decided to agree to the priests' proposal.

"Then I'd be more than pleased to welcome you into my life, Mary," he said with relief. "I hope you will like living in Bethlehem - I'm very fond of the place. And could you just call me Joseph and forget all the 'sir', please? It makes me feel so old!"

Mary burst into a laugh.

"You aren't that old, sir... er... Joseph," she said teasingly. "Compared to those old-timers Hillel and Shammai, you're certainly a big step in the right direction!"

Her cheerfulness was infectious and Joseph was laughing out loud too now. There was a lightness in his heart again when he got up from the bench and held out his hand to her.

"Shall I lead the way, madam?" he said overly politely, with a small bow.

"Thank you so much, my good sir," she replied in kind with a small curtsey, going along with the game and putting her hand in his.

Their eyes met and both felt that they had made the correct decision. Hillel was delighted when he saw the two of them coming along the corridor. They signed the ketubah, the marriage contract, in the presence of the priest. That same afternoon, they went back to Bethlehem together, taking Mary's meagre possessions with them in Joseph's cart. The short journey passed even more quickly as they chatted about all kinds of things. When they reached his street, Joseph pointed his home out.

"Look, Mary, there's my house. I built most of it myself."

To her surprise, Mary saw that it was neat and well looked after. Joseph had made windows that could be closed with shutters. His workshop was next to the house, with a large veranda that gave him a shaded place to work outside as well. When they turned the corner, she saw a small stable with enough room for the donkey and for any visitors' animals. She was pleased that everything was so well cared for and realised with happy relief that she would probably be perfectly able to get used to living here. She smiled and said in admiration,

"It's amazing to think that you built all this yourself. Do you know what? I think I'm going to be happy here."

Her words touched him and he caressed her hand for a moment.

"You can be sure I'll do what I can to make sure you are happy," he promised.

He brought the cart to a halt, hitched the donkey to the fence and lifted her carefully down from the seat. Then he led her into the house. He showed her round the ground floor first: the living room, the kitchen with two separate ranges and a handy stand for all the jugs, and the internal door that led to his.

"This is my room," he said, opening the door for a moment so that she could look round. "And this one will be yours. I thought it might be difficult for you to get used to things at first, so maybe you'd be more comfortable with a room of your own."

He opened the door to her room and she saw a simple bed, a small table with a water jug and an attractively designed cupboard.

"I made that furniture myself too," Joseph told her some-what shyly. "I hope you like it."

Mary turned to him.

"It all looks wonderful," she said, touched. "It's very thoughtful of you to give me a space of my own. Thank you - I'm very happy with it."

She stood on her toes and kissed him on the cheek to thank him. Joseph did not know how to handle that.

"I'll go and fetch your things," he said tersely and went off.

Mary giggled at his shyness. Her cheerful laughter resounded through the whole house, driving away the sorrow that had held sway there for the past year. Her presence continued to bring cheer to Joseph's life up during the days and weeks that followed. They were soon getting on very well together and the days passed happily and harmoniously. Her cooking skills surprised him. She conjured up some delicious meals that he ate with relish. He also noticed all the other small things she did - a basket of fruit on the table, a coat she had made herself - and he was happier than he had been for a long time. And she felt comfortable with him. The age difference was un-important. His loving attention to her and the way he treated her as an equal so that they could talk easily together soon led to her developing a warm affection for him.

One day when Joseph was busy in his workshop, Mary came in with a cup of tea and went to sit on a stool in the corner. She often did that because she enjoyed watching him at work. He handled the wood like a real artist. His hands could make anything his eye could see and he produced some splendid pieces. She was watching him make a small chest of drawers. Using a small chisel, he decorated the fronts of the drawers until it became a thing of real beauty. She drank her tea and let her gaze roam around the workshop, feeling just how familiar it had already become. The rack where his tools hung, the workbench where he could finish off the smaller tasks.

Then, suddenly, something caught her eye, something lying on the ground under the workbench. She bent down and picked it up. It was a figurine of a pregnant woman. Although Joseph had only shaped the piece roughly, it was perfectly clear what it represented. Lots of patient sanding had made the rounded shapes beautifully smooth and he had oiled it so that the wood gleamed softly. Mary let it run through her fingers and felt just how smooth it was. She pressed it lovingly against her cheek. Joseph looked up and saw that she had discovered his small artwork. He was shocked for a moment, but recovered quickly.

"Do you like it?" he asked gently.

"It's wonderful!" sighed Mary. "When did you make it?"

"I think about one and a half years ago," he replied.

He wiped his hands clean and took the statuette from her. His hands caressed the rounded shapes and a shadow of sadness slid over his face.

"I made it for her because she was pregnant. But then, sadly, she had a miscarriage and got sick."

He stopped speaking for a moment and swallowed before continuing in a choked voice,

"We'd so been looking forward to having that baby. A child on the way at last, after all those years of marriage... But instead of that, she died and I was left alone."

Mary saw his sorrow and she put her hand on his shoulder.

"That must have been a very difficult time for you," she said sympathetically. "I can see that you loved her very much."

Joseph nodded. He stroked the figurine again, wrestling with his emotions. But then he put it firmly to one side and managed to conjure up a hesitant smile. He looked at her affectionately and said tenderly,

"But I love you every bit as much!"

His loving words touched Mary deeply. What a wonderful man she had found! He was so good to her. He gave her plenty of scope to arrange her life as she wanted so that she would be happy, never imposing things on her. She did not quite know how to cope with her feelings and stammered,

"I think... I've left something on the fire in the kitchen."

She fled, and this time he was the one laughing at her confusion. He noticed that she had managed once again to make him forget his grief quickly. Whistling cheerfully, he went back to work.

Lying in bed that evening, he thanked God for the happiness that had come his way in the shape of that sweet young woman. Contentedly, he rolled onto his side to go to sleep. But then he heard his bedroom door creak open. He turned and saw Mary enter. He sat up in surprise and said,

"Mary...?"

She did not answer. Silently, she stood next to his bed. Her slender shape could be seen clearly in the soft moonlight that came into the room. Then he watched as she slowly but deliberately undid the ribbon of her nightgown. The garment slid down her body to the floor and she stood naked before him. Her youthful body was breathtakingly beautiful and Joseph could not take his eyes off her. He was overcome by emotion. And Mary whispered,

"Can you make room for me? For I do love you and I don't want to sleep alone anymore."

He immediately parted the sheets and moved aside to make room for her. She curled up close to him, feeling the warmth from his powerfully muscled body. She had never felt so safe before. She turned towards him, found his mouth and cautiously pressed a kiss on his lips. Joseph looked at her young face and the earnestness etched upon it. He hesitated for a moment but then responded to her kiss, feeling just how right it seemed. He took her tenderly in his arms and they embraced one another. And finally, after all those weeks of patient waiting in which he had given her time and space to grow towards this moment, she really became his wife. Their bodies found each other in a shared desire and their lovemaking was both sincere and passionate. And love therefore was the basis of a great and elusive mystery, the continuation of the house of David that would receive God's greatest blessing.

It soon became clear that Mary was pregnant. Unfortunately, though, they were not able to enjoy their happiness for long because Joseph's mother's health was deteriorating fast and his father was no longer able to look after her alone. With pain in his heart, Joseph therefore decided that they would have to move to Nazareth. Building up a new clientele in this new town was hard work, but he still gave Mary every possible care and attention. His concern touched her, particularly because she understood the root cause so well - she knew how often he must be thinking of his first wife's pregnancy and its fatal outcome. She therefore tried to reassure him as much as possible, which was easy enough because she felt so healthy.

As the months progressed it became easier to see that she was expecting a baby. Her breasts became fuller and her belly was more rounded. Joseph's father brightened up now that his son was living so close by. He helped Joseph with jobs around the house and tried to find new customers for him. Mary helped in turn with looking after her mother-in-law, who also perked up a bit thanks to all the loving care. And so the weeks passed.

One day, Mary was resting on her bed. The end of her pregnancy was not that far off and she sometimes needed to lie down for a bit. Today she had even fallen asleep. Her breathing was deep and regular. And she dreamed. She saw herself back in her small room at the temple, with sunlight streaming in through the window. She squeezed her eyes shut because the sun was so bright and when she opened them again, she suddenly saw a figure standing there. Her mouth dropped open in astonishment, because the figure was breathtakingly beautiful and not merely surrounded by light but also radiating light itself. He bowed courteously to her and when he spoke to her, his voice rang pure and true.

"Fear not, Mary, for God is with you and sends His greetings."

His wonderful voice moved Mary deeply. She realised that this must be an angel, a messenger of God. The angel smiled and his wondrously pure voice resounded again.

"Listen carefully, Mary, for I am bringing you tidings of great joy. The Lord will take great care of the son you are carrying. He will be just and wise and the people shall call him Emmanuel, which means 'God be with us'. But you shall call him Jesus. The Lord shall give him the throne of his forefather David and he shall reign for ever and liberate his people from fear and oppression. And God's Holy Spirit shall join with him and help him spread the message of love from God's kingdom."

His words astounded Mary. In confusion, she shook her head.

"How... why... our son..." she asked hesitantly. "Will he really do... all this? Why has God chosen us to... bring up such a special child?"

The angel answered,

"Your husband Joseph comes from the noble house of David. He is a good man and he truly deserves this. And you, with all your wisdom, will be able to support your son in every way."

At which he said farewell and disappeared as suddenly as he had come. Mary woke with a start. For a moment she was unsure whether she had dreamed or whether the angel really had spoken to her. Feeling uneasy, she got up and could hardly wait for Joseph to get back from his work. When she finally heard his familiar footsteps, she rushed outside and threw herself into his arms. She told him everything and they held each other close, realising that all the efforts that the priests had made to bring the two of them together had not been in vain and that their faith would be rewarded. They looked at each other, full of emotion, and thanked God for all the good and wonderful things that were happening to them.

They had been living in Nazareth for a good six months now and would have liked to be able to prepare calmly for the birth of their son. However, the great Emperor Augustus himself spoiled those plans. A decree was issued stating that everyone in the empire had to be registered in the place where they were born. Although Joseph did not particularly want to comply with the emperor's orders - which boiled down to nothing more than a crude tax register - he nevertheless set out for Bethlehem with Mary.

As they travelled they were amazed by the number of people on the road. The entire population of the country seemed to be on the move. They kept meeting people who were on their way to register, just like they were. It did not make the journey any quicker. The roads were busy and, although their donkey kept plodding along, progress remained slow. Fortunately they did get pretty close to Bethlehem after a couple of days and they were expecting to get to the village that evening. Mary was rather quiet. The journey had really been too long for her and bumping along on the back of the donkey was far from comfortable now that she was so heavy. Joseph noticed her fatigue.

"Shall we take a break here, Mary?" he asked. "Or can you still manage?"

Mary smiled, grateful for his concern. Somehow he always seemed to know exactly how she was feeling.

"I'm all right," she replied thankfully. "My back is hurting a bit, but that's all. Let's keep going: the sooner we get there, the better."

Joseph gave her an encouraging nod and added jokingly,

"Let's see if I can't persuade this lazy donkey of ours to walk a little faster."

He prodded the donkey, but it paid little attention to his encouragements. Mary was not only aware of the pain in her back gradually becoming more severe, but also that her belly was regularly feeling uncomfortably hard and tight. It worried her a bit when she realised that these were contractions. Hesitantly, she said,

"Joseph..."

The tone of her voice made him turn his full attention to her at once.

"Joseph, I'm sorry but... I think I'm going into labour."

Joseph was shocked. They were not all that far from Bethlehem now, but there was still no sign of any houses.

"Hold on, darling!" he said lovingly doing his best to hide his concern. "It doesn't usually happen very quickly with the first one, or so I've been told. Are you still all right there on the donkey?"

Mary nodded bravely but the contractions soon became stronger. Joseph tried once again to urge the donkey along, and it did indeed seem to be going a little faster now. Luckily they could now see the first houses of Bethlehem in the distance. Joseph was pleased that he knew his way around the village so well. Despite the deepening twilight, he had no difficulty finding the nearest inn. When they reached it, he helped Mary down from the donkey and, with one arm firmly around her, knocked on the door.

"Yes, yes, just a moment," came a rather grumpy voice.

Someone on the other side of the door slid the bolts back and opened it a crack.

"Good evening, good man," said Joseph in a friendly tone to the innkeeper. "We know it's late, but do you have anywhere we could sleep?"

The door opened a little further and the man looked them up and down, his eyes resting obviously on Mary's belly. He then said brusquely,

"I'm sorry, but we're full. You'll have to try somewhere else."

Joseph felt how heavily Mary was leaning on him.

"Please sir, you can see that my wife can't go any further," he said, urgency in his voice. "Please, I'm sure you can find a spot for us."

The man stuck to his ground.

"I'm sorry, but all that fuss about registering has made it awfully busy in the village. Everywhere is full. I know that's awkward for you, but there's nothing that can be done about it."

He was about to close the door again when he noticed that the young woman was already having contractions. He sighed and scratched thoughtfully behind his ear.

"Very well, why not?" he said, clearly not happy. "There's a small stable in the courtyard. You can stay there tonight, but you'll have to look for something else as soon as you can."

"We certainly will, sir," promised Joseph, relieved that the man was being cooperative after all.

He nodded encouragingly to Mary and whispered to her,

"Just a tiny bit longer, darling. You'll be able to lie down in a moment."

The innkeeper fetched a lantern and led them down a narrow alleyway. A small door took them into the courtyard. What the man had called a stable turned out to be little more than a ramshackle lean-to sheltering an ox. But it offered protection against the wind, and the straw was fresh.

"You'll manage all right here, won't you?" growled the innkeeper as he hung the lantern on a nail. "I need to get back to my other guests now. Good luck!"

Joseph thanked the man and made a quick assessment of the situation. Mary really could not manage any longer and he took their luggage off the donkey as quickly as he could. He improvised a bed from the blankets that they had brought with them, using the straw that was lying in the stable as a mattress. Grateful Mary lay down and was once again completely overwhelmed by the contractions, which were getting more and more intense. Joseph stayed loyally by her side. He watched as she fought bravely through the pain, somehow able to draw on an almost unimaginable primitive strength as she brought their son into the world. The tears ran down their cheeks when they heard him start crying for the first time. They were hugely relieved that everything had gone well. By the light of the lantern they looked at their son. He was absolutely perfect and Mary was radiant. She wrapped the baby in a couple of cloths and held him close to her. Joseph embraced her and wiped the perspiration from her forehead.

"So there he is," he whispered, overwhelmed. "Our little Jesus."

Mary nodded quietly and added softly,

"Our boy king."

Joseph took her hand and kissed it. Then he took both her hands in his own and prayed to God, thanking Him for this beautiful child that had now been entrusted into their care. He also asked Him to give them the wisdom to know what they should do and to take the right decisions for him. Then he lay down next to Mary and, with Jesus safe between them, they soon fell asleep.

They were woken up early the next morning by the baby crying. Mary had all the natural instincts of a mother. She rocked him in her arms and held him to her breast so that he could drink. Joseph tried to make their shelter a little more comfortable. He covered one of the mangers with a blanket so that they could use it as a crib. And after he had washed Mary and given her something to eat, he went off to sort out the tax registration. But to his surprise, the narrow back alley by the inn was blocked by a flock of sheep. A small group of shepherds shuffled hesitantly towards him.

"Excuse me, sir," said one of them, "we're looking for the boy king. Do you maybe know where we could find him?"

Joseph stared at him in amazement.

"How do you know that a child was born here?" he asked suspiciously.

"An angel came and told us while we were out and about watching our flocks last night," replied the shepherds. "And that star showed us the way too."

They looked up. Joseph followed their gaze and to his astonishment saw a star in the sky, so brilliant that it must have been visible from far away. Overwhelmed, he led the men to Mary and their baby, who was fast asleep in the improvised bed. The shepherds fell to their knees, overcome by their emotions, clasping their hands together and thanking God for bringing them the long-awaited king. Only now did it really start to sink in for Joseph: they had been blessed with a very special child and Herod and the Romans would probably be much less delighted with the arrival of a new king than these good folk were.

After the shepherds had taken their leave, he had a serious talk with Mary. They quickly agreed that it was better not to say anything about Jesus' future destiny, certainly as long he was still a child.

At that same time, there was a colourful group of strangers in the streets of Jerusalem, three richly-dressed foreigners who had come on camels to visit the city After seeing the temple and the other sights, they rode to Herod's palace and talked to one of the guards there.

"Good morning, my good man. We've come all the way from Persia to visit your king. Do you think he might receive us? We would like to congratulate him and offer him our gifts."

"I'll see what I can do for you," said the guard and he went inside the palace.

He returned after a short while and bowed to them courteously.

"The king will be happy to receive you, sirs," he spoke politely. "Please follow me. Our stable-boys will look after your animals."

He led them into the palace through a long corridor with splendid columns on both sides. It led to a garden courtyard where burbling fountains and marble statues ornamented the flowerbeds. The whole ensemble was clearly designed in imitation of a Roman model. After they had crossed the garden, there was another long hallway, this time with superb frescoes on the walls. When they got to the far end, the guard opened a huge door and drew a heavy damask curtain aside.

"Your Highness! Your visitors from Persia."

The three foreigners entered the room where the great King Herod was waiting for them. He was actually quite a small man, and clearly overweight from way too many banquets. But he cut an impressive figure nevertheless, with his crown and cloak and his greeting was very friendly.

"Good people, I bid you welcome to my modest home. Come further, please! And tell me: what brings you here?"

The visitors bowed politely and one of them spoke up.

"Thank you very much for receiving us, Your Highness. I am Caspar, priest from the temple at Persepolis and leader of the largest religious community in our country. This is our most renowned scientist, Balthazar. He knows a great deal about astronomy and he was the first to discover the new star in the heavens. And this is our famous philosopher Melchior, an expert in deciphering old writings. He discovered a text by our great spiritual leader Zarathustra stating that the birth of the new king would be announced by a new star in the sky. That is why we have come here, to offer this king our gifts and our homage. But first of all, we would of course like to offer you our sincerest congratulations on the birth of this heir to the throne!"

He held out his hand, but Herod looked at him strangely.

"My dear fellow, er... Caspar, you said? I'm afraid I'm going to have to disappoint you. No heir to the throne has been born in my palace. I think that your philosopher and astronomer have given you some rather dubious information."

Caspar listened to the king's words in astonishment. Then he laughed out loud.

"Surely you are joking, sir? Our culture is centuries old and everyone knows just how advanced our sciences are. You surely do not think that we would have undertaken this lengthy journey if we were not certain of our information?"

The genuine conviction in his words gave Herod a distinctly uncomfortable feeling. He turned his back on the visitors abruptly, walked to a table where a serving tray was waiting and poured himself a glass of wine with trembling hands. A royal child, whose arrival had been seen by these wise men from Persia? That could only mean one thing: the Messiah had been born somewhere in his country! He downed the glass in one go. The tingling warmth of the drink made him feel himself again and he realised that he owed the three visitors an explanation. He forced himself to smile, turned round again and said apologetically,

"Please forgive me for my somewhat awkward reaction. I've been having some problems of a personal nature lately; my wife has left me and I have been living on my own for some time. So your congratulations did touch rather a sore spot. But I do believe that I can help you. It is written in our own books of prophecies that the Messiah, the one who will lead the tribes of Israel, will be born in Bethlehem. I would suggest you go there, and if you do find this blue-blooded baby, please come back here and tell me everything, so that I can go and visit the child myself."

The wise men took his advice and when they got close to Bethlehem they did indeed see the star again. It led them to the stable with Mary, Joseph and the baby, to whom they gave their precious gifts. But they did not return to Jerusalem afterwards. They were unconvinced about Herod's professed good intentions and did not want to endanger the parents or the child. So they avoided the city and went back eastwards via Bethany and Jericho.

Herod was furious when he found out that the three wise men had gone back home without returning to see him. He paced back and forth, beside himself with rage. The idea that the Messiah had been born and might threaten his position drove him to the edge of insanity. It was obvious that he would have to do something. He rang the bell to summon a servant.

"You'd never believe it," he growled with barely contained rage, "but those Persians have deceived me. But I know what I've got to do. Bring me the commander of the Roman guard! I need to talk to him!"

The servant gave a perfunctory, shallow bow and departed. Soon after the Roman commander arrived. The king came straight to the point.

"Listen carefully!" he snapped. "Take a squad of soldiers and march them off to Bethlehem. The people there have been plotting against me and this conspiracy needs to be squashed firmly. I am therefore hereby ordering you to kill all boy children in the town who are less than two years of age. Then I can be sure that we've eliminated the pretender to my throne who was born there just recently."

The commander hesitated. He was by no means faint-hearted and a veteran of numerous campaigns, but this order went against the grain.

"Begging your pardon, sir," he said apologetically, "but I do just want to check I heard that right. Your Highness wants us to kill small children and babies? Isn't that a bit too much?"

If looks could have killed, the soldier would have breathed his last. Herod gave him an icy stare and spoke frostily,

"I don't seem to recall asking you for your opinion. Follow your orders; if you have a problem with that, I'm sure there are plenty of others who won't hesitate to obey me!"

The commander swallowed and then decided he was not going to be intimidated by this king.

"Very well, sir, get someone else then," he declared resolutely. "I'm not having any part of this. I've no problem with fighting, not when it's a fair and honourable fight against worthy opponents. But I can't do what Your Highness is asking now."

Those words cost him his life. Infuriated, Herod sprang to his feet, went over, took the commander's own dagger from its sheath, and stabbed him unhesitatingly in the chest several times. The Roman fell to his knees with an anguished cry, bleeding heavily and with a look of uncomprehending surprise in his eyes. There was one last spluttering breath as he collapsed onto the floor, where he lay motionless, the dagger still protruding from his chest. Herod looked down at the corpse disdainfully. Then he rang again. The servant reappeared. He looked in shock at the dead body on the floor. But Herod did not flinch and his words were cool:

"Maybe now you could find one who will do what I say? And while you're about it, get this mess cleaned up please."

The man nodded, his face deathly pale, and then hurried away. The smell of the blood had made him feel sick. Confused he went to the Roman fortress Antonia and told what had happened. On hearing this, the other commanders proved all too willing to carry out Herod's orders and so it was not long before a large column of soldiers was on its way to Bethlehem to carry out the crazed monarch's gruesome instructions.

Mary and Joseph found they had no option but to remain in the stable. The innkeeper put up with it - after all, they paid him well enough - but his attitude was surly and it was clear he would be glad to see the back of them. Fortunately Jesus was a quiet baby who did not cry a great deal and Mary was feeling stronger day by day. Even so, the return journey would still have been asking too much of her. So they tried to make the best of the situation. Joseph walked to the baker's every morning to fetch bread and the innkeeper brought them some of the leftovers from dinner in the evenings. After eight days they had their son circumcised and he was now officially called Jesus, the name the angel had used. The days passed peacefully enough until the innkeeper came running into the courtyard one evening. He was dishevelled and his voice was shrill as he shouted,

"Listen! You're in danger! Herod's gone completely mad - he's having the whole village searched, trying to find the Messiah. It's awful! Soldiers are roaming the place, killing all the baby boys. But they haven't got here yet, so get out while you still can! Quickly. Take your son with you and get away from here!"

Joseph and Mary were dumbfounded. Exactly what the man had been telling them had not really sunk in yet, but fortunately the innkeeper was more resolute. He untied their donkey and led it out of the stable.

"Hurry up then!" he snarled. "I don't want you lot here when those soldiers turn up. You've been here plenty long enough anyway. So get away from here, now!"

In a flash, Joseph realised just how serious the situation was. He ran to the stable, stuffed everything he could see into his travelling bag and threw it over the donkey's back. In the meantime, Mary had lifted the sleeping Jesus out of his crib. The baby woke with a start and began crying insistently.

"Shush," whispered Mary urgently, rocking him on her arm. "Shhh. Please be quiet!"

The baby seemed to understand her, because it looked at her with big eyes and stopped wailing. Mary hurried out of the stable, where Joseph was waiting with a baby sling. She put it on, placed the child in it and put a blanket round him so that he wouldn't get cold. They then hurried through the narrow back door into the alley, round the back of the inn and out of the village along a small path through the fields. The innkeeper breathed a sigh of relief. He quickly raked up the straw in the stable, fished the last blankets out of the crib and hurried back inside the house. When the soldiers searched his inn and yard a quarter of an hour later, they found no trace of the boy king.

The gentle rocking motion of the sling fortunately soon sent the baby Jesus back to sleep as Joseph and Mary hurried down the little field path. Soon they came out on the larger road, where they could go left towards Bethany or take a right in the direction of Hebron. Joseph hesitated.

"Which way should we go?" he wondered out loud. "If Herod doesn't find Jesus in Bethlehem, will he just start searching the rest of the country?"

"I've no idea," replied Mary, "but I don't much like the idea of following this road. From the South Mountain, you can see for miles along it, both northwards and southwards. Just imagine if we're discovered!"

Joseph nodded. She was right. So what was the best thing to do? Then, suddenly, he had an idea.

"I know what we can do, Mary," he said in relief. "We can cross here and keep going eastwards, towards my people's monastery in Qumran. I'm sure we will find help there."

Mary nodded thankfully.

"Yes, let's do that," she agreed.

They smiled warmly at each other, the frightening situation making them feel even closer. Then they hurried across the road and began following the path that would take them in the direction of Qumran. They walked all night, stopping only to change the baby and feed him. It was nearly dawn when they reached the edge of the woods. The sun came up and they could see the plain below them, stretching all the way to the Dead Sea. The monastery could already by sighted in the distance. They could finally breathe freely again. It seemed as if their escape had not been noticed and that they would be able to get to their destination safely.

They started picking their way carefully down the steep path. Getting down without tripping and stumbling was far from easy, but fortunately they could use the sure-footed donkey for support. After more than an hour, they finally got down onto the plain. They now goaded the donkey into going a little faster so that they would reach the monastery as soon as possible. When they got there, Joseph banged on the gates with his fists as hard as he could. The heavy door swung open almost at once and they saw a brother standing in front of them, dressed in a white habit. The tension finally ebbed away from them and they hugged each other in relief. Then Joseph made the secret sign that only the Essenes knew. The brother smiled,

"We saw you coming. We don't know why you are here, but please come further. Every Essene is welcome here."

Joseph embraced him thankfully and they went inside. They finally felt safe when the heavy gate closed again behind them, protecting them from all the violence of the outside world.

They stayed in the monastery that day and had a long talk with the abbot. They took him fully into their confidence, telling him about the special destiny awaiting Jesus and Herod's fearsome response.

The abbot recommended that they should not remain in Israel but should continue in the direction of Egypt, where they could find a safe haven for a while with a like-minded community in Heliopolis.

That same evening, the brothers helped them along their way, across the River Jordan and southwards down the other side of the Dead Sea. They remained in Egypt for several months, until news reached them that Herod had died. Only then did they dare return to their home town of Nazareth.

Nazareth

The boy Jesus thrived. He was an easy-going, happy child who was able to keep himself entertained. He did not like playing outside so much, preferring to sit at the table with his mother, having stories read to him. He started trying to write down the letters himself when he was only three, with amazing success. Mary and Joseph realised they should give him the opportunity to develop his talents so they asked Rabbi Gamliel at the synagogue to give Jesus lessons. Gamliel really thought the lad was too young but he decided to give it a go anyway. And the boy astounded him time after time. The ease with which he mastered everything was unbelievable. He could already read and write almost perfectly when he was only four.

Gamliel wanted to see what he was capable of so he began instructing the boy in the Torah and the books of the prophets. Jesus studied with an eagerness that astounded the rabbi. His hunger for knowledge seemed to know no bounds and he read everything he could get his hands on. Jesus shared a bedroom with his two brothers and sister. However, Joseph saw that he was increasingly beginning to need his own space and so he put up a dividing wall to create a separate room for him where he could work in peace. Of course Jesus' unusual achievements didn't go unnoticed in their neighbourhood. Despite the effort his parents made not to treat him any differently, Jesus was still seen as being a bit odd and he was often teased when he was out and about. However, this did not seem to bother him much and he quietly went his own way.

One day when Jesus was lying on his bed reading, his baby sister Miriam crawled in. She was six years younger and Jesus adored her. She was just learning to walk and Jesus had been following her attempts with great pleasure. Now, too, she tried to pull herself up by grabbing hold of his bed to stand on her two wobbly legs. Jesus gave her some enthusiastic encouragement:

"Come on Miriam, you can do it! Yes, come and have a look at your big brother!"

Miriam chuckled and clutched at the blanket for support as she tried to stand up. But her hands suddenly lost their grip and she fell backwards with a bump, hitting her head on the floor. She immediately burst into tears, crying inconsolably. Jesus picked her up.

"Oh my little Miriam, what's this all about?" he said soothingly, rocking her lovingly on his knee. "Where did you hurt yourself? Let me take a look."

He gently stroked the painful spot on the back of her head. Suddenly he felt a warm, tingling feeling shoot through his hand. And equally suddenly Miriam stopped crying. Jesus started. He felt confused by the abrupt change from heart-rending tears to this sudden silence and quickly he withdrew his hand. He looked at his baby sister in surprise as she was already laughing again. That was how Mary found them when she came into the room.

"What happened?" she asked, picking up the little girl.

"I don't know," replied Jesus in confusion. "She fell and hit her head on the floor. All I did was stroke her where she had hurt herself and then she suddenly stopped crying. I really don't understand it. I didn't do anything special."

Mary looked at him closely.

"Well, it seems you have hidden talents," she said. "I'll remember this if anything ever happens to James or Simon."

Her response might have been light-hearted but it did not stop Jesus' feeling of confusion. And in the weeks and months that followed, he noticed a number of times that he was able to reduce pain by laying his hands on people. No-one apart from his parents knew about this and they never really spoke about the matter. Apparently it was just something he had. But Jesus realised all too well that it was an unusual gift and he often wondered why he in particular should have this aptitude.

Rabbi Gamliel still enjoyed working with his diligent pupil, even though he was running out of things to teach the boy. Jesus knew the

Torah and books of the prophets off by heart by the time he was seven and was able to recite them without making any mistakes. And if Gamliel quizzed him about what the texts meant, he was astounded by his pupil's level of understanding. In the search for a new challenge he had gone looking for more texts and had found some scrolls in his own library containing wise parables. Jesus was immediately enthusiastic.

"Oh Rabbi, please could I take one home with me to read it there?" he asked hopefully. "I promise I'll be really careful with it!"

"Go on then," laughed Gamliel indulgently. "But make sure you bring it back without any damage, right?"

Jesus nodded and set off home in high spirits with the scroll under his arm. When he got there, he sat at the garden table and spread out the scroll. His eyes sped eagerly over the letters. He always loved diving into texts and Rabbi Gamliel had given him a fantastic scroll. A smile came to his lips. Mary came out to hang up the washing. She looked at his face with affection. She was pleased to see him smiling like that. He was so serious so much of the time, not really carefree enough for someone of his age.

"What are you reading?" she asked curiously.

Jesus looked up.

"Tales of the wisdom of King Solomon," he answered cheerfully. "Rabbi Gamliel gave me the scroll. Isn't that nice!"

Mary put down the basket of washing and sat down next to him.

"Why don't you read one to me?" she suggested.

Although she could read perfectly well herself, she loved hearing her son read aloud. He had a clear voice and wonderful intonation. You couldn't help but listen once he started on a story. Jesus nodded in happy agreement.

"Yes, that'd be nice," he said, pleased at her interest.

He slid the bookmark down in search of a interesting tale and started to read. He put so much life into the story that it seemed to Mary as if she too was part of it. She saw the two brothers before her, each ready to grant the other their father's inheritance as if it had been their own, and now she finally understood what King Solomon meant: that love conquers all. Jesus fell silent. The story had finished. They sat for a moment in silence. Then Mary sighed,

"What a wonderful tale. How much those brothers must have

loved each other."

Jesus nodded wordlessly. Then suddenly a look of sorrow came over him.

"Why can't people always be nice to each other like that?" he spoke sadly. "After all, that's God's will. You know, this Earth of ours is such a beautiful place. I see the sun, the flowers, the animals... But I don't see God here."

He sounded deeply despondent as he said this and Mary saw tears in his eyes. She was taken aback at first but then she recovered and said,

"No, you're right. You can't see God here. But you do feel Him, don't you?"

Jesus nodded.

"Yes, of course I feel Him," he answered as if it was the most natural thing in the world. "I always feel Him. But it's so different to when I was still with Him. I miss that unconditional love that you feel there all the time - I haven't found that here yet. Don't you miss that feeling too, mother?"

Mary shrugged her shoulders hesitantly.

"I'm afraid I don't really remember that feeling anymore," she said gently.

Jesus stared at her in surprise.

"Mother, how can you say that!" he asked wonderingly. "That feeling is so overwhelming! You can't compare it to anything else. You surely can't ever forget something like that once you've experienced it!"

Mary had to pause again. How could she explain to him that he too would lose the memory of that sensation and how difficult he would then find it to get even a faint echo of what he had once felt? She put an arm around him.

"Then I wish you all the best in keeping hold of that memory," she said as cheerfully as she could. "And I hope you can make the people around you feel that overwhelming love too."

She planted a kiss on his cheek and stroked his curly hair. Jesus was already smiling again.

"Yes, that would be wonderful!" he nodded. "And who knows - if everyone feels that love, maybe peace will finally return to our country!"

"Indeed, you never know!" agreed Mary encouragingly. "Keep your mind on that, and no more tears. Right?"

She stood up, picked up the basket of washing and started hanging out the clothes. Then she walked into the kitchen and checked the water pitchers. Unfortunately there was not enough water to last the rest of the day. That meant she would have to walk to the well to draw more water. She reluctantly picked up two empty pitchers and went outside. Jesus saw what she was going to do.

"Oh, can I fetch the water, mother?" he asked enthusiastically. "The path to the well is so pretty. And those pitchers are far too heavy for you to carry."

Mary grinned with relief.

"Please do!" she replied. "To be honest, I'd be only too happy for you to do that tiresome little chore for me!"

Jesus took the pitchers out of her hands.

"I don't find it a tiresome little chore at all!" he laughed. "It's so lovely to be out in the sun!"

He set off in a bright mood. He was still thinking about the interesting story he had just read to his mother. How nice of Rabbi Gamliel to let him borrow that scroll! He was already looking forward to reading more when he got back. He walked along the street, sunk so deep in thought that he failed to notice the group of boys playing further along. But they noticed him.

"Look lads, there he goes again," called one of them. "Take a look at that - our girl's off to get some water."

The group laughed mockingly and another boy called scornfully,

"Come on, let's see whether he needs a spot of help with his girlie job."

They walked up to Jesus and crowded round him.

"So, off to get water, are you?"

The question oozed sarcasm but Jesus did not rise to the bait.

"Yes, as you can see," he said and walked on calmly even though they tried to cut him off.

"Come on, I'll carry that pitcher for you."

One of the teasers, a tall boy, grabbed one of the pitchers from Jesus' hands and rolled it away to taunt him. Jesus pursed his lips but said nothing. Instead he looked intently at the group, the very look that they had come to hate so much.

"So, what are you going to do now?"

They thronged even closer around him and started to push him from one to another to goad him. But Jesus didn't respond to their teasing and so they soon got tired of it.

"Oh come on, let's leave him. He thinks he's too good for us."

They gave him one final big push so that he ended up on his knees. Now the other pitcher rolled out of his hand and he was only just able to grab it in time. The boys laughed scornfully but they did at least leave him now in peace. Jesus stood up and went in search of the second pitcher. Fortunately it had not broken. He picked it up and continued on his way but there was nothing left of his bright spirits. He felt tears welling up. He turned to God, as so often, and asked,

"Lord God, why is it always me they pick on? Why don't I belong?"

There was no answer. Disappointed, Jesus tried to stifle his misery. He was so preoccupied with his thoughts that it took a while for him to notice a huge racket. It was the sound of clopping horseshoes and rattling wheels. A Roman two-horse carriage was turning the corner of the street at great speed and hurtling straight towards him. Jesus had not heard the carriage at all and it was pure instinct that made him jump aside. This saved his life. The horses galloped past only inches from him and he felt the wind from the wheels as they thundered past. His heart was pounding from the shock and he realised that he had been incredibly lucky to escape. But the situation behind him had not panned out so well. Jesus heard a terrible scream. He turned round and saw that one of the boys had not been so quick to get out of the way. He was lying on the ground moaning in pain and clutching his leg. Jesus did not hesitate for one moment. He jumped up and ran towards the lad, kneeling next to him.

"Wait," he said gently to calm the boy. "Wait, I'll help you."

He placed his hands on the leg that was hurting and closed his eyes. He soon felt the relief of the familiar tingling sensation in his hands. The boy felt the pain ease off almost immediately. His jaw dropped and he stared at Jesus in amazement.

"How... how do you... did you do that?" he stammered in bewilderment.

Jesus shrugged a little peevishly.

"It's just something I can," he said tersely. "Let's keep it at that."

The boy felt deeply ashamed. Only a few minutes ago he had been teasing and taunting Jesus and now this same Jesus had helped him. He suddenly pushed Jesus' hands away roughly and got up with the help of two friends. He limped away rather unsteadily, avoiding looking Jesus in the eye. He clearly had no idea how to deal with the situation. Jesus remained seated for a while. Helping the boy had worn him out. His gift was fantastic but it did take a lot out of him and now he was tired. Then he saw his two pitchers standing close by. He sighed. Of course. He had been on his way to fetch water. He got up again reluctantly and picked up the pitchers.

It was the hottest part of the day now and the streets were deserted. Jesus was pleased he could leave the town behind him to take the small road that led to the well. There was not much shade on this narrow path. There were a few bushes and shrubs along the route but they were not tall enough to provide any protection from the sun. But Jesus did not mind. The heat meant he could be almost sure he would not meet anyone on his way. And it was such a beautiful walk. The path twisted its way between the bushes and fields, and he could already see the well in the distance. He felt the weariness slip from his shoulders and he started to enjoy the pleasant walk. His thoughts returned to what had just happened. He was pleased to have been able to help the boy. That the lad had scarcely shown him any gratitude - well, that was no surprise. He had long since learned that some people had a problem with him. They were unable to comprehend why he was different, so they preferred to ignore him. He could even understand that. He laughed somewhat bitterly and said aloud:

"No wonder they don't know what to do with me. No wonder they don't understand me. Even I don't understand it! Why can I do things other people can't? Why can I see and understand things other people can't?"

It was true his mother had once told him that he was a special child, but she had not been able - or willing - to explain what she meant.

"Trust in yourself," she had said. "Just follow your heart, then everything you do will be good."

Jesus thought back to that conversation and said, still talking aloud,

"Yes, it's all very well what my mother says and I would like to follow my heart and do what I think is good, but it makes me different and lonely. And I don't want to be lonely."

Then, suddenly, a voice spoke behind him, saying,

"You'll never be lonely again, Jesus, because I promise you I'll always be with you."

Jesus jumped like a scalded cat and turned round. He had thought he was alone on the quiet path and he had not heard anyone come up walking behind him. But when he looked behind, he was shocked to see the path was empty. It was empty for as far as he could see. Astounded, he turned and looked in all directions. But wherever he looked, there was not a soul to be seen. Then, in a fraction of a second, he realised who it was who had spoken to him. The pitchers fell from his hands and he dropped to his knees. The realisation that he had heard God's voice overwhelmed him so much that his whole body started to shake. And once again he heard the voice and he felt God's calming influence when He said,

"Don't be afraid, My son. There is no need to be afraid because I will care for you like a father. Listen. You are indeed different but you are doing very well. Trust in Me and it will work out for you. Believe in Me and you will be with Me and in Me and I will be in you, now and forever."

Jesus covered his face with his hands. His thoughts were swirling through his head. Then he intertwined his fingers and with a flash of realisation, he said falteringly,

"It's You who lets me take away people's pain with my hands ... You're the one!"

The answer came from his own heart.

"Yes, I'm the one."

Jesus shook his head. This was incomprehensible. Surely this couldn't be true? Was this really happening? And he had a hundred questions he wanted to ask but he could not think straight. The questions came tumbling out but he was unable put them into words. But that was not necessary, for God understood him without the need for words.

"Don't worry," came a gentle voice, seemingly speaking straight to his soul. "Don't worry. You will get answers to all your questions, but only once you are able to truly understand them. Do you have the courage to trust in that?"

These words exuded so much love and warmth that Jesus began to relax. He nodded and his answer came without a sound, his soul communicating directly with God.

"Yes, my Lord. I'm afraid and I don't understand what's going on but I trust You. I will let You be my guide. I'm sure You have my best interests at heart."

And God replied,

"Then I promise you, My son, that I will not betray your trust. And remember - I will be there when you need Me. You only have to look for Me and I will be there."

These words were followed by silence. Jesus wasn't sure which emotion was strongest: he felt frightened, happy, worried and blissful all at once. He decided to keep the memory of God's words deep in his heart and not to mention this to anyone.

But after the evening meal, when Joseph had gone to his workshop to clear away his tools and when Jesus' brothers and sister had been put to bed, Jesus was unable to keep quiet about the incident any longer. When his mother returned to the room after washing the dishes, he asked her with a quavering voice:

"Mother, have you ever heard God speak to you?"

Mary noticed the tremor in his voice and realised that he was asking this for a reason. She sat down opposite him and answered,

"No, I have never heard God speak to me. Not really, I mean."

A tense silence fell. Mary saw her son was very emotional and she asked nervously,

"Why did you want to know that, actually?"

Jesus hesitated at first, but then said,

"Because this afternoon I did hear the voice of God. And no, don't ask me whether I'm certain because I am certain - I just know it was Him."

Mary's heart missed a beat and she closed her eyes for a second. Then she took hold of his hands and stroked them. Her son, her wonderful son! So finally God had revealed Himself to him; what had been promised seven years ago had come to pass. And she started to tell him. She told him everything. That when she had been pregnant an angel had appeared to her telling her that the child she was expecting was a very special child. That he would show people the way to God so that they could come to know God's kingdom of love. And that God's Holy Spirit would help him with this task. She told him more things too. About how there had been a bright star above Bethlehem when he was born. And that three wise men had come from the East to worship him, the new king. About how King Herod had heard about this and had ordered all baby boys to be slaughtered. That they had fled to Egypt and had only returned back home much later.

Jesus listened breathlessly. Suddenly everything seemed clear to him: all the questions he had wanted answered, all those things he had long known in his heart but not been able to put into words, his sensitivity and desire for justice, the way he was so different. When Mary had finished, he rushed over to her and clambered onto her lap. That was how Joseph found them when he came back in from the workshop.

"Well, what's going on here?" he asked in surprise.

Mary looked at him, full of emotion, and said,

"He knows. God has spoken to him so I've told him everything."

Joseph sat down next to them. Full of feeling, he put his arms around his son and told Jesus about the plan that had been waiting for that moment. That they wanted to send him to Qumran, to the Essene monastery, where he would be prepared for the task awaiting him. He would get the best education possible there and he was to take as long as he thought necessary to learn everything he wanted to know.

Jesus was overcome with deep gratitude. He would be going to Qumran, to the monastery that had always fascinated him. Finally he would no longer be the misfit, the target of taunts. He would be able to study in peace and quiet and God Himself would be helping him. When he went to bed at the end of this emotional day, he clasped his hands together and thanked God for everything. For the love of his parents. For his brothers and little sister, whom he would miss. For the trust being shown in him that he hoped was not misplaced. And once again he heard God's voice, but this time it didn't startle him.

He listened attentively and felt God's gentle smile when He said,

"That's good. I see I no longer frighten you. Relax, My son. Relax and have faith. Then everything will be all right."

These loving words made Jesus feel happy and free of worries. Blissfully, he turned onto his side and curled up under the blanket. He soon fell into a deep, dreamless sleep.

In the weeks that followed, God regularly sought contact with Jesus. The boy became increasingly accustomed to His presence in his heart and in his life. Joseph and Mary thought he had changed. He became quieter and seemed unusual calm for his age. He often sat deep in thought, with a glazed look as if he was in a world of his own. At such moments he felt very close to God. As God always called him 'My son', he adopted the habit of calling God his Abba, an affectionate word meaning 'daddy'. He was no longer so keen on the lessons Rabbi Gamliel gave. He had the feeling he had no more to learn there and he was longing to go to Qumran.

Joseph's parents insisted on holding a leaving party for their grandson. They hired an inn and invited all the family and acquaintances. All this attention made Jesus feel rather shy, but he realised this might be the last time he saw his grandparents so he submitted meekly to everything they had organised. After the party had been under way for a while, his grandfather stood up and tapped his cup with a knife. The hubbub in the room subsided and he turned to Jesus.

"My dear child, today you have reached a milestone in your life. You will be leaving the life you have known up to now and you are on the threshold of a new beginning. That is why your grandmother and I would like to give you a present. So tell us what we can give you that would make you happy."

Jesus did not need to think long about that.

"Dear grandfather, I don't want a present because I'm happy with what I've got. But I do have another idea. Would that be all right too?"

"Anything is all right!" cried out Jacob generously. "So spit it out!"

Jesus laughed, pleased at the positive response and he said enthusiastically,

"I'd like a lot more children to be able to enjoy this party. There are lots of boys and girls in Nazareth who hardly have any money and have probably never been to a party. So the best present you could give me is to let me invite the children who are less well off than me to enjoy this party with us."

Jacob's jaw dropped. He felt a rush of joy that the boy had come up with such an unselfish wish. Touched, he said,

"That's a wonderful idea, Jesus! And of course it's all right! Go on and bring as many children as you want."

Jesus didn't have to be told twice. He ran out and spoke to all the children whom he knew were not that well off. He asked them whether they were interested in a free party and soon he had dozens of boys and girls following him back to the inn. In no time, the hall was resounding with the cheerful laughter of children. Everyone was singing and dancing. The children's happiness spread a warm glow amongst all the other guests.

In this way, Jesus' leaving party became an event that people talked about for a long time afterwards. Everyone acknowledged that the unusual integrity demonstrated by the boy could only have come from God himself.

Qumran

The area around the Dead Sea may well be one of the most sinister places on Earth. The lake lies at the lowest point on land on the planet, about twelve hundred feet below sea level. It is no coincidence that it is called the Dead Sea: its' extremely high salt content prevents all forms of life. No fish, no crabs, no water plants - nothing. And the surrounding area for miles around is also empty and bereft of life. No bushes, no clumps of grass, no trees, no plants.

It was here of all places, not far from the village of Qumran, that the monastery of the Essenes was to be found. They had deliberately selected this spot as their base. They abhorred worldly life and the lack of respect with which people so often treated their fellow men. The Essenes preferred the silence of the desert, where they could devote themselves entirely to prayer, study and meditation. Their monastery was an oasis of calm in a dark, hectic world. And they shielded their calm well from the outside world for they were very particular about whom they would let join the order. Candidates had to satisfy strict criteria and be prepared to subject themselves entirely to the rules. This let the monks make sure that their self-created isolation was maintained.

But this day, it was still early, a man on horseback came galloping up to their residence. The guard in the watchtower raised the alarm and sent one of the brothers to the gate. The man dismounted, lifted the heavy knocker and let it fall on the door. A small hatch opened and a brother peered out. He saw a man covered in dust, wearing simple clothes.

"Good morning," he said hesitantly but not inhospitably. "May I ask who you are and what you are doing here?"

The rider replied,

"I'm a messenger from Nazareth. Joseph the carpenter sent me. I have an important message for the head of your order. Please take me to him."

And he made the secret sign that only the Essenes knew. The brother realised he was one of them. He opened the gate and took the rider to their leader who greeted the messenger warmly.

"So, good man, what brings you here?" he asked curiously. "I understand you have come from Nazareth? Here, take a seat."

The courier nodded.

"I come with news from Joseph, the carpenter," he answered. "Joseph says you would undoubtedly remember him. He was here about seven years ago."

"Of course I remember him!" said the abbot. "He came here to protect his son Jesus from the wrath of Herod."

The messenger bent forward slightly and lowered his voice.

"It's about Jesus. It looks like the Messiah we have been waiting for all this time has finally arrived. He is a great joy to his parents and teachers. He is exceptionally bright. Young as he is, he knows all the books of the Torah and the prophets off by heart. And not just that - the ways he can explain them amaze everyone. And now it seems God has revealed Himself to him. That's why Joseph and Mary want to bring him here, so that he can be prepared for the task that awaits him. I think they will be here the day after tomorrow. They wanted to leave Nazareth today."

The abbot stood up and paced back and forth. He was overcome by excitement. Jesus of Nazareth, the child who was to receive the Holy Spirit, was on his way to *his* monastery! What an honour. But at the same time, what a responsibility he would now have to bear. He went up to the messenger and said,

"Thank you my friend, for bringing us this news. We will do everything we can to prepare for the arrival of this exceptional child. And you are welcome to rest here before starting your return journey."

The messenger stood up and gave a small, courteous bow.

"It would be a pleasure if I could join you for your midday meal," he said with a smile.

Joseph and Mary had indeed left Nazareth that morning. They had harnessed the donkey to their wagon and packed only the bare essentials for the journey. Jesus put his parchment scrolls and some clothes under the bench. In fact that were his only possessions.

"Hey, Jesus, don't stay away for too long, right?" called out James. "We're already missing you."

"I'll miss you too!" Jesus called back. "But you can sleep in my bedroom now, remember?"

James nodded and beamed at the thought. A room of his own! They clambered into the wagon and Joseph guided the donkey round the corner. Now Jesus lost sight of his grandparents, brothers and little sister. The journey went smoothly. Jesus took pleasure from the constantly changing scenery. He was looking forward to this new stage in his life.

"Tell me, father," he said as he climbed onto the driving seat next to Joseph, "what does the monastery look like?"

"Well, there's the main building with a big courtyard," explained Joseph. "That's where the monks study, work and eat. And they sleep in little huts or tents. But they also have rooms carved out of the rock."

"Do you think I'll get a room of my own?" inquired Jesus.

"If you want," replied Joseph. "But I guess you'll be staying with your mentor to start with."

"I wonder who my mentor will be," pondered Jesus. "I hope it's someone who gives me loads of new scrolls to read."

Joseph smiled.

"There are lot and lots of scrolls and books there that you've never even heard of," he said. "I think you'll really enjoy studying there. But don't set your hopes too high - it won't be a bed of roses. The land there is dry and barren. And they have strict rules."

"I'm not worried about that," replied Jesus cheerfully. "I really like the idea of learning new things. And I'm sure I'll soon get used to those rules."

They spent the night near the town of Sichar and continued their journey the next day. There was more traffic on the road now as they were getting closer to Jerusalem. Many people were travelling to the holy city to offer a sacrifice in the temple and there were merchants with wagons laden with goods. And they saw more Roman soldiers here, some on foot and some on horseback. Jesus was fascinated by it all.

"Oh father, let's spend the night in Jerusalem!" he suggested eagerly. "I really want to see the temple."

But Joseph shook his head resolutely.

"No, my son," he said in a serious tone. "I'm not sure that would be safe. We haven't reserved a place at an inn. What if we can't find a place to sleep? We might get robbed, or picked up by the Romans. I don't want to run that risk. But I promise you we'll go and see it another time, when you've finished your studies and are a bit older. Agreed?"

Jesus was disappointed but he didn't argue with his father. Joseph avoided the city and took the turning to Bethany, where they spent the night. The next morning they continued further. They were getting close to their destination now and the landscape started to change fast. They descended from the hills onto a flat plain. The lower they were, the hotter and drier it became. Jesus grew quiet now that they were nearing their goal. He was becoming increasingly aware of what he was about to face and how unusual this situation was for a child of his tender age. He sat next to Mary, who put her arms around him and cuddled him. Then, as it got close to midday, Joseph turned round.

"Jesus, look down there, you can see it!" he said, pointing.

Jesus jumped up and sure enough, he could see the monastery in the distance, the big main building his father had told him about with the huts all around. And he could see the rooms carved into the rock face. But the most fascinating part was the enormous aqueduct next to the monastery. Huge reservoirs had been constructed up above to catch the rain. Then an ingenious maze of canals and ditches carried the water down inside the citadel, where lo and behold plants were being cultivated. Jesus breathed a sigh of relief. He was pleased to see some greenery in this barren, desolate country.

They turned onto the narrow path that led to the entrance. As soon as they got to the gate, it swung open. Joseph drove up to the central courtyard where a number of monks were already waiting for them. He saw one or two familiar faces and he jumped off the driving seat. The brothers immediately came up to him and shook his hand enthusiastically. Jesus watched them greeting each other and he was immediately impressed by these men in their splendid white robes. Then he noticed someone striding towards them. The monks made way for the man deferentially and Jesus realised this must be the head of the order. The leader embraced Joseph and said in an emotional voice,

"My friend, it's good to see you after such a long time. Have you all had a smooth journey?"

Joseph nodded.

"Yes, luckily we got here without any problems. And I'd like to thank you for being willing to look after my son. Please follow me, I'll take you to him."

Jesus had already jumped down off the cart. He helped Mary get down as it was so high, then started unloading the luggage. But he was interrupted by his father, who called,

"Jesus, come over here, please. I'd like to introduce you to the head of this esteemed brotherhood."

The boy walked up to the two men rather shyly. He bowed slightly in front of the tall man in his white habit. The abbot held out his hand.

"Welcome to our monastery, Jesus," he said in a friendly tone. "I hope you will enjoy it here."

Jesus shook his hand and answered in a clear voice,

"I have no doubt that I will, as God has arranged for me to stay here."

The brothers gave each other meaningful looks. The little group then went inside, away from the heat.

"You must be hungry," said the abbot. "Come, let's eat."

He gestured towards the table, where a simple meal was waiting for them. They ate, and the three adults talked in low voices. Jesus was not really listening to them. His thoughts were elsewhere. He surveyed the room they were in and saw it was very Spartan. Apart from one or two cupboards containing some clay pots, it was almost empty. He wondered whether he would feel at home in this strict order and he let out a sigh. The abbot heard it. Smiling, he turned to him.

"My dear child, it seems we have rather neglected you. Forgive us, because of course this is really all about you. Is there something you'd like to ask? Because I'll do my best to answer all your questions for the entire time you're here."

Jesus nodded.

"Yes, I would like to ask something," he said. "I'd like to know your name so that I know what to call you."

"My name... ," replied the abbot, then hesitated. "You want to know my name... Unfortunately that happens to be the best kept secret of our order, Jesus. You need to realise that I may well be the biggest enemy of many powerful men in this country. That's why it is better for you not to know my name. It's for your own safety as well. But you can call me Abba if you want. It means 'father', and I intend to be a father to you for as long as you stay here."

But his answer did not please Jesus at all. He stood up and looked at the man fixedly.

"I'm sorry," he said, his voice trembling with emotion, "but I most certainly won't call you Abba. I only use that name for my real father."

Joseph looked up in surprise.

"But Jesus! You've never called me that in your life," he spoke a little reproachfully.

Jesus turned his gaze towards him and said firmly,

"Excuse me father, but it wasn't you I was talking about. I meant my Father in heaven."

An icy silence followed. Then Joseph got up and walked over to his son. He put his hand on his shoulder and said humbly,

"Forgive me, Jesus. I should have realised."

The abbot had also risen and he crouched in front of Jesus so that he could look him right in the eye.

"Perhaps you would like to call me 'master' then, as the other brothers do," he suggested. "Because I hope I'll be able to teach you many things."

But as he spoke those words, he realised it was he who was the apprentice here and that the true master was standing in front of him in the shape of this slight lad. However Jesus nodded in relief and laughed, saying,

"I'll happily call you master, sir, because I'm sure you'll be able to explain lots of things to me."

The abbot gave his hands a friendly squeeze. Then he stood up and said,

"Now it's time to say goodbye to your parents. If they leave now they'll be able to reach Bethany by sundown."

Jesus nodded. He hugged his mother first. Seeing the tears in her eyes, he said tenderly,

"Don't cry, mother. You'll be able to visit me sometimes. And I'll write you loads of letters so that you know how I'm getting on, all right?"

Mary already smiled again. She stroked his cheek and gave him a final kiss. Then Joseph put his arms round his son and whispered in his ear:

"Chin up, my wonderful boy! You won't find life easy here, but I'm sure it'll bring you fulfilment and make you happy person."

Jesus was extremely moved by his words and silently he accompanied them to the courtyard. Joseph helped Mary into the cart, climbed onto the driving box and drove the donkey onto the narrow path in the direction of Bethany. Jesus waved until the great gate closed behind them. Then he turned round. For a moment he felt lost in this strange environment but the abbot took care of him.

"Come," he said. "I'll introduce you to the brother who will be showing you the ropes. He's waiting for us in my room."

Jesus nodded and followed him. But suddenly he had a feeling of unease and he realised immediately why.

"Oh, no" he cried. "My scrolls! My book scrolls! They're still in the cart!"

He ran back to the gate and tried to open it. But the gatekeeper held him back.

"I'm sorry, young man, but they've probably got too far already," he said stolidly.

"But I've got to call them back!" called Jesus excitably. "Those scrolls are my most treasured possessions!"

He looked around him and spotted the stairs that led to the tower. He raced up the steps and looked out over the plain. To his great disappointment, he saw that the gatekeeper was right. His parents' cart was merely a tiny dot in the distance. Tears welled up in his eyes and he felt an intense feeling of abandonment. He started to wonder what on earth he was doing here, why he wasn't just sitting in the wagon with them, going back home. Then he felt a hand on his shoulder and a warm voice saying to him,

"Don't worry Jesus, I got your scrolls from the cart. They're waiting for you in your very own desk."

Jesus spun round. A brother with brown hair and dark eyes stood before him. His face seemed so friendly that Jesus took an immediate liking to him.

"Hello! I'm Matheno," said the brother, introducing himself. "Our master has asked me to look after you. Well, I'd be happy to do that!"

Jesus sighed with relief. He wiped away his tears and said politely,

"Thank you, sir! I could use a friend as everything is so new for me. So could you please show me where you put my scrolls?"

"Of course," nodded Matheno soothingly. "Come with me."

He walked down the steps with Jesus following, crossed the courtyard and opened one of the many doors leading off it. The room they entered was spacious and light, thanks to the windows high up that let in the daylight. Jesus saw that it was a scriptorium, a writing room. There were rows of benches and writing tables on either side of the central aisle. And there were monks at work, bent over their desks and with looks of concentration on their faces. When they heard Matheno and Jesus enter, they stopped their work and nodded at them in greeting. Jesus returned the greeting. He took a look at some of the writing and saw beautifully formed letters with an illustration here and there. He realised these brothers were masters of their trade who put great love into their work. And he drank up the warm atmosphere in this silent room.

"Look," pointed Matheno. "That's your place. I hope the bench is at the right height for you."

Jesus saw that the brothers had put a taller bench ready especially for him so that he would be able to reach his writing desk. He also saw he had been given what was possibly the best spot in the room, under one of the high windows that let in the sun and would give him plenty of light to work in.

"This is fine!" he said gratefully. "Thank you, everyone, for looking after me so well!"

He lifted up the lid to the desk and found his scrolls carefully stored inside. His eyes lit up and he ran his hands over his treasured possessions. And he started to feel more at ease in his new surroundings.

"Would you perhaps like to read something to us?" asked Matheno. "Normally we work in silence here but I think we'd all like to hear you read something. Something from one of your own scrolls, for instance, or from the Torah or the book of the prophets, which is over there."

"Well, I'd prefer something from the prophets," replied Jesus. "I always enjoy reading them."

He went up to the scrolls and Matheno helped him scroll forward to the text he wanted to read. His high-pitched voice rang clearly through the lofty room and the sun shone on his face as he read:

"The people that walked in darkness have seen a great light; they that dwell in the land of the shadow of death, upon them hath the light shined. For unto us a child is born, unto us a Son is given and the government shall be upon his shoulders. And his name shall be called Wonderful Counsellor, The Mighty God, The Everlasting Father, The Prince of Peace. Of the increase of his government and peace there shall be no end, upon the throne of David and upon his kingdom, to order it and to establish it with judgement and with justice from henceforth even forever."

The brothers understood why he had chosen that text in particular and they watched reverently as he carefully closed and tied the scroll. Then Jesus turned to Matheno.

"I feel quite tired from the journey and all the new things I've seen today. Perhaps you could show me to my room so that I could get some rest?"

Matheno eagerly did as Jesus asked. He took the boy to his own tent and showed him the bed that had been put up next to his. Jesus fell asleep almost immediately. While one of the other brothers kept watch over him, Matheno went in search of the abbot. He told him about the text the boy had chosen to read and how moved they had all been to hear him read that text in particular. Aware of their responsibility, they turned to God and thanked Him for this priceless gift they had been chosen to play host to. And the abbot gave Matheno free rein to look after Jesus.

When Jesus woke up the next morning, he was not sure where he was for a moment. But he soon remembered that he was now finally in Qumran, the place he had been looking forward to for so long. He got up and went outside full of expectation. The sun had already risen and was shining brightly on the plains surrounding the monastery. Apart from the other monks' huts and tents, there was little to see. The plateau the monastery was built on was encircled by barren mountain slopes, and steep rock faces descended to incredible depths.

Jesus saw that steps had been carved from some of the cliff faces, leading to caves hacked into the rock and now being used as dwellings. On impulse he walked down one set of steps and peeped into one of the rock-face rooms. He was lucky. The room was empty and seemed to be unused so he was able to go inside and have a look round. It was pleasantly cool. The cave was facing east and the walls arching over him made him feel strangely secure. When he looked out he could see the Dead Sea far beneath him. His father had told him about this unusual lake, where the water was so salty it kept you afloat whatever you did. The morning sun lit up the cave and covered him with its warm glow. Jesus felt overwhelmed by the immense views and the exceptional opportunity he had been given to stay here. He knelt and his prayers went up to God, whose greatness he recognised in the nature surrounding him, the mountains, the rocks and the sun. And he knew he wanted a room like this very much. For what could be better than being kissed awake by the sun in the mornings and greeting each day afresh like this? He decided he would ask Matheno if he could be allowed this.

He carefully climbed back up the steep steps again and went off in the direction of the main building. He soon met Matheno.

"Well, young man!" he said, giving Jesus a friendly greeting. "Did you have a good sleep?"

Jesus nodded and immediately felt a bit embarrassed.

"Should I have got up earlier?" he asked bashfully. "If so, please tell me because I really want to keep to your rules."

"We always get up at sunrise," explained Matheno. "Then we get together in the prayer room for the morning prayers. Come along, I'll show you where it is so you can join us tomorrow."

He showed Jesus the prayer room: it was empty apart from some benches along the walls. Then the monk showed him the rest of the complex. Jesus got surprise after surprise as there was much more to the monastery than he had expected. As well as the prayer room and the scriptorium he had seen the previous day, he was shown a pottery workshop, a place where paints were made, a mill to grind corn and a dining area with the kitchen leading off it. Then there was the garden where medicinal herbs were grown. Bordering the garden on one side were the stables, which housed no less than six horses.

There were monks hard at work in all these areas, and all of them gave the boy a friendly greeting. Jesus shook a lot of hands, getting to know everyone a little bit at least. Matheno was taken by the serious manner in which he absorbed each new piece of information. When the tour of the monastery was complete, he brought Jesus to the abbot.

"And Jesus, what do you think of it here?" the leader asked curiously. "Did Matheno show you everything?"

"Everything except the library," replied Matheno. "I thought you would like to do that yourself."

Jesus looked up in surprise.

"The library!" he called. "Matheno, why didn't you show me that first? I love reading and I've been so looking forward to reading all your scrolls. Please master, could you take me there straight away?"

The abbot laughed heartily.

"Well, it sounds as if I don't have much choice in the matter! All right then!"

He went into the corridor and opened the door directly opposite his room. The library was not large but there were bookcases along all the walls. The abbot opened one and Jesus saw that it was stuffed full with books and scrolls. His heart jumped with excitement.

"Dear God, thank You for giving me the opportunity to experience all this!" he said enthusiastically.

He looked excitedly at the leather volumes with titles he had never heard of before and which immediately aroused his curiosity. He touched them lovingly for a moment. Then he asked the abbot,

"There are so many books here - how do you find your way around? Where should I begin?"

The abbot smiled at his keenness.

"Let's start by concentrating on the Torah and the prophets, Jesus. Then we can move on to the Vedic hymns or the Greek philosophers such as Plato and Socrates."

Jesus was confused for a moment because he knew the Torah and the prophets but he had never heard of the other books the abbot was talking about. But he was not about to let this put him off. On the contrary! His face broke into a laugh and he said eagerly,

"I can't wait! After all, that's what I'm here for! Though I do wonder how long it's going to take me."

His enthusiasm was catching and the abbot had to laugh too.

"We've got all the time in the world, Jesus," he said cheerfully. "We'll start at the beginning and we'll see where that takes us. And is there anything else, any other request you have at the moment?"

Jesus did not know what to say at first. But then he remember the room carved from the rock and how much he wanted to be able to sleep there. He told them about this and the abbot was delighted to get such an unusual request. He saw it as a clear sign that this was no ordinary boy. For what other seven-year-old would choose to sleep in a bare cave? But Jesus had felt the spiritual bond with nature there and had responded to it. His master gave Matheno instructions to prepare the cave and Jesus was able to sleep in his new room that very same night.

In the weeks that followed, Jesus learned how to keep to the order's rules. As soon as the first sunbeams lit up his room, he got up and join the other brothers in the prayer room. They spent two hours praying in silence, followed by a ritual cold bath. Then it was time to have breakfast. Only after breakfast were they allowed to speak and went each their own way.

Jesus was usually to be found in the library where his master had always put out something for him to read. His mind was like a sponge. He could easily recall everything he read. In the quiet hours around midday, he let the texts sink deep into his heart, and tried to grasp their true meaning. After lunch he was given various jobs, such as helping brother Levi in the garden. The monk told him enthusiastically about the medicinal powers of the herbs growing there and the illnesses they were capable of healing. Jesus loved listening to Levi's wise words. He also helped copy out important texts in the scriptorium. Sitting at his desk he wrote patiently and full of concentration. His handwriting was elegant and a pleasure to read.

Within a few weeks, he was completely at home. He followed the order's daily rhythm, cheerfully did all the jobs assigned to him and felt quite content, even if he did find the strict observation of the

Sabbath a little trying sometimes. He had even found it quite easy to hand over his scrolls. The order did not allow the monks to have possessions of their own, which was why Jesus' scrolls were now stacked with all the others in the library. He also had to hand in his clothes. Now he too was wearing his own white habit. But he did not seem bothered by this either. The abbot was pleased to see how easily he adapted and he savoured the time they spent working together in the library. But today his mind was wandering. The fine weather outside was tempting, so he said,

"What do you reckon, Jesus, shall we have a walk and see how the herbs are doing in the garden?"

Jesus jumped up straight away.

"Yes, please!" he replied happily. "The lavender smells so lovely at the moment! And I want to know how the camomile is doing. Brother Levi told me all about its healing powers. Isn't it wonderful, the way God makes sure we can find everything we need in nature?"

The abbot smiled, affected by the boy's childlike enthusiasm.

"It certainly is wonderful, Jesus!" he said and rested his hand on the boy's head for a moment.

They walked outside, crossed the courtyard and opened the gate to the garden. Levi was weeding. He gave an amused smile when he saw the two of them, their leader, tall and solid, next to the little boy so vulnerable and touching in his white robes. They walked along the flowerbeds and Jesus chatted freely about everything he had learned.

"Look, these are marigolds. If you make tea from them, they will cure a headache. And if you boil water with camomile and put your head over the steam, that will help cure a cold. And look here, the lavender is flowering even more nicely than yesterday!"

"I can see you've already learned quite a lot," said the abbot, complimenting him. "I'd like to hear you talk more about what you know. Let's go and sit in the shade over there."

When they had sat down, he asked,

"Tell me Jesus, you know the Torah inside out, don't you? So what were the ten commandments Moses was given up on the mountain?"

Jesus did not hesitate for a moment: he recited the text in question off by heart with not a single error. The abbot nodded approvingly.

"I can see you don't have any problem with that. But tell me, which do you think is the most important of the ten commandments?"

Jesus frowned and thought for a moment. Then he answered,

"I don't see any of the ten commandments as being the most important. But I do see a common theme running through all ten, making them into a single whole. And that theme is love - it's there in all of them. Because if you love someone you won't kill him and you certainly won't lie to him. And why would you steal or covet what someone else has got? After all, if you're full of love, the only thing you can is honour God and your fellow man."

The abbot was astounded by his answer. He recognised in the boy's words the wisdom he had been given by God.

"Your answer reveals a deep understanding, Jesus. Tell me, who taught you this truth?"

Once again, Jesus paused for thought before answering:

"I don't know. I have the feeling no-one taught me but the truth has always been revealed to me, even though I may not always have been able to put it into words. And I think that when people open up the windows to their soul, they too will be able to receive the truth. Because the truth can get in through any gap, any window or any open door."

"But how are people supposed to be able to open that window?" asked the abbot. "Which hand do you think is strong enough to open the windows and doors to the soul and let the truth enter?"

And Jesus said,

"I think that love, the common theme linking the ten commandments, is strong enough to open any door and let the truth in so that people will understand the secret of God in their hearts."

The older man nodded and they sat in silence for a moment. But then he questioned Jesus again. He looked at the boy and asked gently,

"And Jesus, what do you think your role is here?"

He saw Jesus become pensive and a shadow passed over his face. And it was a while before he answered, his voice trembling:

"I don't know what role God has in mind for me. I feel He is trying to come into contact with me and He puts wise words in my mouth. But it's not clear to me how or why."

He wiped his forehead with a weary gesture and continued,

"I don't understand how I could do anything when I'm just a small boy. I just know it makes me feel uncertain and even a bit scared sometimes."

He smiled shyly at his master because this was quite a confession. The abbot put an arm around his skinny shoulders.

"Perhaps we can help you with this," he said cheerfully in the hope it would encourage the boy. "You clearly don't need any more Torah lessons. And we can leave the writing in the scriptorium to others as well. What would be good for you is learning how to meditate. Meditation will bring you closer to God and that will certainly help you understand what His intentions are for you. And it will undoubtedly stop you being afraid. After all, as you said yourself, it's love that links the ten commandments. Well, that love must come from God Himself! And if God is love, surely there's no need to be afraid of Him?"

But now Jesus replied without hesitation.

"But maybe there is," he said decidedly. "Too much love can be smothering and stop you feeling free. I hope that I, Jesus, won't end up trapped by God's good intentions."

Once again the older man was amazed at the boy's insight.

"You're right," he admitted reluctantly, "But that is still what He is asking of us. There will only be room for Him once you put your own wishes to one side. So if you want to know what He has planned for you, you'll have to learn to listen to Him alone rather than your own ego. That's quite an order, I know. But that's why we are here to help you. Because it's definitely not God's intention for you to feel trapped. And that won't happen either. I can assure you that the closer you come to Him, the more you will feel His love. So, what do you think? Are you ready to take on that challenge?"

Jesus nodded in relief, pleased that he did not have to face this on his own.

"But I would like to carry on working in the garden!" he then said. "And Nathan promised he would teach me how to ride a horse. I'll still be able to do that, won't I?"

"Of course," laughed the abbot. "If that's what you want, go ahead and do so!"

The monastery's meditation room was an intimate space hewn from the rock. Jesus liked spending time there as the serene silence helped him achieve the calm he needed to find God in his heart. The presence of his Father consumed him and sometimes he would feel His energy from the tips of his fingers down to his toes.

He had now been living in the monastery for two years and Nathan had willingly taught him how to ride a horse. From the very first lesson, Jesus had shown he could relate to the horses in a special way. He had natural authority, which made it easy for him to win their trust and he mastered the art of horse riding in no time. He liked all the horses but was particularly fond of the handsome grey mare Bianco. He would regularly take her out and ride with Nathan on the plain surrounding the monastery. His attempts at pottery were less successful. He was unable to get the hang of it, despite the patient assistance of brother Michael. He would turn the wheel too fast, or too slowly, and the clay would worm its way between his fingers and mutate into all kinds of shapes. Often, his shrieks of delight reverberated through the workshop when he managed once again to produce some fantastic monstrosity. His happy presence warmed the hearts of the monks.

His master had taught him Greek and Latin and now that he knew these languages, he was starting to read the Greek philosophers Plato and Socrates. The way in which Socrates talked about the divine spark he felt inside made Jesus feel a genuine connection with him and when he read that he had been condemned to drink the cup of poison, tears came to his eyes. Plato's theory of ideas also intrigued him. It seemed related to his memory of God's overwhelming love, which he still cherished even if he never mentioned it to anyone. He could really understand what Plato meant: that this world was but a feeble reflection of the real world.

On his parents' last visit, his father had told him more about the three wise men who had visited him shortly after he had been born in Bethlehem. As one of the men had been an expert on the teachings of Zarathustra, Jesus had asked his master if by any chance there were writings by Zarathustra in the library. To his great surprise, the abbot was indeed able to bring out some books. Jesus had started reading them the very same morning. He was immediately gripped by the beauty of the texts and in some strange way it felt as if he had seen them before. He lost track of the time. The abbot noticed he was missing at lunch and went to the library afterwards. There he found his pupil totally absorbed by his reading.

"Are you still studying Zarathustra?" he asked curiously.

Jesus started. He had not heard the man come in. Then he nodded.

"Yes, that's right. I'm reading the Gathas at the moment. Those texts are so beautiful! They are a perfect description of my feelings for my Father. Here, listen to this!"

And he read:

"I, your steadfast pupil, who have followed
The straight path of truth and justice,
And who will learn from Your wisdom,
How I can best do that which must be done,
I ask you, my Lord: Bless me with Your vision,
Honour me with Your presence.

Come to me as You are, oh Lord,
Come unmistakably, oh Greatest one,
And inspire me with Your truth and wisdom,
Let my message spread beyond the boundaries of my land,
And let me carry that message with the help of Your spirit.

And I offer to You, my Lord, my life's work as a sacrifice,
And even myself and the most essential of my thoughts,
And I shall obey and devote myself to the truth,
In word and deed, with all the strength of mind I possess."

There was a moment's silence when he had finished reading. Both let the words enter their hearts. Then, in a voice that betrayed both wonderment and a little disbelief, Jesus said,

"What do you think? This is about me, isn't it?"

And he suddenly started to sob piteously. His shoulders shook and his face was drenched in tears in no time. The abbot got up in a flash, rushed over to the boy and embraced him lovingly. His comforting helped Jesus. He soon regained control of himself and said apologetically,

"Sorry for breaking down like that. But for some reason this really moves me! And I'm not crying because I'm sad, even if it may seem that way; no, I'm crying because I'm happy! I always thought I was the only one who had such a special bond with God. And I just couldn't work out why He chose to anoint me of all people with His light, from this infinite cosmos that is His. But now I've found a brother. Because Zarathustra must have felt the same thing too. It almost seems like our souls are one. But how can that be? After all, he lived so long ago."

The abbot took his hands and squeezed them.

"It may well be as you say, Jesus," he said encouragingly. "We believe at any rate that when you die, your soul returns to God, but not necessarily for eternity. You may also return to Earth if you feel you still have unfinished business or because your presence can help bring about God's kingdom. Perhaps I came back because I was supposed to get to know you and teach you this. And perhaps Zarathustra's soul really does live on through you."

He saw Jesus withdraw into himself and become pensive, a familiar habit ever since they had met and something he admired so much in the boy. Always he was able to digest new information and work things out for himself. He never rejected anything out of hand. The boy's mouth showed the beginnings of a cautious smile and his eyes glowed warmly.

"That's a lovely thought," he said with a sigh. "And in more ways than one. Because it not only makes me feel honoured to be so closely connected with Zarathustra but it must mean that I really have lived with my Father before and have felt His love."

"More than that!" said his master. "I suspect your soul has been there several times and has lived here on Earth several times before. That's the only way I can explain that you have been given perhaps the most important task of all to carry out. God would never impose that burden on you if He didn't think you were up to it. But apparently He thinks the time is ripe now, after what may be centuries of preparation."

He squeezed Jesus' hands again and continued:

"Perhaps you can consider, Jesus, whether you ever feel homesick for something that you can't really put your finger on. If you recognise that feeling, that is undoubtedly because you have been there before, in the spirit world."

Jesus had to hold back a cry of surprise and he called out,

"Of course I recognise that feeling! I've felt that so often. If ever I see something that really seems so unjust, for instance. Then I feel - no, then I *know* - that I've been somewhere where there's no injustice and where respect and love are self-evident. That must have been there, when I lived with God!"

The abbot smiled.

"That is unquestionably the case," he agreed. "And then you will probably recognise the feeling that there is a huge chasm between that world and this world."

Jesus nodded at once.

"Yes, I see that chasm," he said earnestly. "And sometimes I barely know how to bridge it. I even sometimes get the feeling I'm a stranger here. I look around in amazement, like a visitor to a strange city who doesn't know the way and doesn't understand the customs."

Now it was his turn to squeeze his master's hands as he said,

"Thank you for telling me all this and for understanding what it feels like for me. I haven't been able to talk to anyone about this up to now. Hopefully now I'll be able to read these beautiful texts without bursting into tears!"

He rubbed his cheeks dry, then burst out laughing.

"Did I really miss lunch? No wonder I'm so hungry!"

His master laughed too. He jumped up and said,

"Well, come on then! Let's see if we can find you something to eat!"

He extinguished the oil lamp and together they left the dark room, emerging into the bright sunlight outside as they made their way to the kitchen.

One day, Jesus and his master were sitting in the monk's room working at the table. Jesus was reading new parts of the Vedas and the older man was copying a text, deep in concentration. But Jesus was unable to keep his attention on what he was reading, which was very unusual for him. His mind kept wandering and after a while he gave up and put the book to one side. He looked at the head of the order and listened to his quill scratching busily on the parchment. He saw his familiar face and the wisdom it expressed. And breaking the silence, he said,

"Can I ask you something?"

The abbot looked up.

"Of course you can," he said and he put down his quill.

"It has to do with something you said to me when my parents brought me here," continued Jesus. "I remember I asked you your name. And you said it was safer if I didn't know it as you could well be the biggest enemy of many powerful men in this country. I've never forgotten that, because you have always seemed to me to be a gentle, sympathetic person. How could anyone see you as an enemy? Whose enemy are you and why? I don't understand."

The abbot stood up and paced back and forth, deep in thought. Then he asked Jesus a question of his own.

"Tell me, Jesus, what picture do you have of the task that awaits you? What do you think the message is that God wants you to spread?"

Jesus replied without hesitation,

"That people should open up their hearts to God's light. That they should reflect on things and put their egos to one side so that there is room for God's word. And if people hear that word and understand it, they will meet God face to face and experience perfect happiness and perfect love. And then the kingdom of God will have arrived."

His master nodded, moved by the words.

"How beautifully you express this, Jesus!" he said, warmly. "But that message also contains the threat that my enemies are so afraid of. Because as you just said, people can rely on their own strengths to achieve this, can't they?"

Jesus nodded hesitantly. He was not sure where his master was headed.

"So they don't need any priests for it," added the abbot. "They don't need to go to the temple to make sacrifices. They don't need to put money in the offertory box or pay temple taxes. Do you understand what the threat is, Jesus? That clique of priests in the temple who think they are so important and earn a packet at the expense of the poor; your message will make those priests... redundant. Worse than that - you will be showing them up for what they truly are! You see why they'll do anything to make sure that doesn't happen!"

Jesus absorbed what he had just said. Then he added seriously,

"You know, I can see even more happening. For that problem with those priests, well, that's nothing in the grand scheme of things. Because if people only feel love, that will set the Roman Empire quaking on its foundations. People will no longer accept that loveless occupation. And if people are no longer interested in material gain, that will mean the end of the economic order too."

"You are quite right," nodded the abbot. "The coming of the kingdom of God will indeed lead to an unprecedented revolution! So your message will meet a lot of resistance."

He sat down again and took hold of Jesus' hands.

"I don't want to frighten you," he said earnestly. "But you must be brave enough to face the truth. They will try to oppose you with every means at their disposal. They will call you a liar, threaten you and accuse you of blasphemy. They may even try to kill you. That is why we have tried to make you resilient so that you will be willing to stand your ground. And you have learned not to be too attached to this world so that it will be easier for you to take leave of it when you have to. I can only give you one good piece of advice: do what the voice of God tells you in your heart. Remain true to yourself and faithful to Him. That's the only way to keep your credibility, to project it and be able to achieve things. Let God decide when you need to start your work. Do nothing that goes against your con-science. Then it will turn out fine."

He looked at the boy and saw that his words had made a deep impression on him. For a moment he felt sorry for that slender child sitting so quietly opposite him. The boy was eleven now. Other kids of his age were playing in the streets, but he was bearing the happiness and future of the human race on his shoulders. He squeezed his hands and said, in an attempt to break the tension,

"We'll end our lesson there for today, Jesus. What do you think? Might Levi need your help in the garden?"

"I suppose he might," replied Jesus in a subdued tone. "But first I'd like to think about all what you've said. If you don't mind, I'll go to my room. And I would like to be excused from lunch. I don't have that much of an appetite today."

He stood up and left the room. Contrary to his usual demeanour, he appeared rather depressed. His master shook his head. Was this responsibility perhaps too great for those small shoulders to bear? Was it really fair to ask so much of him when he was so young? And he turned to God and asked for the wisdom to take the right decisions in his supervision of this special boy.

Jesus did not appear at dinner that evening. Matheno, who always used to collect him, had not found him in his room. And he was not there for evening prayers either. The abbot sent a few brothers to search the monastery. But they returned empty handed. It seemed as if the boy had disappeared off the face of the Earth. Their leader bit his lip and cursed himself. Should he have spoken so openly? Should he have given the boy such a burden to bear when he might not yet be up to it? He remembered how depressed Jesus had looked and he could have kicked himself for having misjudged the situation so badly. Matheno saw his unease.

"Come now, I'm sure he can take care of himself," he said encouragingly, but he did not sound too convinced.

Dusk had now fallen and none of the brothers felt like going to bed when they did not know what had happened to Jesus. But the abbot ordered them to retire to their rooms. And he asked Nathan to keep watch. Nathan nodded in assent. After everyone had gone to bed, he decided to take one more look round the monastery. Perhaps his fellow brothers had overlooked something. He lit a lantern, walked through the garden and opened the heavy door to the stables. The horses shifted around restlessly. They were not used to seeing him at this time of day. He calmed them and stroked his own mare on the nose. Softly he whispered,

"You don't know either where Jesus is, do you? What a pity!"

He walked past the stalls and filled up some of the mangers. Then, all of a sudden, he realised that one stall at the end was empty. The grey horse Jesus always liked to ride was gone. In dismay he stared at the empty stall. He slowly grasped that Jesus had taken Bianco with him. And that meant he could be anywhere now. He spun round and ran back across the garden, through the courtyard to the abbot's room. He carefully shook the man's shoulder to wake him up.

"Sorry for disturbing you," he said frantically. "But I was in the stables and Bianco is gone. Jesus must have taken her with him!"

The abbot was silent for a moment as he absorbed this information. Then he said with relief,

"Good! I think he made a wise decision in taking Bianco with him. He will be less vulnerable with Bianco and now the nights are so cold, the horse will keep him warm."

He shook Nathan's hand.

"Thank you for bringing me this message. I don't think I'll be able to get back to sleep tonight so I'll take over the watch for now. You go to bed. We'll see about things tomorrow."

Nathan nodded and retired to his room. And the abbot waited up in the hope that Jesus would soon return.

After the conversation with his master in the morning, Jesus had gone back to his room. He felt downcast and confused. Until now he had experienced the contact with God to be loving and inspiring. It was not always easy, but he had had a positive feeling about it. It was no coincidence that he had got into the habit of calling Him his Abba. He was convinced that God had his best interests at heart, that they stood for something together and that His Father was going to make sure his mission was successful no matter what. But now the words his master had spoken, had put everything in a very different perspective. It was not going to be as straightforward as he had thought. And even God's protection was apparently no guarantee of success. The abbot's words reverberated in his head: 'They will call you a liar, accuse you of blasphemy, even try to kill you!' Restlessly, he searched for a candle in his chest, put it on the table and lit it. Then he knelt in front of it. He turned to God and submitted all his fears and doubts to Him in the expectation that God would put him at ease. But God's reply was very clear.

"Did I ever promise you that it would be easy, Jesus? I believe I promised you that I would look after you, and I certainly will. But there will be difficulties. Your master was right."

His words cut through the boy's heart. Suddenly, the foundations for all the confidence he had had, all his former motivation, had gone.

"Surely that won't happen if You are looking after me?" he called out wordlessly. "You call me Your son, I call You my Abba. And then this is what awaits me?"

And once more he heard his master's words reverberating in his head: 'Liar, blasphemer! Liar, blasphemer!'

Still agitated, he stood upright and fury welled up in him. Why had God not made this clear to him before? He had been here four years now. He had worked hard for four years - but what for? To be branded a liar? To be threatened? He had invested four years of his young life in a mission, the success of which now seemed far from certain. In a fit of anger, he kicked his table and the candle rolled onto the ground, the flame dying out slowly on the cold stone floor. And Jesus ran outside in a rage. The sun was high in the sky. It was midday and his fellow brothers would be eating their lunch. This meant he was able to reach the main building and cross the courtyard unnoticed. His steps took him in the direction of the stables. For there was only one thing he wanted: to get away from this place where he had wasted so much time, valuable time that he could have spent doing other things. He opened the heavy door. His favourite horse Bianco lifted her head and whinnied in recognition of him. Touched, he stroked her neck, lay a blanket across her back and saddled her. He picked up a leather water skin, filled it with water and hung it over his shoulder.

"Are you coming, girlie?" he whispered tenderly, on the verge of tears. "Will you take me to... I don't know where? To somewhere where I can live with no cares and where I can just be myself again?"

Bianco inclined her head as if she had understood his words. Jesus opened the back door that led directly outside the complex, avoiding having to cross the courtyard again. This let him leave the monastery without anyone noticing. He mounted the horse and rode off, with no plan of what he was going to do or in which direction he was heading. He set Bianco galloping fast and soon he was far away, leaving the monastery and the life he had lived there behind him. The wind whistled in his ears and the rhythmic thud of Bianco's hooves was the only other sound he wanted to hear. But God had no intention of letting him escape so easily.

"Are you giving up so soon? I'm disappointed. Don't you trust Me?"

Jesus ignored the voice and carried on riding. He rode for a long time for a long way through the inhospitable landscape and time passed. After having ridden for what seemed like hours, he began to feel tired. It had been hot all afternoon and he was thirsty. He dismounted close to some rocks, sat down and drank from the water skin. He poured a little water into his hands and gave Bianco something to drink as well. It seemed for a moment as if he was just having a trouble-free day out. But God soon dashed that illusion because Jesus heard His voice again.

"Come on Jesus, surely you're not going to give up that easily? What have you been learning these past four years? I thought you were so tough and resilient. But it doesn't look that way now!"

Jesus stood up and stretched his muscles, which had become stiff from the long ride. He still refused to obey God's call to him to turn back. But God persisted,

"What are you actually planning on doing, Jesus? Are you really thinking of quitting? Have I been so wrong about you?"

Finally, Jesus could no longer take it.

"Stop it!" he screamed. "Stop it! I don't always have to do what You say! I'm here too! And yes, you're right. I am indeed giving up. Too right! It seems I'm not as fantastic and tough and resilient and whatever else I'm supposed to be after all. How terrible: You made a mistake! Jesus just wants to be Jesus, isn't that terrible!"

And he ran off, away from the voice in his head, away from his doubts, away from everything. God's voice sounded shocked when He answered,

"I'm quite sure I did not make a mistake, Jesus! And I am also quite sure that you are making a mistake now. Because you can't avoid your calling. Believe Me, if you give up now you will regret it later, I'm convinced of that!"

But Jesus had no intention of being influenced by the sound of God's voice. He pounded his temples with his fists and screamed,

"Go away! I don't want this anymore! I never asked for this anyway. Go away, go away!"

God saw that he was serious and in His infinite wisdom He withdrew. Jesus suddenly felt a gap in his heart. God left behind an emptiness he had not known before. But instead of feeling relieved, he felt bewildered. How was this possible? Was he - a mere boy - able to send God packing just like that? Surely that was impossible! He could only do that if... if... He dared not think further. But a tiny voice in the back of his head would not leave him alone, teasing him, saying,

"Where does that God of yours actually come from, Jesus? If you can just send Him away like that, could it be that you also summoned Him yourself? Or did you really think you were so special...?"

Once again, Jesus beat his fists against his head.

"Shut up!" he cried desperately. "Shut up! I don't want to hear any more! I don't want to hear any more and I don't want to know! I'm not mad, am I?"

These last words sounded very uncertain and Jesus no longer felt in control. The teasing little voice would not go away and suddenly he started to doubt everything: the voice he had heard, which obviously had not been the voice of God at all but just a mere figment of his imagination; his memories of his previous life in the spiritual world, which had clearly been something his own spirit had fabricated; his bond with Zarathustra that was completely baseless. The only thing he actually knew for certain was that he wanted to go home, to the familiar surroundings of Nazareth, to his family and his bedroom in the house on Marmion street. And all at once he could smell the scent of freshly sawn wood and could see his father clearly in his mind's eye, hard at work in the workshop.

He looked at his habit and felt suddenly repulsed by the thought of having to wear it. He tore open the neck and pulled it roughly over his head. He flung it away, for it belonged with a life he no longer wanted to lead. And he whistled to Bianco. The faithful mare came up to him immediately. He mounted the horse and brought her to a brisk trot in the direction he thought Bethany must be. But darkness was falling fast by then and it soon turned cold. The wind cut through the thin shirt he always wore under his habit. He shivered. He had never spent the night in the desert before and he had not realised that it could be so chilly at night when it was so blisteringly hot during the day. He noticed Bianco was slowing down. It was now so dark that he could barely see his hands in front of him and he began to feel a little sorry for deciding to take off so impulsively. He pulled on the reins, brought Bianco to a halt and considered the situation. What should he do? Another shiver ran down his back. It was getting extremely cold now so he decided to at any rate turn round and look for his habit. He turned Bianco and they went back to the same spot, at a gentler pace now. He soon found the place where he had pulled off his robes and it was still lying there, a pale white shape on the ground, just visible. Pleased that he had been able to find it back so easily in the darkness, he dismounted and quickly pulled it back on. However it did not make him feel much warmer and his teeth started to chatter.

He looked around him and saw the vague contours of some rocks in the distance that would protect him from the wind. He led Bianco there by the reins and once they got to the rocks, he took the saddle off her back, grabbed the blanket from underneath and wrapped it around himself. The blanket was warm from being next to Bianco's body and he felt a little better. He stroked the horse on the nose, whispered in her ear and gently pushed her until she lay down. He curled up next to her and pulled the blanket around him. He lay there warm and sheltered. But his heart felt like a stone in his body, cold and empty. Gradually he began to consider the consequences of his action. He would have to live further without the comforting illusion of a God who cared for him. For a moment he felt torn apart. But at the same time he was determined to show that he could very well manage without!

He snuggled down deeper under the blanket in the hope that he would fall asleep. But his thoughts were too agitated. He realised he would first need to inform his master of his decision before returning home. Having established this course of action, he began to relax. And soon he dozed off to sleep with the plan in his head to look for the way back to the monastery the next day.

The following day, the abbot was working in his room. However he was unable to keep his attention focused on his text. His mind kept wandering. He thought about Jesus and wondered where he could be. He had hoped the boy would return in the morning but it was late afternoon now and they had still seen no sign of him. He sighed and wondered if he should do something. At the same time, he knew he had to trust in God and have faith that He would take good care of the boy. He rested his head in his hands and tried to concentrate on his book, but without success. Suddenly he heard a strange commotion. Excited voices could be heard in the corridor and someone abruptly threw the door open. It was Matheno. He was beaming as he called,

"The guard on the tower! He's seen them. Bianco! With Jesus! He's coming back!"

The abbot jumped up.

"Thank heavens!" he sighed with relief. "Well, don't stand there like that! Go to the gate, quickly!"

Matheno nodded and ran off. He soon returned, bringing Jesus with him. The abbot was shocked at the sight of the boy. His habit was dirty and torn. His face was pale with dark rings around his eyes. And his voice sounded bitter as he said,

"I have taken a decision. I want to go back home. I think I've spent long enough here."

The abbot walked up to him and made as if to put a hand on his shoulder. But Jesus stepped back and said, pushing him away,

"You don't need to try and change my mind. My decision is final."

His attitude was unbending. But his master was not one to give up that easily.

"Come and sit down first, Jesus," he said in a conciliatory tone. "You can't have had much to eat. I insist you get some food inside you first. And please, let's talk about it."

"That's not necessary," replied Jesus coolly and his words increased the distance between them even further. "I've already discussed this with my Fa... with God. He knows my opinion on the matter. There's nothing more to say on the subject."

The abbot shook his head, appalled at what the boy had said.

"You can't mean this, Jesus!" he said in dismay. "I thought we had developed a bond these past few years. You can't just ignore that by behaving like this."

He noticed that his words were having some effect. Jesus was hesitating slightly.

"Come now," he insisted. "You need to eat."

He went over to the cupboard, retrieved some bread and fruit and put it on the table. He sat down and gestured in invitation. Jesus was clearly struggling inwardly. His face betrayed great emotion. The abbot said nothing and waited. And Jesus fought a lonely battle. Once again he experienced the struggle he had gone through the night before with God and with himself. Sending his Abba away like that and renouncing his destiny had had more of an effect on him than he was willing to admit. Now he had made that difficult choice, he was not prepared to be talked out of it just like that. But neither did he want to make his master sad.

"Just eat something then," he said curtly and he sat down at the table.

He ate in silence and the abbot said nothing either. Until the silence became painful and Jesus started to feel uncomfortable. Fortunately his master helped him out by saying,

"I was so pleased you took Bianco with you! The nights are very cold here. You might not have survived if you had been on your own."

Jesus was deeply touched by his friendly words. He could no longer eat because of the sudden lump in his throat. And the abbot continued,

"I should offer you my excuses, Jesus. I made you face up to what might happen to you because I thought you would be able to cope, but I was wrong. Please forgive me."

Jesus pushed his plate to one side and shrugged testily.

"None of that matters anymore," he replied impassively. "I'm not going any further with this anyway. I now know for certain I was only imagining it all. How could I have been so arrogant to think God had chosen me for such an elevated task? I think I rather lost my way. But now I know where I stand again. I'd like to go home and start my apprenticeship as a carpenter."

"That's fine," nodded the abbot, showing his great wisdom.
"We'll arrange that tomorrow. But first you should get a good night's sleep."

He stood up and called Matheno.

"Matheno, will you make sure Jesus gets a nice hot bath? And please put up a bed in your tent. He will be sleeping with you tonight."

"Of course, master!" nodded Matheno. "I'll sort that out."

And he took the boy with him. Despite everything, Jesus took intense pleasure in the bath. Normally, only ritual cold baths were allowed in the monastery and hot baths were considered an unnecessary luxury. But now the warm water drove out the cold that had taken hold of his bones the night before, and he emerged from the tub pink all over. On top of that, when they got to Matheno's tent, his friend produced a jug of wine.

"Don't tell anyone, will you!" he said conspiratorially, pouring a small cupful for the boy and a large mugful for himself.

Jesus smiled and shook his head. That Matheno! They sipped at the tart wine and when Matheno had emptied his mug, he poured himself a second one.

"You know what, Jesus," he said, the drink having made him more expansive. "Everyone has a period of doubt at some point in their life. Everyone wonders occasionally whether God really exists. Isn't that something we all struggle with? In fact, as soon as we start believing He exists we immediately start doubting it again. That's a normal, human reaction. But I'd never expected it from you. You always seemed so sure."

Jesus shrugged. He was not really in the mood to discuss the matter.

"Yes, I know," he replied reluctantly, and really only so as not to disappoint his friend. "But who is to say it wasn't just my imagination? I think you can only be sure after you die. Only then do we really know whether He is indeed waiting lovingly for us. But it could equally be the case that we have been fooling ourselves all along and that there isn't anything at all."

Matheno shook his head, disconcerted. Then he leant a little closer to the boy and whispered confidentially,

"But I do know for sure that there is something, Jesus! And I'll prove it to you by telling you something I have never told anyone else apart from our master. It's a very precious memory but I'm willing to share it with you because I think you... will appreciate it."

His voice sounded increasingly impassioned and Jesus looked at him in surprise. He had never seen his friend getting so emotional. Matheno swallowed. Then he said:

"Once when I was a boy I fell in a deep ditch filled with water. I nearly drowned but luckily a local boy was able to pull me out of the water just in time. A fairly ordinary story so far, you could say. But when I fell in that water and sank deeper and deeper, I had the strangest experience! The only way I can explain it is to say that I was outside my body, though I've no idea how. I entered a dark tunnel but I wasn't frightened at all because at the end of the tunnel I could see the most unimaginably beautiful light! I was sucked through that tunnel incredibly fast until I became surrounded by that marvellous light. And I was enveloped in pure love. Everything was filled with understanding, respect and appreciation. I was overwhelmed by all that loving attention. I had never felt so totally happy before. But all of a sudden it ended. I was promptly pulled back through the tunnel by an invisible hand and dropped back inside my body. The first thing I saw when I opened my eyes was the boy who had saved me."

His voice stopped and Jesus saw tears in his eyes. He too felt tears welling up because what Matheno had told him was so familiar to him and intensely he missed God's love. Fervently, he took Matheno's hand and kissed it.

"I understand so well what you mean," he stammered. "If only you knew how homesick I get sometimes! But now I'm back to being Jesus again, carpenter's apprentice and nothing more."

Matheno heard the determination in his voice and in a surge of emotion, he put his arms around the boy.

"Still, that isn't the right choice, Jesus. After all, you are our promised one. We've been waiting for you to come for so long. God Himself will look after you and be waiting there to greet you, I'm sure of that."

Jesus was deeply touched by his words. And he realised that the suit of armour he had surrounded himself with was just a thin shell. He assiduously extracted himself from Matheno's embrace.

"I'm off to bed," he said, avoiding Matheno's eyes. "Thanks for confiding in me. Your story is safe with me... but you knew that anyway."

He undressed and curled up in his blanket.

"Sleep well, Matheno," he said, yawning. "And don't drink too much wine - that's not good for you."

Matheno sighed, then said calmly,

"Good night, Jesus. And no, I won't do that."

Jesus turned over and soon fell asleep. Despite his promise, Matheno drank the entire jug of wine, only then getting into his own bed.

The following morning the abbot called for Jesus. The good night's sleep had done the boy good, but he was still determined to stick to his decision. He sat there rather reluctantly, not really prepared to get into conversation.

"So," said his master, "was the wine good?"

Jesus looked up in surprise. He could feel he was blushing slightly. But he asked innocently,

"Wine? What wine?"

The abbot burst out laughing.

"You are a reliable friend, I see," he noted with satisfaction. "Don't worry. Matheno told me everything, including what you discussed. I understand his story made quite an impression on you."

"It was recognisable in some respects," said Jesus blandly.

"Ever experienced anything like that yourself?" asked the abbot with an air of nonchalance as he poured a cup of water.

"Not in that way," replied Jesus evasively, wondering in the meantime where this conversation was headed.

"As it happens, you can get an out-of-body experience like that sometimes in meditation," explained the abbot as he moved to sit opposite the boy. "So you might have. It's happened to me once. But I did have the help then of the person who was leading the meditation."

He lent slightly towards Jesus.

"I can help you if you want," he offered. "I would be happy for you to experience this and it may help you find a way out of this impasse."

Jesus saw that his master meant what he said. His body tensed nervously. The idea that he could take a look in God's world excited him.

"Have you done that before?" he asked hesitantly.

The abbot nodded.

"Yes, a few times."

"And did it always work?"

The monk nodded again.

"Yes, it works if you are prepared to relinquish control."

On edge, Jesus stood up and paced round the room a couple of times agitatedly. The desire to find his Father again burned passionately in his soul. And the thin shell of armour was pierced. He turned to his master and said in an emotional voice,

"I think I need to thank you for this opportunity. I'm not sure what I will find but I'm willing to take the chance."

"Then let's take the bull by the horns," smiled the abbot and he too stood up.

Jesus followed him and the two of them went out through the gate. They walked a long way in silence until they came to a small spring. There, they sat down.

"Are you ready, Jesus?" asked the abbot in a friendly voice. "Then close your eyes and listen carefully to my voice. Visualise everything I say. Don't think of anything else, just try to concentrate fully on what I am saying, all right?"

Jesus nodded. He closed his eyes and let himself be transported to a wonderful lake with not a ripple on the surface and that was not set in motion by any thoughts. He felt himself sink into a pleasantly relaxed trance and the abbot's voice seemed to become part of him. Now he was walking up stairs, higher and higher. At the top of the stairs was a door. He opened it, curious to see what was behind it.

And all of a sudden a wave of energy swept over him like a hurricane. He lost all contact with the Earth from one moment to the next and was hurled into another dimension. He no longer sensed his body and the waves rushed through him and over him. He was being carried in a purple sea of love and happiness, with a shining light ahead of him, sparkling like a jewel, erupting with golden gleaming stars like a ball of fire, and radiating energy: powerful, empowering, overpowering. It enveloped him on all sides, surrounding him and permeating him, tingling, vibrating, pulling, tempting.

He was like a ship, a mere plaything of the waves. There was no longer any up or down and time too lost its meaning. He sped along with that shining light in front all the time and he felt that all was good: benefaction, peace, space, love. There was nothing more being asked of him and he let himself be carried, in complete surrender. Then, all at once, he heard God's voice in his head.

"Welcome, Jesus. I'm pleased you are here again!"

Jesus' heart missed a beat of happiness. He realised how important that voice was to him, how much his contact with God meant to him. And God spoke,

"The energy you feel is that of my Holy Spirit, who is on his way to help you with your task. He has already descended through many spheres and the reason you can feel him now is because he is already close to Earth. But your time has not yet come. You are still young and have a lot to learn. That is why your decision to leave the monastery is a good one. You will learn more outside than cloistered within its walls. So follow your intuition and seize the opportunities that come your way. And remember that I will be watching over you and will give you the strength you need to carry out your task. Well, what do you think - will this help you continue? Do you have the courage to do that?"

Jesus felt that he was completely at one with the overwhelming energy surrounding him while the sense of security given by God filled him to overflowing. Touched, he nodded and wallowed deep in this loving attention. He had never felt so perfectly happy before. Then he heard the abbot's voice in the distance calling him back. Reluctantly he detached himself from God's warm embrace. He wiggled his toes to regain contact with his body. This brought him back.

The abbot saw how he beamed. And Jesus was full of what he had experienced. So full that he had the feeling he would burst unless he gave some expression to the deluge of impressions welling up in him. He jumped up ecstatically and trying to put his feelings into words and unload that enormous charge of energy, he called out,

"I have to ... I have to ... run!"

He rushed off at once and sprinted across the plain. The abbot watched as he threw his arms into the air while he ran, as if he wanted to embrace heaven itself, then running in wide circles with his arms outstretched like wings and twisting and turning like a bird in the wind. And he ran and ran and ran. It was a long while before he was standing in front of his master again, panting but still beaming. Then he hugged him and said,

"I now know everything and I have learned everything I need to continue further. If possible, I would really like to go back home. I know my mother misses me and my father has a lot of work, so he could do with my help."

The abbot nodded with a smile.

"We'll start the preparations for your departure tomorrow," he said.

Jerusalem

Jesus found it wonderful to be home again after his lengthy stay at the monastery. He enjoyed being able to sleep in his own room, which James had relinquished for him, albeit with very poor grace. He took great delight in helping Miriam with her first attempts at learning to read and write, and he proved to be a patient teacher.

Joseph went to work energetically about making a skilled carpenter of his son. They worked together in the carpentry workshop every day and Joseph taught him all the tricks of the trade. Jesus was pleased to be doing some honest physical work again. His slender boy's body developed rapidly into that of a muscular adolescent and Mary realised that his leaving the monastery had signalled the end of his childhood days. Joseph soon made a useful handyman of him and took him along when he went to work at the customers. In fact, he had soon become so useful that Joseph wanted to reward him for his efforts. So he called him over one day and said,

"I reckon I still owe you that visit to the temple, Jesus. Remember? Well, it's nearly Passover. How would you like to go to Jerusalem with me? We can celebrate Passover there together."

Delighted, Jesus embraced his father round the neck.

"Oh, father, thank you so much!" he exclaimed. "Now I'll finally be able to visit the House of our Lord that Solomon built so lovingly!"

He started counting down the days until it was finally time to go.

It was incredibly busy in Jerusalem. People were streaming to the holy city from all over the country to commemorate their nation's flight from Egypt. Joseph first found the inn where they were going to be staying the night and they dropped their luggage off there. Only then were they able to find their way to the temple complex. Jesus' heart was pounding with excitement. When they reached the famous building, he stood there, stunned, looking up at the tall and graceful pillars. It seemed to him that they were reaching right up into the heavens and when he put the palm of his hand on one, it felt as if he had a direct connection to God. Joseph saw how moved he was. Understanding perfectly how he felt, he took the boy by the arm and said gently,

"Come on, son. There's a lot more to see here yet. Let's go inside and make an offering."

They went into the forecourt and Jesus was taken aback for a moment by just how busy it was. Joseph set off self-confidently in the right direction, though, and Jesus was pleased that his father was with him. As they were walking, Joseph told Jesus what all the buildings around the square were for. They exchanged some money for temple coins and bought a dove from one of the merchants to take to the altar. Jesus held the animal carefully. He could feel the warmth of its small body and how its heart was beating. Tenderly he stroked the feathers.

They now respectfully entered the actual temple building through the Beautiful Gate. Silently they took their places by the altar and knelt to ask God's blessing for their sacrifice. There were other people in the prayer room who had already given their sacrificial animal to the priest who was authorised to perform the ritual slaughter. Although Jesus was aware of what happened during the offering ritual, this was the first time that he had actually seen it in practice. He saw that the priest took a long, sharp knife and slit the throat of the sacrificial animal in a single clean stroke. The blood of the poor beast coloured the ground of the altar red and a sickly smell permeated the room. Jesus started to feel nauseous. A haze passed over his eyes and he did not see that the priest kindled a fire on the altar. He only realised what had happened when the pungent odour of burning flesh reached his nose. His mouth fell open in astonishment. The wonderful feeling that he had been experiencing up to that point was gone, instantly. Disillusioned, he looked at the dove in his hands and his whole being rebelled against this cruel state of affairs. He nudged Joseph and whispered,

"Father, why do these poor animals have to be killed like that? I can't imagine that God really approves."

Joseph shrugged.

"It's a ritual that's been performed for centuries," he said gently. "It seems to be something that people can relate to. Surely there's nothing wrong in that?"

But that answer did not satisfy Jesus. His heart was pounding with indignation and, on a whim, he threw his dove into the air. The bird flapped through the gate and escaped outside. Relieved that he had been able to save it, Jesus watched it fly off. Then he walked over to the altar and spoke bluntly to the officiating cleric.

"Please tell me: why are you killing these poor animals? Why are you burning their flesh for God? Are they not His creatures, just as we are?"

The priest looked at him examining. It was clear that he did not take the boy's remarks very seriously.

"The Torah says it clearly enough, young man," he replied somewhat condescendingly. "The sacrifices will atone for our sins. God Himself instructed us to do it this way. He said that these sacrifices will wash our sins away."

Jesus refused to be brushed aside like that, however, and said self-assuredly,

"So you claim that a sacrifice such as this will atone for our sins? I think that God means that the people should sacrifice themselves, that they should devote their lives to Him. After all, only then is it possible for a person to live without sin. And did not King David teach us that animal sacrifices are barbaric? Which it also says in the book of Isaiah, by the way."

The priest was clearly getting irritated by his words.

"My child, you do not know what you are talking about. Do you think you know more about God's laws than we do, the priests of Israel? Off with you, back to your father. This is no place for boys who just want to show off how smart they are."

He turned his back on him contemptuously. But Jesus did not give up so quickly. He ran out of the prayer room and Joseph, who had hardly dared to breathe as he listened to the whole scene, could do nothing but follow him. He saw his son head very deliberately for the building where the High Council sat and then go inside.

Jesus knocked on the first door he came across and opened it. He saw a priest who was sitting reading at a table.

"Excuse me sir for just barging in like this," he said politely, but with an icy undertone to his voice, "but I'm looking for the head of the High Council. Could you perhaps tell me where I can find him?"

The priest looked up at the interruption and scrutinised the boy. Then he said,

"Well, you've come to the right place. I'm Hillel, head of the Sanhedrin. So you want to speak to me?"

Jesus nodded vigorously.

"Yes, I do," he said with indignation, "because I'm upset about the service that's being held right now. I thought that the temple was the house of God, where love and goodness hold sway. But surely you can hear the bleating of those poor lambs and the frightened doves cooing that are about to be killed there for not good reason. And just smell the awful stench of all that burnt flesh! How is it possible that cruel acts like that are being performed in the house of my Father? I'm certain that God does not approve of these practices: for the God I have come to know is a God of love. But that's clearly not the God who lives in this temple!"

Hillel had not expected words of wisdom such as these from such a young boy. He looked at him, bewildered.

"I can see that you're very concerned about the fate of these animals," he said in a friendly tone. "I'm glad that you think that way about it, because it shows the purity of your heart."

His voice faltered for a moment, as Jesus' words had affected him more deeply than he wanted to admit. He stood up, walked over to the boy and put his hand on Jesus' shoulder. Touched, he said,

"My dear child, I know for certain that there is a God of love and if you think that He does not reside here, let us go forth together and search for that loving God."

But Jesus replied,

"I don't understand you. Why should we have to go anywhere to search for God? Isn't He everywhere? Don't we just have to open our hearts to Him and discard cruel and bad thoughts, so that we ourselves become temples where this loving God can live?"

Hillel, the grand master of the Sanhedrin, stood there tongue-tied. He looked at the boy opposite him in astonishment once again and he realised that he was looking at the master and expert on higher laws, a role he had always believed to be his own.

"Tell me," he inquired curiously. "Who are you, actually, and how did you get involved in this?"

"I'm here with my father Joseph," explained Jesus. "We've come here from Nazareth to celebrate Passover. My name is Jesus and I've been looking forward to visiting the house of God my Father all my life. I'm eleven now, and I was finally allowed to come. And then I see this! So you can imagine my disappointment!"

Hillel's heart skipped a beat when he heard those words. In a tense voice, he asked,

"Then your mother must be Mary, who lived here in the temple when she was a girl?"

Jesus nodded.

"That's right. But it seems that a lot has changed since then, because she always talks with the utmost respect about the priests who serve here. Unfortunately, it's not an opinion I share. It seems as if my master in Qumran was right to warn me about the things that go on here."

Hillel listened to him with mixed feelings. On the one hand, he understood that everything he had set in motion in preparation for the arrival of the Messiah had not been in vain for he recognised God's hand in the wisdom of Jesus' words and it seemed certain that this boy was being guided by God Himself. Nevertheless, Jesus' criticism of the customs at the temple confused him.

"Tell me, Jesus," he said. "How would you like to study at the temple school here for a while? It sounds to me as if you could learn a great deal about our traditions and why we do things the way we do."

Jesus looked up in surprise. He knew the Torah inside out and backwards - what could they teach him?

"Well, I'm not so sure that would be a good idea," he answered firmly. "After all, I haven't been very complimentary, have I?"

Hillel gave him an encouraging smile, though.

"Perhaps that's exactly why you should join us! I mean, a critical voice is more useful to us than somebody who can't add anything new. Come, let's ask your father what he thinks about it."

Jesus hesitated visibly, but did eventually follow Hillel from the room. They almost tripped over Joseph, who had sat down by the door waiting for his son to return. Hillel greeted him as an old friend and invited him cordially into the room. After they had caught up on each other's news, he asked,

"What do you think, Joseph? Would it be a good idea for Jesus to come and study at the temple school for a while? Given his destiny as a king from the line of David, he actually belongs in Jerusalem."

Joseph gave Jesus a questioning look.

"Have you already discussed this?" he asked, intrigued.

Jesus opened his mouth to answer his father's question, but Hillel spoke first.

"I've suggested it to Jesus," he said with a smile, "and I reckon he thought it was a good idea, didn't you, Jesus?"

Shocked, Jesus looked at him.

"Absolutely not!" he reprimanded the man sharply, without considering who he was speaking to. "In fact, I said quite clearly that I was unsure. And anyway, father, what's he talking about? I mean, I'm certainly not going to be a king like our forefather David once was? At any rate, God has never put it like that to me. I'm here to spread His message of love. That's surely something completely different?"

Joseph looked at Hillel.

"It seems clear enough to me," he said neutrally. "Jesus will just be coming back home with me."

The disappointment in his voice was clear as he added,

"I thought you were different, Hillel. That's how I remember you, anyway. When did you start letting those conservative followers of Shammai tell you what to do?"

For a moment, Hillel did not know how to handle that. Then he said apologetically,

"Maybe you're right, Joseph. Maybe I go with the flow a bit too much. Even so, I'd like to ask you both to reconsider my suggestion. It can't be right that Jesus won't accept his own traditions?"

But Jesus had no intention of letting the man manipulate him. Clearly irritated, he said,

"We've already said that we aren't at all keen on the idea. And now you dare to say that I'm denying our traditions – but you don't know the first thing about me! I don't know what your plans are, father, but I'm leaving. I don't see why I should stay here a moment longer."

He stood up, gave Hillel a brief nod, and then walked out of the room. A very uncomfortable silence remained. Joseph fiddled with his coat in embarrassment and Hillel did not seem to know what to do either.

"Don't get me wrong, Hillel," said Joseph at last. "I do trust you. But I'm worried about all the others here, the ones who think differently than we do. I genuinely believe that letting Jesus find his own way is the more sensible course of action. Please let's just give the boy a chance to come up with something really new. After all, the old way didn't bring us what we hoped for. Isn't it God's hand that we're now able to hope for a new start?"

Hillel was silent, painfully aware of the fact that Joseph was clearly right. He raised his gaze and looked Joseph in the eye. They stared at each other and realised that they understood one another. Then they went their separate ways. Joseph went looking for Jesus and finally found him with the merchant from whom they had bought the dove earlier in the day. He had bought three more doves with his last temple coins and Joseph watched as he released them with obvious delight.

A year passed by and Jesus, now aged twelve, worked with pleasure as carpenter's assistant. One day as he was planing planks with his father, he said suddenly,

"I'd like to go to Jerusalem again soon, father. I think that I should have a bar mitzvah, just like the other boys. So I would like to pick up my text for it so that I can prepare."

Joseph could only admire the fact that his son did not want to be any different from other boys.

"Why should you need to prepare?" he replied, however. "Isn't that completely unnecessary in your case?"

"It is," said Jesus with a sly grin, "but I'm interested to see what text they'll pick for me. And I want to show Hillel that I really do care about our traditions. I think it would be a good idea to teach that man a lesson!"

Joseph looked at him in bewilderment. He saw the twinkle of suppressed enjoyment in Jesus' eyes and burst out laughing.

"So that's the game, is it?" he said, surprised. "Right then. If that's what you want, we'd better pay them a visit soon."

Four of them made the trip: Joseph, Mary, Jesus and James. As they travelled, they joined up with others who were on their way from Galilee to the holy city. While James and Mary waited in the outer courtyard, Joseph went with Jesus to the Sanhedrin. Hillel's heart missed a beat with excitement when he noticed them among the other bar mitzvah candidates. He had not reckoned on ever seeing the boy again and feverishly, he and the other priests discussed which text they should select for him.

The texts were handed out at a special service on the Sabbath. The prayer room was busy. Just like Jesus' family, many parents had come with children who were visiting the temple with an eye on their coming bar mitzvah. They looked for a place to sit and then the service began. Jesus waited for a sign from Hillel that he should come forward. He squirmed about on the bench impatiently, feeling rather nervous after all. Hillel led the service punctiliously and finally the moment arrived for the texts to be handed out.

Hillel beckoned him forward, gesturing that he should come and stand behind the lectern. Jesus saw that they had laid out the book of prophets ready for him. His heart pounded with tense expectation. These were some of his favourite writings! Hillel browsed through the book. It seemed to Jesus that he was turning the pages torturously slowly. But finally he found the right text. He beckoned the boy over, saying in a loud voice,

"Jesus of Nazareth, we have selected the following text for you. You are allowed to prepare it, as you know. After all, your bar mitzvah isn't until next year. But you may read it for us now too, if you think you are up to it."

Jesus stepped forward. His eyes ran swiftly over the letters and he was relieved to see it was a text he knew. More than that - he had discussed it more than once with his master in Qumran. His tenseness disappeared.

"I would very much like to read it now, as you are giving me the opportunity," he stated confidently.

And he began to read.

"Woe to Ariel, to Ariel, the city where David dwelt. For a multitude of enemies shall descend upon thee as clouds of dust. Thou shalt be visited of the Lord of Hosts with thunder, and with earthquake, and great noise, with storm and tempest, and the flame of devouring fire. See, this people have deserted Me. Forasmuch as this people turn to Me with words and do honour Me with their lips, but their hearts are far removed from Me. And I shall blow a breath of ill wind over My people Israel; the wisdom of their wise men shall perish. Yet it shall not always be so, and the time shall come that the fruitful field shall become as a forest. And on that day shall the deaf hear the words of God, and the eyes of the blind shall read God's mind. The sufferers shall be relieved and they shall have joy in abundance; and all those who lack things shall be satisfied and it shall come to pass that all those who were foolish shall become wise. The people shall repent and shall honour the Holy One and they shall respect Him in the very depths of their souls."

His voice died away and the priests were amazed for he had read the difficult text without making a single mistake. Jesus closed the book and looked at them.

"May I ask something?" he said boldly, his voice carrying clearly through the big room. "I've read the text now... but what is it actually all about? Could one of you perhaps explain the words of the prophet?"

The priests looked at one another in confusion. The question had caught them by surprise. Then Hillel stood up.

"I have thought about you a lot over the past year, Jesus. And you read so beautifully just now. So why don't you have a go at explaining the text yourself?"

A tingling of tension ran through Jesus' body. How was this possible? Hillel, the respected leader of the Sanhedrin, was asking him to explain the text? He put his hand on the book and stroked the leather binding for a moment. Then he nodded.

"That's all right. The prophet is talking about our own city, Jerusalem. When he wrote this text, all that time ago, he had already foreseen what it would be like in our time. He saw that the lawgivers and priests would oppress the poor while living in luxury themselves. The sacrifices that are offered here are an abomination in God's eyes. The only sacrifice that He requires us to make is in fact... ourselves. And if our people will not listen to the voice of God, foreign conquerors will take Jerusalem and destroy our temple. Our people will be scattered over the whole world, like sheep without a shepherd. But this will not be for all time, for God will cause his sheep to return to the fold and they will then live in peace. And those who did not want to listen at first will hear God's message; those who did not want to look will see the light; those who were sick will be cured and those who can break free of the desire for material goods will see that they are happier without. And the messenger who had long been predicting this and who had been seen as a fool, will be recognised as the true king and they will worship God and His messenger."

After he had said this, he nodded briefly to the priests and then went back to sit with his family. All eyes were now on him and you could have heard a pin drop. The priests realised that they had to respond, but seemed not to be able to agree what to say. They whispered animatedly and tempers began to fray. Finally, Hillel was once again the one who stood up and spoke for them.

"Our young friend here has shown that he is already more than ready for his bar mitzvah. Jesus, come forward for a moment, please. I would like to say the words of the priest's blessing for you."

Jesus stood up again. He walked between the benches and knelt on the ground in front of Hillel. Despite the sharply disapproving looks of this fellow priests, Hillel laid his hand on the boy's head and pronounced the traditional blessing. His voice caught just a little, because he was perfectly aware that the long-awaited Messiah himself was there in front of him.

"Jesus of Nazareth, may the Eternal One bless you and preserve you. May the Eternal One turn His radiant face toward you and be merciful to you. May the Eternal One keep watch over you and grant you peace."

Then he reached a hand out to Jesus to help him stand up. They looked at one another, the powerful leader and the young boy. Jesus saw tears glistening in Hillel's eyes. He swallowed as he was touched as well. Then Hillel said softly,

"Stay here a little while after the service Jesus, so that we can have a chat."

Jesus nodded in agreement.

"That sounds good. I'll tell my mother and father that I'll see them again shortly."

And he stayed behind in the temple and talked to Hillel for a long time. When Hillel had finally withdrawn to his own room, his heart full of questions, Jesus was about to go and look for his parents when a man came up to him.

"Excuse me, Jesus," he said, politely requesting the boy's attention. "May I introduce myself? My name is Lamaas Brahas. I was at the service and I'd like to compliment you on your performance. I really am very impressed!"

He shook Jesus' hand and added,

"I'd very much like to talk to you sometime. My country, India, is another one where the priests have a great deal of power and animal sacrifices are performed. And I too am finding that increasingly hard to stomach. That's why I came to your country. I'm a priest of the Brahmins, and I was very curious about how you - descendants of the patriarch Abraham - put your religion into practice."

Jesus looked at the man in astonishment.

"You came here all the way from India?" he asked. "To learn about our religion? That sounds like quite an undertaking!"

Lamaas smiled.

"Yes, it certainly was," he replied. "But I thought it was worth the effort if it would let me study your patriarch Abraham. After all, he appears in our writings too. It's no coincidence that his very name reflects the fact that he was a follower of the god Brahma. But when severe drought affected our country, he left with his flocks, heading westwards and ending up in Canaan. And although we do worship many gods, including Brahma, I am convinced that there is only one God and that we experience the same manifestations of Him wherever we may be in the world."

Jesus was all ears. He had never previously heard about the possibility of a link between his Jewish roots and the deity called Brahma in India. Excited, he said,

"I'd really love to read the writings you're talking about! Abraham has always fascinated me too. I think it's such a special story - he heard a voice and off he went. Think how much faith you need for that! I hope that I too will feel that confidence as I make my way in the world. And what do your holy texts say about our Abraham? Oh, I've got to read this!"

Lamaas dampened down his enthusiasm a little though, by saying,

"Most of our writings are in Sanskrit, Jesus. I don't believe you know that language, and learning it would take a long time."

Jesus was hugely disappointed. He had learned Greek and Latin in Qumran, but he did indeed not know Sanskrit.

"Can't you teach me that language?" he pleaded. "I'd be more than happy to go to your country with you, so that you can teach me. And then I'd learn a bit about your religion and culture too."

"Well, it seems as if you're just as adventurous as me!" laughed Lamaas. "And in fact I think that sounds like an extremely good idea! I mean, I know already that I'll be able to learn a great deal from you too. Come on, let's see if this madcap plan of yours is a possibility. And perhaps you can tell me a bit more about yourself while we're at it."

He led Jesus to a quiet spot in the temple where they talked for an hour solid. Jesus told him about God's voice, which he - like Abraham - had heard, and about the time he had spent in the monastery. And Lamaas admitted freely that he actually felt a bit of an odd one out within his own order and that he was ready for a new step in his life. A strong affection was soon developing between them and Jesus' desire to go with the priest so that he could learn Sanskrit grew more and more intense. And he forgot the time. It was only when twilight began to fall that he realised that he should have returned to his parents ages ago. He jumped sharply to his feet.

"I'm sorry, Lamaas, but I really do have to go now. My parents won't have a clue where I am."

Lamaas got up too.

"I'll walk with you," he said. "I don't want you to be going outside on your own in the dark."

They crossed the temple courtyard together. It was quiet there, as most people had already gone home. Jesus' parents were nowhere to be seen either.

"Oh no!" sighed Jesus guiltily. "They won't be at all pleased about this... But your stories were so fascinating! And time really does fly then..."

"You can stay in my room tonight," offered Lamaas. "We'll try again in the morning."

Jesus hesitated for a moment, but then realised that there was not really any other option. He followed the priest to his room and Lamaas gave him the bed, while he himself lay down on a sleeping mat on the floor. Jesus was fast asleep in no time, for the day had been full of exciting impressions and he was tired.

He returned to the temple the next day with Lamaas. Many of the people who had been at the service the day before complimented him and wanted to talk to him. Lamaas was astounded by his knowledge and insights. He gave self-assured answers to all the questions and Lamaas was increasingly beginning to wonder just who his new companion was. Hillel came over to him again as well. He greeted the boy amicably and suggested,

"Come on, let's go for a stroll."

Jesus went with him, his curiosity piqued. He felt that the priest was in a strange frame of mind and he wondered what he wanted to say. They crossed the temple courtyard, went under the colonnade and turned left into the park around the fortress of Antonia. It was quieter there. After they had strolled through the park for a while, Hillel stopped and turned towards Jesus. With a serious look on his face, he said,

"There's something I'd like to show you, Jesus."

Out of the voluminous pockets of his priestly robe he brought out a piece of parchment. He stood there for a moment with the sheet in his hand, embarrassed. But then he spoke resolutely,

"This is my letter of resignation, Jesus. I have decided that it would be better if someone else were to be the high priest. You've opened my eyes. What I've been doing for the last few years was not good. I haven't stuck to my principles enough and I've gone with the flow too much, conforming with what other people think about things. That wasn't right. After Shammai's death, I thought that I needed to let his followers have a say too. As a result, I've strayed too far from my own ideals. You've shown me that. That's why I wanted to tell you this in person."

Jesus stared at him, perplexed.

"I think it's a brave decision," he said finally, "although staying on and making sure that your own voice is heard from now on might be even more courageous."

Hillel smiled uncertainly.

"You've got a lot more courage than I have, I fear," he admitted reluctantly. "You dared to say exactly what you thought. And in the lion's den at that! To be honest, I shrink away from that."

Jesus gave an embarrassed shrug.

"That's not how it felt to me," he replied modestly. "And there's no comparison, anyway. I mean, you're in a completely different position than I."

"Well, I'm free of it now, thank God!" laughed Hillel. "I'm going back to where I was born. I'm sure I'll be able to find work in the synagogue there."

They walked back and Hillel shook Jesus' hand once they had come back to the temple.

"I hope all goes well for you, Jesus," he said softly. "Follow your heart and stay true to your ideals - don't do what I did. And be brave - you're going to need that."

For a moment, he hesitated as if he wanted to say far more but then he turned on his heel and walked out of the temple complex, never to return.

In the meantime, Joseph and Mary had already long left the city. They had set off happily enough, believing that Jesus had clambered into the tilt-cart along with James. They only noticed his absence in the evening when they were about to put up their tent. Joseph asked around among the people they knew but to no avail and he returned empty-handed. Because it was already twilight, they decided to sleep first. They went back to the temple again the next day and spoke to the guards.

"Have you by any chance seen our son? A lad with dark blond curly hair and blue eyes, twelve years old?"

One guard nodded immediately.

"Yes, definitely. He's here in the temple. There were people here just a moment ago who'd been talking with him."

Joseph and Mary thanked him and hurried inside, where they found Jesus accompanied by Lamaas. Mary rushed over and hugged him, saying slightly reproachfully,

"Oh, Jesus, why did you do this to us? For all we knew, you might have had an accident!"

Jesus looked back at her guiltily.

"I'm sorry, mother," he said, ashamed. "Please forgive me. But I honestly don't know why you were so worried. You must surely have seen that this is where I would be, busy with my Father's work?"

Lamaas, who had kept clear of the conversation until this point, held out his hand to Mary.

"Please let me offer you my apologies, madam," he said politely. "I'm afraid that I must also shoulder some of the blame for this situation. I was talking to your son and we just kept on chatting without realising, didn't we, Jesus?"

Jesus nodded vigorously.

"That's right, mother. He's told me all sorts of things about his country! Did you know that our very own patriarch Abraham lived in India and worshipped an Indian god there, Brahma? I'd never heard about that. And Lamaas is convinced that this deity is the same god as my Father. Their holy writings talk about Abraham and his links with Brahma. And well, if that's true... if Brahma really is the same as our Yahweh in the Torah, then I absolutely have to read those texts, you must surely understand! So please, mother: may I go with Lamaas to learn his language so that I can read those texts?"

Mary's consternation grew as she heard his words. He was so hugely excited that she was afraid that there would be no way of talking this plan of going to India out of his head. Lamaas intervened in the conversation once again.

"I do understand that your son has dropped this idea onto you out of the blue," he said sympathetically. "But I too have observed that you have a most exceptional child and I would very much like to take him under my wing - with your approval - to teach him about our language and religion."

Jesus nodded enthusiastically again, unable to hide just how keen he was on Lamaas' idea.

"Please mother, may I?" he begged. "I learned a great deal in Qumran. But now I see that there is still a much more to learn, and Lamaas is offering me that opportunity. Please - give it your blessing!"

Mary and Joseph looked at each other. The idea of not seeing their son for another lengthy period was not one that they found particularly attractive. Yet at the same time, they understood that it was no coincidence that had made his path cross with that of the Indian priest.

"I would first like to get to know you better," said Joseph. "I'm sure you understand that I'm not going to let my son go off with whoever he just happens to meet, even though you make a good impression on me. Come on, let's go to an inn so that I can talk with you."

They left the temple and went to find a quiet spot in the city. Joseph and Mary talked to Lamaas in great depth, because they wanted to be certain that they could entrust their son to him with confidence. They were soon deeply impressed by the integrity of the man and it did not take long before he had won their trust. They therefore consented to Jesus going with Lamaas, on the condition that he should send letters home regularly. Despite the fact that he could undoubtedly have become a skilled carpenter in Nazareth, they realised that his calling lay elsewhere. After a fulsome farewell from his parents, Jesus left for India with Lamaas and his life took a new direction.

India

When Jesus had rather impulsively expressed that he wished to accompany Lamaas, he had had no idea what to expect. He knew it would be a long journey but he had not realised they would be on the road for months before they got to India. And while he thought it interesting to see all these places that were mentioned in the Torah, such as Babel and Ur, he found the journey rather a drag.

It was quite the opposite with Lamaas. He was enjoying the trip because it meant he spent every day in the company of Jesus. He was constantly touched by the natural manner in which the boy displayed his wisdom. Lamaas was increasingly aware that this boy was a very special individual and he realised that Jesus was far ahead of him. So one day he asked him,

"Jesus, would you mind if I sometimes quiz you on your thoughts about certain matters? After all, we often get stuck in a certain way of thinking and it can be difficult to let go of particular preconceptions. It might also make the journey pass a bit more quickly for you if we spend our time debating this and that."

Jesus looked at him enthusiastically.

"Oh, you mean like Socrates used to do?" he answered eagerly. "Well, that sounds really interesting! It would force me to think things over too!"

Lamaas stared at him in amazement. He had read Socrates? His admiration for the boy grew even further.

"Well, I'm not sure that I'll be able to think up such sharp questions as Socrates did!" he said modestly. "But I'll do my best."

And he decided he would try to formulate penetrating questions that would challenge Jesus to the limits of his understanding. They were travelling through Babylon now and to start their Socratic diversion Lamaas asked,

"Tell me, Jesus, what are your views on judging?"

Jesus smiled with delight. He realised Lamaas was out to test him thoroughly and he felt excited at the challenge. It would certainly mean an end to his boredom if all the questions were like this! And he replied,

"You should not judge another because you don't know what you would do in his situation. And the worst kind of judging is prejudging, because that means you are condemning someone without having even heard or seen his case."

Lamaas' heart jumped for joy. If this was a taste of what was to come, he would be happy for the journey to take twice as long! They rode past the Sea of Chaldea and Lamaas asked,

"Jesus, what do you think sin is?"

Jesus replied without hesitation,

"Sin is not taking account of your fellow men properly. Because if you take proper account of your fellow men, you will try to avoid hurting them or doing them wrong."

They reached the border with Persia and Lamaas asked,

"What do you see as wickedness, Jesus?"

Jesus replied firmly and without pausing to think,

"Wickedness is a weakness of men. If you try to overcome that weakness, eventually you will conquer your wickedness. Because nobody chooses deliberately to be a wicked human being."

They passed through the famous city of Persepolis and Lamaas asked,

"What are your views on people's sense of guilt, Jesus?"

Immediately Jesus replied,

"A sense of guilt is an excuse to do nothing about the wrong you have done to someone. Whereas if you have done something wrong, whether it was big or small, you should simply go to the other and tell him you're sorry. For if you really intend to harm someone you would not feel guilty about it. So a sense of guilt shows that you are basically a good person."

They continued their journey eastwards. They passed through the southern hills of Persia and Lamaas asked,

"Jesus, why do you think man has to suffer?"

Jesus was even able to answer this question after only a brief pause for thought.

"Suffering makes a person milder and stronger and gives him greater understanding. Someone who has not suffered does not understand what it means to be without suffering. Someone who has not known sorrow does not understand what it means to know joy. Someone who has never been unhappy does not understand what it means to be happy. Someone who has not experienced despair does not understand what it means to have hope. Someone who has not known pain does not understand what it means to be without pain. Someone who has never been sick does not understand what it means to be healthy. You learn the one side of the coin by experiencing the other side."

Lamaas was astounded by the wisdom in this answer, as indeed in all the answers Jesus gave. It was hard to believe this boy was only twelve years old! He noticed that Jesus himself was also clearly enjoying answering his questions. So they carried on with their game. When they reached the border with India, Lamaas asked the boy,

"What are your thoughts on fear, Jesus?"

Jesus replied,

"Fear is the most dangerous emotion there is. Everyone gets frightened at times, but the important thing is not to let fear take over because then it has you in its clutches. And you can conquer your fear! If you are capable of letting your fear go and observing it from all sides, you will recognise it for what it is and see through it. And that which you recognise and see through can never take over, then you will have won."

They travelled through the Thar desert. The heat was scorching and the sand got into their eyes, mouths and clothing. And Lamaas asked,

"How should someone deal with grief?"

Jesus answered,

"You can experience grief just as you do joy. It is something that happens, that you feel, experience and come through. Then it is something you have processed and it becomes part of you but it doesn't destroy you."

They left the desert and Lamaas asked,

"Jesus, what in your opinion is the most important thing in life?"

"Knowing yourself is the most important thing in life," replied Jesus adamantly. "If you don't know yourself, you will never be able to know another. If you don't love yourself, you will never be able to love another. If you don't have faith in yourself, you will never be able to have faith in another. If you cannot provide support for yourself, you will never be able to support another. If you don't have any of this, you are spiritually dead. So you must dive deep inside yourself and learn to live with yourself, with your good traits and your bad ones. Only when you have learnt to live with yourself will you be able to live with another."

They crossed the Ganges and Lamaas asked him,

"Tell me, Jesus, what does wealth mean to you?"

Jesus gave a warm smile and answered full of conviction,

"Wealth is a blessing because it means you can share it out! You can feed the hungry, give drink to the thirsty, clothe the naked, provide a place to sleep for the tired. But you can only give if others are willing to receive. Receiving is also a service to the other. And receiving is much more difficult than giving. Because if you are given something, you feel it to be a debt to the person giving and you think you have to repay him. But the only thing you need to do is to receive with grace so that the person giving experiences inner joy."

His answer moved Lamaas. The end of the journey was now in sight. It was not far anymore to the city of Benares where his order's temple stood. And Lamaas asked, bringing their game to a close,

"What does belief mean to you, Jesus?"

For the first time, Jesus took some time to think. Then he spoke, his voice sounding warm,

"Belief is feeling that a part of God is present in you and that you can find support and strength there. And if you have found that, you won't need anything else. Then you feel part of the bigger whole, of the universal force that is in you and that you are an element of. And any individual person can gain that."

That was how they arrived in Benares. Lamaas was amazed at Jesus and all the things he had said and the way he had behaved. Because it was not just their Socratic game that had made a deep impression on him. He had regularly seen Jesus praying during the journey, seeking contact with the God, whom he called his Father. And he had witnessed how he seemed to be bathed in a great light at such moments and how close the bond between them was. When they reached the temple, he made sure Jesus got a room of his own and they spent the first week resting to recover from the long journey.

The priests of Brahma welcomed Jesus graciously. As disciples of Brahma they were a minority in India's richly diverse religious scene and they felt honoured that this Jewish boy was interested in their beliefs.

Although Jesus had difficulties here too with the sacrifices, he was prepared to put up with them in order to learn Sanskrit and he paid dedicated attention to Lamaas' lessons. It cost him a great effort to learn this new language. While it had only taken him a year at Qumran to learn both Greek and Latin, he found he needed to put a lot more work into mastering Sanskrit. They studied together every day except for the Sabbath, which Jesus continued to observe here, and Lamaas was impressed by his perseverance. As the language lessons could get rather tedious, he would sometimes offer the boy other texts, such as the Ayur Veda, as a diversion. There had been a few fragments of the Ayur Veda available in Greek in Qumran. Jesus had already been fascinated back then by the medical knowledge described in these fragments and he was incredibly enthusiastic when he heard Lamaas had the complete version for him in Greek.

The idea that illness was due to an imbalance between the body and the spirit particularly appealed to him and he was determined to become proficient in the study of herbs that could be used to restore that balance. That was why he could often be found in the temple's herb garden in between lessons. And occasionally, Lamaas would tell him tales of wisdom, simple stories that revealed the meaning of religious beliefs. He also had one ready for him today.

"Tell me, Jesus," he asked. "Have I already told you that story about that father and his son?"

Jesus looked up from his book expectantly.

"I don't think so," he answered, his curiosity awakened.

"Then that will be today's one," laughed Lamaas and he told, "One day, a father said to his son, 'Put some salt in this water and wait until the morning'. The son did as his father had said. The next morning his father said, 'Now bring me the salt'. The son looked in the water, searching for the salt, but he couldn't find it because it was dissolved. The father now said, 'Taste the water, my son. What does it taste like?' 'Like salt,' replied the son. 'Exactly,' said the father. 'The Divine is just like that. You might not notice it but it's in everything, just like the salt in this water. And that is the truth and soul of belief.'"

"What a lovely story!" sighed Jesus. "It's so wonderful, how you can really get to the heart of the matter with such a simple tale. Perhaps I should use that as a way of getting my message across later on too. I'll suggest this to my Father."

As so often, Lamaas was struck by the natural manner in which Jesus referred to God as his Father. And he asked a little shyly,

"Forgive me for asking such a personal question, Jesus, but do you always discuss things first with your Father? And... are you really the son of God?"

Jesus burst out laughing.

"No, of course not!" he answered with amusement. "Of course I'm not the son of God. At least, no more than you are. But God always calls me His son and that's why I decided to call Him 'Father'. And naturally also because what I feel can only really be compared to the love a father feels for his son. Do you understand what I'm saying?"

"Perhaps..." nodded Lamaas hesitantly. "That's not a feeling I've experienced, but I can more or less picture what you mean. But how do you discuss things with Him, how do you know His opinion on matters?"

"Sometimes I hear His voice," explained Jesus. "But that's quite rare actually. More often it's..." he struggled to find the right words, "...as if I get a clear thought in my head but I know it wasn't my thought. It might sound weird but that's what happens. For example, I just knew what I had to say during the service in Jerusalem and when you were asking me all those questions during the journey. I don't know... I never have to think it through. So I assume it'll go something like that when the time comes for me to really spread His message."

"That must be so nice, to be so sure of your future," sighed Lamaas. "Lately I've felt so... as if I'm still searching. I often wonder if I should stay here."

"Well, you can't go yet!" joked Jesus. "After all, you've still got to teach me Sanskrit!"

Lamaas smiled for a moment, but then continued in a serious

voice,

"No, seriously Jesus, I'm not joking, I mean it. I find it quite difficult to decide what is the best path for me to take. It was these doubts that led me to go on that journey and that's how I bumped into you. But to be honest, what I have seen and heard from you makes me even less sure. The way you experience your God is so different to my experience. I really don't know any more what I should do next."

"Well, I'm sure you didn't 'just happen' to bump into me," said Jesus adamantly. "Nothing happens without a reason. It's clearly the intention for me to help you with your quest. Well, I'd be happy to do that, given all the effort you've put in to teaching me. I think that if we just wait and see what happens, we will both automatically find what has been destined for us. And shall we go further with the lesson now? The sooner I master this the better, so it seems."

Lamaas hesitated. He would really have preferred to spend a little longer discussing the matter with Jesus, but at the same time he realised the boy was probably right: he needed to learn to live in the moment and not be constantly trying to work out his future. And at that particular moment they were studying Sanskrit together.

"All right then," he said, yielding. "Where had we got to? Oh yes, lesson six, page seventy-four."

He found the right page and the two of them bent over the book in fraternal harmony.

After a long period of drought, the monsoon arrived. One day it suddenly started raining, bursting the skies open to release a deluge of water. Jesus, who had been working on a copy of the Ayur Veda, rushed to the window and his jaw dropped in amazement. Of course it occasionally rained in Israel but this was quite new to him. The rain drummed a beat on the roof and made a huge racket. In no time great puddles had formed in the courtyard. Even the thick canopy of leaves on the trees was unable to prevent the water getting through.

Then, all at once, he spotted a boy defying the downpour. He was dancing in the rain, completely unconcerned by the fact that his clothes were getting soaking wet. He jumped blithely into the puddles and held up his hands cupped to catch the rainwater. Jesus burst out laughing. He was overcome by a strong desire to join the boy in his antics and without hesitating he ran outside. In the blink of an eye, he too was soaked. The water streamed down his hair, flowed over his face and gushed out of his shirt sleeves. He dashed across the courtyard, stamped his feet in the puddles and opened his mouth wide to taste the water. He enjoyed the moment to the full.

The other lad seemed a little shy and stayed out of his way but Jesus ran up to him, grabbed his hands and took him with him. Surprised, the boy let himself be led and they were running hand in hand now, turning round each other and dancing and jumping in the puddles, laughing at each other joyfully. Then they went looking for something they could use to catch the rain. They soon found two bowls and started trying to chuck water over each other, at the same time cutting crazy capers to avoid being drenched by the other one. Both were roaring with laughter, their eyes sparkling with pleasure, until they finally collapsed on the veranda out of breath. Panting, Jesus turned to the boy with a cheerful look and asked,

"Who are you exactly? I don't think I've seen you around before."

"I'm Rajiv," replied the boy, still gasping for breath as well. "I don't normally ever come here. But when I was playing I ended up here by mistake. I hope the priests won't have seen me, will they?"

Jesus shrugged nonchalantly.

"I've no idea," he said. "But that doesn't matter, does it? Come, let's go to the kitchen then I'll get you something to eat. And I'll give you some of my clothes. Yours are soaked through."

Rajiv burst out laughing.

"And yours aren't?" he teased. "And you really don't need to give me anything - I'll get wet again anyway."

Jesus laughed, a little embarrassed.

"Silly of me," he admitted. "Unfortunately I can't make it stop raining. But you will be able to dry off a bit at any rate."

He took Rajiv with him to the kitchen, found some towels and gave him something to eat. The boy tucked into the simple meal with great gusto.

"Are you that hungry?" asked Jesus, amazed at the speed with which the food was disappearing into Rajiv's mouth.

"I haven't had anything for a couple of days," explained Rajiv, still chewing. "So this tastes pretty good!"

"How's that possible?" asked Jesus sympathetically. "Don't you have any parents to look after you?"

A look of sorrow came over Rajiv's face.

"I do," he said quietly. "But my father can't find any work so we don't have enough money to buy food. And we don't have a house either, but that's the case for most of us. Usually I just roam around and try to earn a few coins doing jobs for people. Not that I mind. You get used to living on the street. But it can get a bit tricky during the monsoon."

Jesus had been listening with an increasing sense of indignation.

"But why are so many people living on the streets?" he asked in wonder. "Is there nobody trying to help you people?"

Rajiv was on the point of answering his question when they were interrupted by one of the priests coming into the kitchen. As soon as he caught sight of Rajiv, he let out a shocked cry and snapped in a tone of revulsion,

"What on earth is that boy doing here!"

Jesus stared at him, not aware he had done anything wrong.

"I brought him here," he explained. "We were playing outside in the rain and now we're sitting here to dry out a bit."

Full of disgust, the priest looked at him.

"Where did you get such an idea!" he lashed out. "Can't you see he's an untouchable and impure? I hope you didn't actually touch him?"

Jesus listened in astonishment. What was that man talking about? Not understanding what was going on he turned to Rajiv. He was surprised to see that the lively, confident lad who had just been sitting next to him had changed into a submissive, lethargic puppet. Worried, he put his hand on Rajiv's shoulder.

"What's up? Don't you feel well?"

Rajiv wanted to say something but the priest's shrill voice stopped him.

"Don't touch him!" he cried out and pulled Jesus roughly away from the table.

He shook him furiously and hissed viciously,

"How could you do this? Go to your room at once and stay there until one of us comes to you!"

He pushed Jesus out of the kitchen and then turned to deal with Rajiv. But the boy had already escaped. The priest saw him through the open door running off, carefully avoiding the puddles he had so recently been dancing in, until he disappeared among the bushes.

In the meantime, Jesus stood irresolutely in the corridor, still not sure what error he had committed. He did not like the idea at all of being sent to his room like a small child. Because what on earth had he done wrong? The rainwater was still running down his back but the sense of pleasure he had had with Rajiv had evaporated. That was how Lamaas found him.

"Oh, why are you standing here looking so lost?" he asked in a friendly voice. "Is something up? And you're so wet!"

Jesus looked at him in relief.

"Nothing's up in my opinion," he replied indignantly. "So I hope you can explain to me what I've done wrong."

He reported Lamaas what had happened. Lamaas gave him a worried look.

"I think I need to explain something to you," he said in a serious voice. "Come, let's go to my room."

He gestured to the priest, who came out of the kitchen to check if Jesus had gone up his room, to show that he had everything under control and led Jesus off. When they reached his room, he gave the boy a cloth to dry himself with. Then he invited him to sit next to him on a bench.

"I can quite understand that you don't think you did anything wrong," he said sympathetically. "Because this wouldn't have been wrong in your country. So how could you know it was such a sensitive matter here?"

And he told Jesus that long ago, a foreign people had invaded India and made the original inhabitants, the Dravidians, their subjects. Even today the Dravidians were considered to be second-rate citizens. They did not belong to any of the castes and were known as the untouchables. They often lived in desperate conditions but no-one was able to do anything to improve their situation, as consorting with these people was strictly forbidden because they were considered impure.

Although he had never intended this, Jesus had made the kitchen impure by bringing Rajiv there and apparently the priests would now have to clean the place in accordance with strict rituals to prevent a calamity. And Jesus too would have to ritually cleanse himself before he could even be allowed to enter the temple again. Jesus listened to his story in astonish-ment. When Lamaas had finished talking, he asked,

"Why didn't you tell me this before, Lamaas? I've been here so long but you never mentioned this."

Ashamed, Lamaas shrugged.

"I'm not proud of this aspect of our culture," he replied diffidently. "Knowing you as I do, I was afraid you wouldn't want to continue with your studies if you'd known this. And that would have been a pity because our religion has so many good aspects too, and so far they have been enough to make me decide to stay here. But everything will be fine as long as you cleanse yourself now."

He took Jesus to the bathing area. Jesus subjected himself resignedly to the lengthy ritual, purely so as not to disappoint his friend. But his sense of injustice was burning inside. For how on earth could you become impure simply by touching another person? Once they had finished, Lamaas urged him,

"I think you should go to the kitchen now and offer your help. I fear you are going to have to make amends."

Jesus looked at him sullenly.

"I'm quite happy to help with the cleaning," he said impassively. "But don't expect me to offer any apologies. In my eyes, everything you have told me is unjust and I have no intention of changing my behaviour to comply with that!"

Lamaas saw the boy's determination and he started to worry that Jesus' idiosyncratic attitudes might rile the priests. Jesus followed Lamaas' advice and went back to the kitchen. To his great surprise, the priests had already started systematically cleansing everything. They were washing the cupboards and thoroughly scrubbing the floor. The chair Rajiv had been sitting on had been broken into pieces and was now being burned outside. Jesus started to realise that Lamaas had not been exaggerating. This really was a sensitive matter! He decided he would go along with this for the time being and helped as best he could. But the priests no longer treated him in the easy-going way they had adopted up to then; from that day forth they kept a close watch on him.

It took Jesus nearly a year to truly master Sanskrit but his reward was great. Finally he had access to the mystic Indian literature such as the epics of Mahabharata and Ramayana. It opened up a new world for him. While he was surprised by the diversity of the many gods, he was affected at the same time by the teaching of the transmigration of souls and redemption, which offered people the prospect of growth, getting closer and closer to God until you could finally be taken up in the Divine itself. He was deeply moved by the realisation that this was a long and difficult path for most people while he himself was already so close to God, and he felt the bond with his Father tighten even closer.

Now that he understood Sanskrit, Jesus turned to the deity of Brahma to see whether he could discover the connection with Abraham and Yahweh that Lamaas had spoken of. He soon felt deeply disappointed. While Brahma was also described as the creator of the universe, he could not see any other similarities between him and his Father. In many texts, Brahma was depicted as a duplicitous figure who was in love with Shatarupa, his own daughter no less. In drawings, Brahma was shown as having five heads, which had grown when he turned his lustful gaze on his daughter. The supreme god Shiva had chopped off his fifth head as a punishment for his incestuous behaviour. The Brahmin priests' temple he was in now had been built on the spot where this had occurred.

The story of the creation of the world by Brahma also seemed nothing like the creation story in the Torah, one of his favourite tales. He was amazed at how the creation of the human race was described and how that had led to the caste system that he felt to be so unjust. He had regularly walked through the city with Lamaas and had seen the consequences of this system with his own eyes. He had been shocked by what he had seen. The people in the lowest caste, the servants, seemed to have no rights at all. It distressed him greatly that they did not even dare look at him because he came from the temple. And he had also seen the conditions Rajiv and his kind had to live in: life was even more difficult for the untouchables, who lived as outcasts in slums, if they had a roof over their heads at all.

One day, Jesus was sitting with the priests in the prayer room. Thinking about the story of the creation by Brahma and all he had seen in the city, he could not help asking,

"Could you be so good as to tell me more about the castes? Why are people not all equal before Brahma? I don't understand that."

One of the priests stood up.

"I would be happy to explain that to you," he answered. "When Brahma created man, He did as He thought right and it is not for us to complain about it. The first man came out of his mouth. He was like Brahma himself and so was called a Brahmin. Brahma made him the priest, who would act on His behalf in all earthly matters. The second man came from His hand. This man was created to be the king, or ruler or warrior, and his main duty is to protect the priest. Out of Brahma's thigh came the third man. His task is to farm the land and tend to the sheep and cattle. Finally, out of Brahma's feet came the fourth man and he is the servant of the human race. He has no rights that others have to respect. He is not allowed to listen when the holy scriptures are being read and he is forbidden to look at the priest or the king. If he does then he must die, and death alone can free him from his state of servility. This is still the way in which our society is ordered. Each has his own task and knows what that is. I don't see what is wrong with that. We can't all do the same tasks, can we? And if you manage to perform your task well in this earthly life, you might be reincarnated in a different, higher caste and so improve yourself."

Jesus had listened in amazement. When the priest had finished speaking, he too stood up and said in a harsh voice,

"I think all of this does a great injustice to a large group of people. Because why shouldn't people be able to improve themselves during this life? After all, everyone has the right to get to know God! I cannot see Brahma as a just deity because of the way he has given some a high and others a low position. And you didn't even mention the untouchables! I know why - as far as you're concerned they don't even exist! But how can that be just?"

And he knelt and in an intimate voice he prayed,

"My dear Father, who was, is and always shall be, You are justice itself. In Your infinite love, You have created all men as equals. The priests, the kings, the farmers and the servants are all equal in Your eyes. And everyone, even the untouchables, can look at You and say 'Our Father who art in heaven, hallowed be Thy name. May Your kingdom come and may You, the true God of love, reign forever."

The priests listened to his words with rising irritation and their frustrations culminated in an outburst. They all rose up at once and grabbed hold of him. Jesus was startled. He had not expected such a fierce reaction. He felt their fury and their hands were hurting him.

"Ow! Why are you doing this? Let go of me!" he cried and he tried to break free of their clutches, but he was unable to.

Luckily Lamaas intervened, saying in a sharp voice,

"I urge you brothers, don't do this! You don't realise who you are dealing with. But I know the God this boy prays to. I have seen him in prayer and I saw him bathed in a light more beautiful and brighter than the sun itself. So think about what you are doing, for his God could well be more powerful than Brahma!"

The priests looked up in confusion. They were not pleased at the fact that Lamaas was so brazenly standing up for this child. But his words had an effect because they let go of Jesus for now. The boy gave his friend a grateful look and rubbed his arms, realising that he would probably end up with several bruises. Meanwhile Lamaas continued in his efforts to persuade his brothers,

"Friends, isn't tolerance one of the cornerstones of our religion? Surely we can't force Jesus to keep silent about these things. And if he is wrong then his words won't have any effect anyway. After all, the truth always triumphs in the end."

But the priests did not give up that easily. Lamaas may have been an authoritative figure within their order but that did not mean he alone decided matters.

"Why should we listen to you, Lamaas?" said one of them indignantly, " And why did you bring this boy here anyway? If you think this God of his is so wonderful, what are you still doing here? Aren't our laws clear? Whoever insults Brahma - in here of all places, his own holy place - must die!"

His inflammatory words met with approval and before Jesus knew it they had taken hold of him again. The state of affairs had not really improved and his heart was beating wildly from fear. Lamaas saw how serious the situation was. He rushed up to the brothers and said vehemently,

"Brothers, please don't do this. We can't kill this boy just because we don't agree with what he says! Why are we unable to critically examine the message we spread ourselves? Because what if he's right? How will God judge us if we kill him just like that?"

The priests hesitated. They had often been surprised at how firm and convinced Jesus seemed and they were frightened at the thought that they might bring the wrath of his God down upon their heads. They took a brief look at each other, then let go of him. Both Jesus and Lamaas breathed a sigh of relief. But one of the priests snapped brusquely,

"Listen Jesus, we'll spare your life this once, but we don't want you living here any longer. You must pack your things and leave immediately!"

They pushed him off into his room and watched as he packed his few belongings into a bag, his hands trembling. Lamaas was deeply shocked. Ignoring his brothers, he embraced Jesus warmly and whispered in his ear,

"Look for Rajiv. I'm sure he'll help you. And don't let this silence you! Stay true to what you believe in!"

Moved by his friend's courage, Jesus flung his arms around him. Then he nodded to show he was ready. They took him outside the temple complex and left him there to his fate. Jesus took a final look at the place where had after all spent several years of his young life. Then he turned round and, with pain in his heart, went on his way.

He reached the city around evening. He decided to take Lamaas' advice and go in search of Rajiv. He tried his luck in the slums, where most of the untouchables could be found, doing their best to build up something of an existence. He searched for the boy among the rickety shelters people had created from old rubbish. His search was fruitless, until a man sitting on an ancient stool asked him,

"Can I help you? You don't look like you're from round here."

"Perhaps," replied Jesus. "I'm looking for someone called Rajiv, a young man about my age. Do you know if he has a home here?"

"A home, indeed!" laughed the man sarcastically. "Well, if you want to call it a home... If you walk further up to that rubbish tip and then turn right, you'll find a woman who's got a son named Rajiv."

Jesus thanked him effusively and followed his instructions. He soon found a small structure made up of slats with a couple of sheets serving as a roof. A woman was sitting in its shadow, chopping carrots.

"Excuse me," said Jesus, addressing her. "Is this where I can find Rajiv? I met him once in the temple."

The woman looked up. Jesus recognised the similarity with Rajiv at once. Without thinking, he cried out,

"This has got to be the place! Rajiv is the spitting image of you. You must be his mother!"

The woman laughed.

"Yes, that's right. Everyone always says we look alike. But I'm afraid Rajiv isn't here. He left more than a year ago to go to Nepal and join the Buddhists. He'd got fed up of being treated like dirt. The Buddhists will have nothing to do with the caste system. That's why many of our people live there now."

"Oh..." replied Jesus in surprise. "I thought Buddha was one of the gods in Hinduism? At least, that's what I was taught. Isn't he an... what do you call it... an avatar? An incarnation of your god Vishnu?"

"I can imagine that's what you might have been taught," answered the woman. "But it's not the truth. Buddha is not a god. He was a man who found enlightenment. He lived and preached close to here in Sarnath. His followers try to find enlightenment just like he did."

Jesus was silent for a moment as he absorbed her words.

"How lovely," he then said. "After all, self-realisation is the best path to God. What a good move of Rajiv to go there. It must have taken quite some courage!"

His mother nodded with pride.

"Yes, it did take courage," she agreed. "But I suspect you had a part in his decision too. Aren't you the Hebrew boy who once gave him food even though you knew the priests wouldn't approve? That must have taken courage too! So you set the right example."

"Well, it wasn't quite like that," confessed Jesus. "When I did that, I didn't know anything about the caste system yet and in fact I couldn't understand why the priests got so angry. Now I know better and I told them clearly what I think about it. That's why I've been expelled from the temple. To be honest, I'm glad I'm still alive to be standing here in front of you, because I think the priests might well have killed me if a good friend hadn't stood up for me."

His voice trembled; the whole episode had affected him more

than he had been willing to acknowledge. The woman looked at him compassionately.

"So you've got nowhere to stay," she inferred.

Jesus nodded.

"That's why I was looking for Rajiv. I was hoping that he would have some tips for me. But that's an end to that idea."

He looked around him irresolutely. For the first time in his life he did not know what to do. Rajiv's mother saw his confusion.

"Sit down a moment," she said in a friendly voice. "I'll get you something to drink."

She stood up and offered him her only chair. Jesus smiled in gratitude. After she had gone, he pondered what he should do. He could travel north to find Rajiv among the Buddhists. He was intrigued by the teachings of this Buddha and he would surely feel more at home there than in the Brahmins' temple. Or he could return to Galilee. He had been away from home for more than five years now and his mother would undoubtedly be pleased to see him again. But was that the best option?

He stood up, stretched and surveyed the woman's meagre lean-to with his carpenter's eye. His hands itched to get working, as he could see that a few simple alterations would improve it quite a bit. In a burst of enthusiasm, he delved into his bag and retrieved the set of tools his father had put in it back in Jerusalem. He had been wondering for years what he was supposed to do with it but now it could prove its worth. And his decision was made. He would stay in India for the time being. At any rate he wanted to give Rajiv's mother a better place to live. And after that he would see.

When the woman returned with a bowl of milk, he asked her if he could spend the night there. And the following day he started work on her shelter. He searched through the rubbish that lay all around and found an old cart. He sawed planks from it and used them to strengthen the lean-to's walls. Then he went down to the river and cut as much reed as he could carry. He wove them skilfully into a sturdy mat and attached that on top of the sheets to give a watertight roof. Rajiv's mother was in seventh heaven. People came and watched him as he worked.

"Why are you doing this?" asked one man, curiously.

"Why not?" replied Jesus simply.

"Because nobody ever cares about us," said the man in a resigned tone.

"And I don't think that's right," answered Jesus. "After all, everyone has the right to a decent life. And God has given me the task of making people happier. So that's what I try to do."

The man looked at him in surprise.

"Are you doing this in the name of your God?" he asked. "And who is this God then?"

"My God calls Himself Yahweh," explained Jesus. "But I call Him my Father because He loves me like a father. And He wants to be your father too because everyone is a child of God. Whether you are an untouchable, a priest or a farmer, my Father loves everyone. Because He is the God of love."

The man stared in amazement. He had never heard of anything like this! Another person said,

"We have many gods but we haven't heard of this God, Yahweh. How can we get to know him?"

"That is very easy," replied Jesus. "Because He lives in your own heart. He speaks there with His soft, loving voice. So be quiet and you will hear Him. And once you have found Him, you must honour Him. You honour Him by honouring and helping the people around you because what you do for another, you do for God."

"So in helping this woman now, you are honouring your God?" asked the man.

"Exactly!" nodded Jesus. "And I enjoy doing it too! So if you have any more jobs for me, please let me know."

The man looked at him in amazement. Then he burst out laughing.

"Well," he said. "My stool is pretty unsteady. I'd be very happy if you were to give it a couple of new legs!"

"No problem," smiled Jesus. "I'll come along in a while."

And that evening he repaired the man's stool. He became quite well known in the slums in the weeks that followed. Many people asked him for help and everywhere he came, people were impressed by his integrity. He was popular with the untouchables because of the way he talked to them with no trace of reluctance, and his popularity spread through the rest of the city and beyond. Even if they did not have a job for him, people would still come to him to hear what he had to say. Jesus felt God's approval of his actions deep in his heart. He felt intensely happy even though he had no permanent home and was roaming from place to place. He was always able to find a place to sleep and some food, and every evening he thanked his Father that he was able to give so many people hope for a better life, before falling contentedly asleep.

But one night he was rudely awakened. Someone banged loudly on his window shutter and he woke with a shock. He got up still half asleep and drowsily opened the shutter. To his amazement he saw Lamaas standing there.

"Lamaas? What are you doing there?" he asked in surprise. "It's the middle of the night! Anyone in their right mind is asleep at this time. Or is something up? Wait, I'll open the door for you."

But Lamaas interrupted him and whispered fervently,

"Don't worry, I'm fine. But I've come to warn you. The priests are furious. Fewer and fewer people are visiting the temple and they blame you. And now I accidentally heard that they plan to hire an assassin to murder you. So you must flee before it's too late!"

Jesus, who was still not properly awake, stared at his friend. Then his message slowly started to sink in. Piqued, he said,

"Flee? You can't be serious! I'm not going to run off like a criminal! I haven't done anything wrong and anyway I can be of help to the people here. So forget it - I'm staying put!"

Lamaas stifled a doubting sigh.

"Please, Jesus, now is not the time to be stubborn about things," he said in an urgent tone. "Of course you haven't done anything wrong. But surely you don't want to end your life here? So be sensible. I'm not joking! Or do you really want them to succeed in eliminating you and hiding your body so that no one ever hears of you again?"

Jesus hesitated. He realised his friend was serious and that he would not have come looking for him unless it was absolutely necessary. He sighed deeply. Then he collected up his things and got dressed, though with great reluctance. He grabbed his bag and climbed out of the window. Lamaas embraced him with relief.

"My dear, dear boy," he said emotionally. "I've grown so attached to you and I will miss you so much. I hope things go well for you. Please be careful. And try to get out of the country as soon as possible. Will you promise me that?"

Jesus nodded silently. Tears were in his eyes for Lamaas had been such a good friend to him all this time. He asked quietly,

"What about you, Lamaas? What will you do?"

"I have decided to go to Nepal to join the Buddhists," replied Lamaas. "The temple didn't feel the right place for me anyway any more, as you know. And I feel this is the path I need to take."

"Yes, that's a good decision," nodded Jesus. "I wish you lots of luck. And who knows, perhaps you will meet up with Rajiv. If so, give him my regards."

"I certainly will, Jesus!" promised Lamaas. "And now off you go - that will give you a good head start!"

They embraced once more, then Jesus disappeared off into the dark night. Lamaas thanked God that his young friend had escaped unharmed and he asked Him to keep this pure soul safe from everything he would have to face later on in his life.

Persia

After travelling for some weeks, Jesus reached Persia, where he felt safe. While crossing the barren border country, he had taken the opportunity to reflect and he realised how much he had changed. He had only been a child when he had set off with Lamaas, heedless and naive. How much wiser he was now, at the age of eighteen. He had already discovered that the abbot had been right: his message did provoke resistance. But he had also found that he was able to face that.

Now that he was in the land of Zarathustra, he was keen to learn more about this kindred spirit. As the real experts on ancient writings were to be found in Persepolis, he decided he would go to that famous city. More and more people joined him on his journey; impressed by his personality, they wanted to travel with him. Jesus felt honoured by the great faith they had in him, yet at the same time he felt unsure how to deal with this situation. Whereas the people in India had treated him as an equal, the people here were inclined to put him on a pedestal. When they got close to Persepolis, he gathered his fellow travellers around him and said,

"I thank all of you for having so much faith in me that you have decided to join me on my journey. But to be perfectly honest, I also feel rather embarrassed. I mean, why do you look up to me so much? I'm just a simple lad, who was once trained to be a carpenter. So please, don't honour me: honour God my Father - He is the one who deserves your honour. As for me, well, I'm just Jesus of Nazareth. Perhaps I may say things from time to time that you find useful and can help you. But that's only because God is helping me do this, because I consented to be His instrument. And you can do that too. Turn yourself into a temple in which God can live; then you will experience His unconditional love."

His words must have hit home because someone called out,

"Tell us, Jesus, what do we have to do to become such a temple?"

Jesus, pleased with this positive response, replied in his melodious voice,

"Search for silence, because it is in silence that you will encounter God. And if you encounter God in your own soul, you will be filled with wisdom, love and power."

However his answer was clearly not enough as someone else asked,

"But where can we find that silence? Where should we look for that quiet place?"

Jesus answered patiently,

"You can't describe that place. It's not a town you can go to, marked out by the walls surrounding it. No, you carry that holy place inside you. It's within yourself that you can meet God. It doesn't matter where you are - at the top of a mountain or deep in a valley, at a market or just at home - you can always open the door to find the silence and enter the house of God that is in your soul."

The people absorbed his words. They were joined by a wise man from the temple of Persepolis. He had gone for a walk that morning and had noticed the group gathered outside the city. Intrigued, he had asked a man who was trying hard to pick up what Jesus was saying,

"What are you all doing here?"

The man gave him an irritated look and hissed,

"Shhh!"

The wise man apologised and tried to get closer. Some of the people in the group recognised him as Caspar, the leader of their country's religious community, and they whispered,

"We're listening to that young man there. We've been travelling with him for a while and he really is something special! He must be a prophet because he says such wonderful things, we've never heard anything like it!"

Caspar stood on tiptoes to catch a glimpse of the boy they were talking about. As soon as he saw him, he felt impressed by the wisdom and strength of his face.

"Who is he?" he asked quietly.

"A Hebrew lad called Jesus of Nazareth. He's come from India and is on his way to his home country."

Caspar was unable to suppress a cry of surprise. With increasing interest, he pricked up his ears and heard Jesus continuing,

"Don't let yourself be distracted by your work or what others may think of your quest. Persevere. Look for a quiet place to pray and meditate. Let go of your rational side and let your own will be subsumed in the Divine. Experience perfect happiness and perfect love in the presence of God!"

He fell silent and a wave of emotion passed through the little group. Caspar too was moved. Young Jesus had turned into a true spiritual master, it seemed. The crowd now dispersed, realising that Jesus had finished speaking. Caspar seized his opportunity and went up to the young man. He put his hand cautiously on his shoulder and said meekly,

"Excuse me, Jesus. I understand you might want to be on your way but I would like to ask you something, if I may."

Jesus gave a friendly nod.

"Of course," he smiled disarmingly.

Caspar looked at him expectantly.

"I'd very much like to renew our acquaintance, with your permission. It's been so long since I last saw you and I'm really delighted to run into you again like this!"

Jesus raised his eyebrows, unsure what the man was referring to.

"I'm afraid you'll have to help me," he said candidly, "as I can't remember having met you before."

"No, you wouldn't," answered Caspar at once. "After all, you were only a baby and I was just one little incident in your life. But I'm Caspar, one of the three wise men. We followed the star, which took us to Bethlehem. Unfortunately, my two travelling companions have now passed away. But I have been granted the honour of meeting you and hearing your wise words, God be thanked!"

Fervently, he took Jesus' hand and kissed it. Jesus looked at him in happy surprise.

"How wonderful!" he cried out. "I'm very pleased to be able to get to know you better. I see from your clothes that you must be connected to the temple at Persepolis. That's just where I wanted to go, because I've heard you have lots of books about Zarathustra. And apparently you even have some even rarer texts written by

Zarathustra himself. I'd love to read them one day."

"I'll arrange personally for you to get access to our library," promised Caspar. "And could I invite you to be my guest? I'd be happy to tell you everything you want to know. And I can be your guide if you'd like to explore the city and surrounding area."

"Well, that's not an offer I'm going to refuse!" laughed Jesus and he followed the priest to his home.

When they arrived, Caspar ordered his servant to prepare a celebratory meal. It was a long time since Jesus had eaten so well. Caspar had put candles on the table and laid out his best dishes. One course after another was served up. While they were toasting one another, Jesus said,

"Who'd have thought it - us sitting down together after all these years! You can't have imagined this when you saw me all those years ago in that stable!"

"No, definitely not!" replied Caspar. "But it can't be a coincidence that our paths have crossed again now."

"I agree," said Jesus. "At any rate, now I can finally ask what I've been wondering for so long. Because how is it that you three were able to see that star back then, Caspar? I can appreciate now how far from home this is and I can hardly imagine how the star's light could have reached this far."

"We might not have noticed it if we hadn't been prepared," nodded Caspar. "But we were naturally waiting in anticipation because of the prediction Zarathustra had made."

"A prediction?" asked Jesus curiously. "I've never heard about that."

"Some time ago a text was found by Zarathustra that made this prediction," explained Caspar. "I'll give it to you so that you can read it. He talks about his return to Earth and says a star will be the sign that he has come back. From that point on, our astronomers scrutinised the heavens closely. And that is how I was led to you."

"Isn't it strange how God directs our lives in such a way that we are able to serve His Kingdom?" said Jesus with a sense of awe. "It's clearly His intention for me to stay here a while and learn more about Zarathustra. So I would very much like to see that text now, Caspar, if that's all right with you."

"Of course!" laughed Caspar. "Let's finish our drinks, then I'll take you to the library."

No sooner said than done. After they had finished the pitcher of wine, Caspar took Jesus to the library, and looked for the text they had been talking about. Jesus waited impatiently and when Caspar finally laid out the precious scroll on the table for him, his eyes sped over the words.

"And after me shall come he who is called Christ and I command you to offer him gifts. And when he is born, a star shall appear that is visible not just at night but also during the day and that can be seen from afar. Yet you, my children, shall be the first of all the peoples to see its arrival. When you see this star, you must set off and follow it wherever it leads you. You must worship the child and offer him gifts, for the child is the Word - the logos - and Christ himself who is in Heaven. And he shall be of my lineage. I am him and he is me. He is in me and I in him. And when his arrival is made known, great signs shall appear in the heavens and his splendour shall surpass the splendour of heaven itself. And you, children, must keep watch and pay heed to what I say: wait for the promised one. Guard this secret, guard it as a treasure within your soul. And when the star of which I spoke rises, you shall send emissaries laden with gifts to worship him. For this king is the king of kings. And I and he - we are one."

Jesus felt deeply moved, just as he had done in Qumran when he had first felt this connection with Zarathustra. He read the text three, four times before eventually making a request to Caspar:

"Would you ask one of your scribes to copy this text for me please? I would like to take it home with me to show my master and my parents."

Caspar made sure his wish was granted at once.

The next day, Caspar gave his servant orders to make up one of the rooms on the ground floor for Jesus' use. Meanwhile, he took Jesus on a walk through the city. Persepolis was beautyfully laid out with broad streets, parks and palaces. Quite different from shabby, chaotic Benares.

"What is that building there, Caspar?" asked Jesus, pointing to an imposing structure.

"That is the palace of King Darius," answered Caspar. "He was one of the greatest kings our country has ever known. It is true he fought many wars, because he wanted natural borders for our country. But he was a just ruler."

"Yes, I think I may have heard of him," said Jesus thoughtfully. "Didn't he conquer Israel?"

"Yes, that's right," Caspar nodded. "And he was favourably disposed to your country as well. He gave you the money to build your temple in Jerusalem, for instance."

"Really?" cried Jesus in surprise. "What did he do that for? He must have had his own religion. Why would our god matter to him?"

"You're wrong there, my friend!" Caspar admonished him. "Darius also believed in one god only and he saw all the other gods in the world as different manifestations of that one supreme being. Allegedly he was even a follower of Zarathustra but we have never been able to find any written proof of this."

"I'm sorry. I shouldn't have been so quick to judge," apologised Jesus. "But I didn't know that the idea of there only being one god was around so long ago. I'm actually quite surprised that you are so good at keeping the teachings of Zarathustra alive."

"Fortunately, we have usually had honourable rulers who have done good work for our society," said Caspar with a certain amount of pride in his voice. "Take Xerxes. He was the first to start paying slaves and craftsmen for their work. And when a slave was unable to work anymore because of an illness or accident, Xerxes would make sure his family was cared for. That's why our city is full of such wonderful buildings. Craftsmen came from far and wide to work here because they knew they would be treated with respect."

"Could you show me the palace of Xerxes as well?" asked Jesus, full of curiosity. "I'm sure it must look splendid too."

"Unfortunately not," replied Caspar sadly. "Alexander the Great plundered it and then set fire to it. Legend has it that he needed a hundred beasts of burden to remove all the treasures. But we can have a look at the palace of Darius from the inside. Be careful with the stairs - the steps are pretty shallow."

He took the young man inside the huge palace and Jesus looked around in awe. The roof above the huge rooms was supported by hundreds of columns. The walls were covered with marvellous reliefs showing scenes from life in the times of King Darius. Caspar proudly showed him round. When they had seen everything, they descended the stairs again. The steps were indeed unusually shallow and, although Caspar had been up and down them many times in his life, this time he misjudged his step. He twisted his ankle and fell down hard, tumbling a good five yards to the bottom of the stairs, where he landed with a thump on the street. Shocked, Jesus rushed down after him.

"Please, let me get through to him!" he cried urgently to some bystanders who had hastened to the priest.

He exuded so much authority that the people immediately moved to one side. He knelt next to Caspar.

"Are you all right?" he asked in a concerned voice, at the same time looking to see whether the man was seriously wounded.

Caspar groaned.

"My head," he whispered almost imperceptibly.

"Don't worry," said Jesus in a calming tone. "Don't worry, I'll help you."

He placed his hands on Caspar's head and closed his eyes. It had been a long time since he had used his gift but he soon felt the health-giving tingling sensation in his hands. Caspar felt the pain ease off almost immediately. He sat up carefully and stayed sitting, still a little dizzy. The bystanders looked at one another in amazement. Who was this youth? And what had he done to make the old man recover so quickly? One of them whispered,

"Isn't he that prophet from Galilee? This means he really must be a messenger from God! How else could he have had the power to do this?"

Jesus heard his words. He looked at the man and said modestly,

"Good sir, I would appreciate it if you didn't talk about this. Many people think I'm different from them and I'd prefer it if people didn't see me like that. So please just continue on your way. We'll be fine."

The man looked at him in surprise. Then he shook his head and went off. The others soon followed his example. Jesus turned his attention back to Caspar.

"Are you all right again?" he asked, holding out his hand to the man. "Come on, let's see if you can stand."

Caspar got up, still a little unsteady and leaning heavily on Jesus' arm. He took a few hesitant steps. Then he gave his friend a grateful look.

"Yes, I can," he said, smiling with relief. "Thank you! And even though I'm not allowed to say this, I'm going to anyway: you are a very special person! You could achieve so much already!"

Jesus shrugged, embarrassed by his words.

"Oh, I don't know about that," he said quietly. "That depends on so many things."

And that was the end of it as far as he was concerned. They walked slowly back to Caspar's house where the servant had now prepared the room for him.

Jesus was happy to remain in Persia. He felt incredibly inspired by the thought that he was following in the footsteps of Zarathustra. He went off more and more to talk to people or visit the sick. Fortunately, Caspar's accident left him with nothing worse than a bump on the head and he would sometimes accompany Jesus on his expeditions. He never ceased to be surprised by the impact this young man had on people. If he talked to a sick man or woman, you could see the change in that person. Was it the words he used, or the sound of his voice, or did it perhaps have nothing to do with what he actually said... Caspar did not know. But he saw how people forgot their misery and felt much better for that reason alone.

Jesus regularly used his gift of the laying on of hands. And he also gave herbal remedies using herbs he had picked himself. Some he dried while others he crushed to make into oil. Caspar loved being in his company, and given that Jesus seemed to be in no hurry to return to Galilee, he took the opportunity to show his friend the most beautiful parts of his country.

One day, when they were out riding near Persepolis, Jesus saw a great crowd gathered around a pool. He turned to Caspar and asked,

"Why are all those people sitting there? It seems as if they are waiting for something."

"They are," replied Caspar. "This is a spring with healing powers. Their deity descends once a year and gives the water its powers. If the sick wash themselves in the water immediately afterwards, they are cured. But no-one knows exactly when the deity will come. So that's why they're waiting."

Jesus looked at the sick waiting resignedly for their god to come and his heart went out to them. He dismounted, gave the reins to

Caspar and walked up to them. A lot of them appeared tired and he could see from their eyes that they were beginning to doubt whether their god would ever come at all. Filled with pity, he looked around him until he spotted a rock. He went over to it, climbed up and called,

"Good people, why are you waiting here for a sign that will not come? Why do you think this water needs a special blessing from God? Do you really not know where the healing power actually comes from?"

The crowd looked up in surprise. Who was this man and what was he talking about? Jesus was pleased he had been able to get their attention and he continued steadfastly:

"Listen! Surely you don't believe God is biased in the way He hands out His gifts? Why would He bless this spring today but not tomorrow, so that anyone who happens to come along tomorrow won't find a cure? Believe me, the power in this spring is not a special gift from God! Your own faith is the power that's in the water. If you believe with all your heart that you will be healed by bathing in this pool, then you will be healed. And that means the spring will be able to do its work every day."

The people were enthralled by his words and there were murmurrings among the crowd. One or two of them ventured into the water - and were cured. The others watched in bewilderment. Then they too rushed to the spring, afraid that the divine power would have disappeared before they could be healed as well. In no time at all, nearly everyone was in the water. Jesus shook his head in dismay at such lack of faith.

Then he saw a little girl sitting some distance away. The child was too weak to walk to the water on her own and no-one had thought to help her. Jesus jumped off the rock and went over to her. He knelt down next to her and said in a friendly voice,

"Hey, little one, why are you still waiting here? Don't you want to go in the water? Look at all those people washing themselves and getting healed!"

But the girl replied,

"I'm not in a hurry. Why should I be? You just said yourself that God's blessing in the water isn't just for today. Well, that means His power will still be there in a bit! So let me wait here. Those people are only afraid they won't have enough faith. But once they've gone, the spring will still have the same power for me and then I can enjoy the water in peace."

Jesus was so moved by her words that he could not speak for a moment. Then he took hold of her hands and said in a voice full of emotion,

"You've understood me! If only all these people had a fraction of your faith!"

He leaned over and picked her up. She was as light as a feather in his arms. He smiled down at her and, with his head close to hers, he whispered confidentially in her ear,

"Shall I tell you a secret? It's not just the water that has healing powers, even the air here does. So if you have faith, take a deep breath and you will be cured! You know - why don't we do this together?"

The little girl nodded enthusiastically and Jesus saw an optimistic twinkle in her eyes. They looked at each other like two conspirators and Jesus counted quietly to three. Then they both took a deep gulp of air and she was cured at once. The people around them looked on in astonishment. And Jesus said to them,

"Do you understand now how it works? It wasn't me who did this, it was her. Because true strength comes from love and true healing from faith."

He kissed the girl and carefully put her down again.

"Run along home now," he said tenderly. "And be careful, all right?"

Then he gestured to Caspar, who had been following the entire affair from a distance. They mounted and spurred their horses on. Soon they had left the spring and the people there far behind them. They rode side by side in silence, each deep in his own thoughts. Caspar was so overwhelmed by what he had seen that he could not find the words to express his feelings. Jesus himself was also impressed by what he was able to do thanks to God. He felt the power he was being given becoming stronger all the time and he was moved by the thought that he had been chosen to be God's instrument. At the same time he wondered why he in particular had been selected for this task. And he was pleased Caspar was with him.

The good man always treated him the same as everyone else for he understood that despite everything, he was still just Jesus of Nazareth. After they had been riding like this for a while, they arrived at an inn.

"It's such lovely weather today, Caspar," said Jesus, breaking the silence. "Let's stop here, relax, have some food and drink a good pitcher of wine."

Caspar nodded in agreement. They dismounted, tied up the horses and sat down at a table outside. It was a lovely place to stop, right in the middle of a wood. The sunlight was filtered by the leaves and the wind murmured gently through the branches. Jesus savoured the moment. He looked at Caspar sitting opposite him and felt a warm affection for the old man. Of course the fact that he had been there at the start of his life created a huge bond between the two. And Jesus was very appreciative of the way he was taking him all over the country despite his advanced age.

The innkeeper brought them a pitcher of red wine and some bread and they ordered two bowls of soup. Jesus wished he could make time stand still so that they could remain sitting there for all eternity. They toasted each other and drank. Soon the innkeeper returned with the soup. Not wanting it to go cold, they ate it straight away, enjoying the flavours.

"You know, Caspar," said Jesus in between two mouthfuls. "It's so different being here compared to back home in Galilee. Your people have really absorbed the teachings of Zarathustra and you see that in everything. I feel so at ease here. Now I think about it, there's a huge amount to be done back home!"

"The situation in your country is not easy, of course," observed Caspar. "It's an occupied territory and there are a lot of political interests at stake."

Jesus nodded and remained deep in thought for a moment. Caspar saw the relaxed look in his eyes disappear, to be replaced by a certain unease. He asked sympathetically,

"Are you afraid to follow your calling?"

Jesus shrugged.

"I don't know," he replied quietly. "I don't think it's fear as such, more a feeling that it seems so inevitable. I can feel God's power becoming stronger in me and I wonder what the future holds in store for me. Many people in Israel are hoping for the Messiah to come and I'm a member of the house of David. But that's obviously not my mission. But how can I make that clear to people? And how will I still be able to remain myself when the Holy Spirit unites with me? How much of myself will I have to sacrifice in order to do God's will?"

Caspar nodded with understanding and Jesus continued to speak from the heart.

"Do you know, Caspar, what I find most difficult? That God never asked me first if I wanted all this, at least, I can't remember that ever happening. Everyone makes plans for the future and has expectations about how their life will turn out. But I never had all that. I feel I've been destined for this ever since I was a small child and I sometimes wonder whether I want to continue doing it. But there doesn't seem to be a way out."

"And if you had been able to choose for yourself, Jesus, what would you have done differently?" asked Caspar, thereby hitting the nail on the head.

Jesus had not been expecting this question. He thought for a moment, then admitted,

"I don't know. I'm actually very happy at the moment. God fills my soul. Knowing Him is the greatest prize a human being can have. His energy supports me in everything I do. My wish is that everyone can experience this and live united with God."

"Then keep hold of that feeling in everything you do," advised Caspar. "And who knows, if God wills it then your wish will be granted! And surely it'll be fantastic if you can play a part in achieving that!"

He raised his cup and said cheerfully,

"Let's drink to that, Jesus! To your wish being granted!"

Jesus laughed to chase away his unease, and picked up his cup too. They toasted one another again and finished their soup. And it was good, sitting there and enjoying life.

While Jesus had only intended spending a few weeks in Persia, the weeks turned into months, then into years and before he knew it he was coming up to his twenty-sixth birthday. He decided to give a big party to show his gratitude for all the understanding he had found in this country. Naturally, Caspar was invited, along with the other wise men from the temple. But Jesus had not forgotten the ordinary folk, which meant farmers were sitting next to priests and bakers next to temple officials. A group of musicians provided lively entertainment and people were laughing, singing and dancing.

Jesus was relishing the occasion. After finishing the meal, he mingled among his guests. He saw the table where the wise men had gathered, sat down with them and said contentedly,

"My brothers, I know for sure that you have the blessing of my Father. Your master Zarathustra has done so many good things that have brought you closer to God. Because he was right when he said that God created heaven and earth, the sun, the moon and the stars. There is really only one aspect of his teachings that I do not agree with. Because Zarathustra said God also produced an evil power. I wonder how God, who is love and love alone, could have produced evil. Perhaps one of you can explain this?"

The wise men were embarrassed by his question and Caspar said somewhat reproachfully,

"Well, Jesus, that's a very tricky question you've come up with! And on a day of relaxation like today! Why don't you let that matter rest and pour us another cupful?"

But one of the others responded,

"No, no, Caspar, we won't just brush him off like that. After all, we do acknowledge that there's evil in the world. And if God didn't create that evil, where did it come from then?"

Caspar felt he was being called upon to reply so shrugging his shoulders, he said,

"I wouldn't like to say! But Jesus," he continued in a teasing tone, "you've put us in a quandary but now I'd like to pass the challenge back to you. Tell us what you think about the matter, instead of putting us in a tight spot like this!"

The others applauded. In support of Caspar, they called out merrily,

"Yes, come on Jesus. Tell us the answer! After all, that was where you were heading, wasn't it?"

Jesus laughed and he stood up to tackle the challenge. Everyone listened with bated breath as he spoke,

"Whatever God makes is good. Everything that comes from the hands of Him, is good. Now everything that is created has its own sound, colour and shape. But some sounds, however good and pure on their own, can sound harsh and dissonant in combination with others. You will have noticed that when you pluck the strings of a harp. Each note on its own is perfect and pure. But if you play a wrong chord, it jars on your ears. So evil is such a dissonance in the colours, sounds or shapes of good.

Now God in His infinite wisdom gave man his own will when He created him. After all, He prefers to have creatures that choose to do His bidding from their own free will and with all their heart rather than dumb puppets. But this also means that man has the power to mix God's good things in all kinds of combinations, thus leading to dissonance and evil every day. So it is man, and no-one other than man, who has caused all the evil and it is man only who can drive it away again!"

When he had said this, he sat down again and his audience were speechless. Caspar, who had after all seen a great deal of him already, was amazed once again by what his Hebrew friend had to say. He cried out ecstatically,

"Let's drink to our host, friends! Because God's wisdom that was introduced to us by Zarathustra has come to us once again!"

They all raised their cups, toasted Jesus, patted him on the shoulder and showered him with compliments. And Jesus laughed and drank - finally staggering into bed at the end of the party, feeling rather giddy from the wine.

He woke up the following morning with a pounding headache. His temples were throbbing and the light hurt his eyes. He groaned, pulled the sheets over his head and cursed himself for having drunk too much. In marked contrast to his usual routine, he remained in bed and dozed off. Until he realised that the pounding was not just coming from his head; there was someone knocking on the door. His befuddled brain only vaguely perceived the sound and it took a while for him to grasp that he could not stay lying in bed for ever - he would have to see who was at the door.

"I'm coming!" he called and got up slowly.

This was a difficult move. He had never got drunk before and now he was feeling nauseous and dizzy. He stumbled towards the door, opened it and leaned against the doorpost, afraid he would lose his balance otherwise. A humbly dressed man stood before him with a letter in his hand.

"Good morning," he said, giving Jesus a critical look. "Are you Jesus, son of Joseph the carpenter from Nazareth?"

Jesus nodded.

"Yes, I am," he replied in a rather shaky voice.

"I have come from Galilee to look for you," continued the man in a serious tone. "I have a message from your mother. Unfortunately, I have to tell you that your father has passed away after a short illness. You can read all about it in this letter."

He wanted to hand him the letter, but Jesus stared at him absently. The man's words had not really sunk in yet.

"Did you understand what I said, sir?" asked the man, surveying his pale face with concern. "This letter is for you, from your mother!"

Jesus looked at him vacantly. He took the letter as if in a trance. It was only when he read the addressing and recognised his mother's handwriting that the message got through to him.

"Please excuse me," he apologised. "I'm not feeling so well today. But I did understand your message. Thank you for having gone to so much trouble to find me. I'll read the letter at once. Where can I find you to give you my reply?"

"I'm staying in the inn around the corner for the time being," answered the man. "And I certainly won't be going back today so there's no need to rush."

Jesus thanked him again and closed the door. He sat down on his bed and opened the letter with trembling hands. He was touched at the sight of his mother's familiar handwriting as he read:

My dear son,

I am writing you this letter in the hope that one day you'll read it. Not knowing whether you are alive or dead is a real burden on me, especially now that your father is gone. I should tell you that you father passed away in full confidence that you are fine. He has encouraged me in this regard and so there is still a small spark of hope in my heart that this will reach you.

Your father's death was the result of an accident at work. He let his attention lapse for a moment and cut his hand with the saw. At first it seemed to be all right but then the wound started to fester and in the end that was what killed him. Our master from Qumran has tried to stop the infection with herbal compresses, but unfortunately they had no effect. What a pity you weren't with us. Perhaps you could have done better. But anyway, that wasn't the case.

I hope you are doing well and that you think of me from time to time. I miss you and long to see you again. So if you have an opportunity to drop in on us, I would be very pleased to see you.

Your mother, Mary.

The letter's sombre tone weighed heavily on Jesus and he was overcome by a strong feeling of impotence. Indeed, why had he not been there at his father's side in his final hour? Why had he abandoned his mother to her grief? Why had he not thought of them more often, of their goodness in entrusting him to Lamaas like that, not knowing when they would see him again, all because of his calling that he had to follow?

A silent tear ran down his cheek. In a vain attempt to express his impotence he cried out, grabbed the jug of water that he always had next to his bed and threw it savagely across the room. And he wept. His head was still throbbing, his hands were trembling, he was nauseous and he had never felt so unhappy in his entire life. He had helped so many people, in India and here in Persia. But he had neglected his own father. How bitter this felt. And he silently reproached God. Why had He not let him know his father needed him? But at the same time he realised that he should not put the blame on God. After all, it was he who had decided to stay such a long time in Persia because he felt so at ease here. Even though he knew that his actual task lay in his home country with the people of Israel.

He felt sickened by his egotism and the fear that had prevented him from returning home. But how was he to deal with his friends, acquaintances and neighbours? How could he ever explain his relationship with God to them and what God wanted him to do? How could they understand that and would they be able to accept that he would be taking such an unusual path? He realised all too well that all these doubts had kept him in Persia. Ignoring the mess, he crawled back into bed and hid under the sheets, hiding from his own lack of confidence.

That was how Caspar found him when he came to see what was going on, bothered by the strange noises. He was shocked when he saw Jesus. Was this the same young man who had spoken so eloquently yesterday at the party? The bundle of misery he saw now seemed a different person.

"Hey, what is it, Jesus?" he asked with concern and he sat down on the edge of the bed.

Jesus came up and put his arms round the old man. A little embarrassed, Caspar hugged him. They sat there in silence until Jesus faltered, realising the route he had to take,

"I can't hide away here any longer, Caspar. I have to go back home and really do what it was God has called on me to do."

He gave him his mother's letter to read. Caspar nodded silently.

"You're right," he said based, "It's a pity. I'll miss you."

They looked at each other and Jesus could see that Caspar knew exactly how he was feeling. They embraced again and Caspar whispered in his ear,

"Don't be afraid, Jesus. I have seen what you are capable of. You can do it and you know that. Trust in God. He loves you more than anyone else. And rightly so, because I have never met such a wonderful person. Thank you for letting me be your friend. I will be thinking of you and praying for you. And now you must write back to your mother and send the letter with the fastest messenger, so that she knows you are on your way. That will make her so happy! That thought ought to cheer you up, I should think!"

Caspar's reassuring words revived Jesus and he began to feel a little better. He smiled hesitantly, then asked,

"Would you please help me first to clear up this mess? And I'll buy you a new pitcher."

Caspar burst out laughing.

"There's no need for that," he said indulgently. "There are pitchers galore in this house!"

Together, they gathered up the shards and dried the floor. Then Jesus sat down at the table with ink, pen and papyrus. After thinking for a moment, he wrote:

My dearest mother,

Thank you for letting me know that father is no longer with us. I am sorry I wasn't able to do anything for him. But mother, you do know that God is looking after him now. So let us look back in gratitude on his life. And please don't cry anymore, because your tears won't take away your grief. It is better to care for those who are still alive. Then you will be able to enjoy the sun again and the dew in the fields, the birds singing, the flowers and the stars. I know for certain that father will be waiting for you when your own life comes to an end.

I will soon be returning home and I will bring a gift for you more valuable than gold or precious stones. I hope that James and Simon are looking after you properly and that you soon feel better. For now I am with you in my thoughts, until we see other again in the flesh. Please give my love to Miriam and I look forward to seeing you soon,

Yours, Jehoshua.

When he had finished writing, he went in search of the messenger and found him in the inn. With some difficulty, he persuaded the man to set off back home that same day. So it was that his letter was on its way to Nazareth that very afternoon to make his mother happier than she had been for a long time.

Galilee

Now that Jesus had finally taken the decision to return home, he wasted no time in making the actions match the words. He bought things he would need for the journey and Caspar gave him one of his horses to take with him, nonchalantly waving aside Jesus' objections to such an excessively valuable gift.

He left Persia behind him with mixed feelings. He was looking forward to seeing his family again. At the same time, he was going to find it difficult to meet them again after all these years. James, just a boy of eleven when he left, was now a grown man and probably long married. And how would things have turned out for Simon? Would he really have become a farmer, as he had always wanted? And Miriam, his sweet little sister, was quite possibly already a mother.

It was an emotional moment when he reached the River Jordan a number of weeks later and saw the familiar landscape. It made him want to get back home as quickly as possible. He decided to keep riding through the night and so he was able to arrive in Nazareth late in the afternoon the next day. It brought back all kinds of old memories - hardly anything had changed. Excitedly, he turned into Marmion Street and he was in front of his parents' house in no time. It was exactly how he remembered it: the porch where he used to saw planks with his father, the modest vegetable garden, the fence he had once built. He had the feeling that his entire youth was flashing before his eyes in just a few seconds, and there was a sudden clear image in his mind's eye of his mother, laughing and playing with him. He was all but overcome with the need to see her again after all this time. He hurriedly hitched his horse's reins to the fence, ran to the door and pushed it open.

And there was his mother. She was standing with her back to him, folding the linen, but she was startled by the door being thrown casually open and turned round. Jesus bounded across to her. Impetuously, he threw his arms around her and, overflowing with emotion he stammered,

"Mother, my dearest mother!"

The emotions overwhelmed him. He felt his voice catch in his throat and he began to weep. Mary was unsteady on her feet, so surprised by his sudden appearance that she almost fell. But Jesus held her tight and said in a choked voice,

"Mother, I'm so sorry that I stayed away for so long. I know - I should have written to you more often. Please forgive me... But you did get my last letter, didn't you?"

Without waiting for her answer, he kissed her impulsively on her cheeks and stroked her hair. He saw that it was now streaked with grey, making him feel even more ashamed that he had left her alone for so long.

"Is everything all right with you, mother?" he asked. "Has James looked after you well? And are you in good health?"

Once again, he hardly gave her any opportunity to respond. He felt as if he had years of catching up to do and he eagerly drank in the sight of her. He was relieved to see that she looked well - older of course, but that somehow made her even more beautiful than he remembered. Mary was bemused by it all. His unexpected presence completely overwhelmed her and she was unable to utter a word. Jesus saw her confusion. He took hold of her arm lovingly and said,

"Come, let's sit down for a moment."

On the bench, he drew her close, an arm still around her protectively. It was only then that Mary found her voice again.

"Yes, I got your letter. You can't believe how glad I was to hear from you. I've been so worried so often, and missed you so dreadfully!"

Jesus took her hands and planted a firm kiss on them.

"I'm not going away for now," he assured her. "I'm going to stay here a while first, until I know what I have to do."

He looked around and saw that the house was clean and tidy. Mary followed his gaze and said,

"Your sister Miriam still lives with me and helps me with everything. She's been my greatest source of support all this time. I mean, your brothers are both married and can't spare all that much time to look in on their mother. Wait, I'll call her."

She disentangled herself from his embrace and went into the kitchen. One moment later, Miriam was standing in front of him. Her brother seemed to her to have changed so much that she hardly recognised him. But Jesus recognised her at once. He embraced her and thanked her for looking after their mother so well. And later that day, he told them about everything he had seen and done. How he had denounced the caste system in India. That he had then had to flee but had found a safe haven in Persia. About what a good friend Caspar had been to him and how he had come closer to God. They saw just how inspired he was and realised that this was only the beginning and that he would be capable of much greater things yet. Delighted that he was there with them, they made up his old room for him. When Jesus went to bed that evening and saw the familiar view from the window, he realised just how good it was to be back home again. Fatigued by the journey, but blissfully delighted nonetheless, he stretched out on his bed. It seemed as if he had never been away; he was fast asleep in next to no time.

After the euphoria of those first few weeks, in which Jesus had taken great pleasure in rediscovering everything about Nazareth, the small town began to feel oppressive. He was unable to settle into any kind of rhythm and restlessness set in. He missed his father, who had always been the glue that held the family together. And although God was always present, He had not yet made clear what was expected of him.

Waiting and not knowing what he was supposed to do made him impatient and so he put all his efforts into his work as a carpenter. Mary often heard him sanding and sawing until late in the evening. The physical work distracted him from his thoughts and he was extremely productive, making beds and tables for nothing for the poor people of the area, as well as helping with other jobs.

His brothers were pretty scornful about it all. They did not understand him in the slightest and their attitude was distinctly condescending. When they found out that he had come back from his travels without bringing any money or other valuables, they were unable to see him as anything other than a worthless adventurer. They accused him of having been indifferent to their fate and only having sought his own fulfilment. Jesus was deeply hurt by the way they treated him. Whereas he had told Miriam and his mother in great detail about everything he had done, he stayed resolutely silent on the subject with his brothers. He did not feel any obligation to justify or defend his actions. They in turn perceived this as indifference, which annoyed them even more, all the more so because Mary was clearly delighted to have Jesus back home. She did see that he was feeling ill at ease, though, and one day she said,

"You've been working so hard lately, Jesus. Why don't you take a bit of a break? You could go to Jerusalem or visit your friends in the monastery."

Jesus looked up in surprise.

"To be honest, that's one of the things I've been thinking I might do," he admitted. "But I don't want to leave you alone again."

"Are you mad?" said Mary, waving his objections away. "I'll be just fine! Although I have been wondering exactly what's bothering you. Those brothers of yours aren't getting to you, are they?"

Jesus smiled.

"No, that's not it," he reassured her. "But I am finding it tough, not knowing what God wants from me."

And with still enough of a sense of humour he added jokingly,

"Most of Nazareth has new furniture by now, I reckon! I really don't know what I can keep doing here to make myself useful for much longer."

Mary burst out laughing.

"That's why you should go," she repeated. "As long as you agree that you'll be back when Reuben and Miriam get married. Then you'll have something nice to look forward to."

Jesus nodded in relief. He wouldn't want to miss his sister's wedding, of course! He was so pleased that she had finally met the man of her dreams. The next day, he saddled his horse and he decided to go and visit the monastery first. After a couple of days, he saw the familiar buildings before him - an emotional sight. What a wonderful time he had had there! Expectantly, he raised the big door knocker and let it resound on the gate. To his great delight, it was Matheno who opened the door. Although they had not seen one another for nearly twenty years, Matheno recognised him at once.

"Jesus?!" he cried out in surprise. "How can it be? There you are, right in front of me all of a sudden!"

He examined him from top to toe and saw that his friend was still the same confident and honest figure as always. And he could also see the enormous charisma that the young man was exuding and sense the almost physical power radiating from him. He put his arms round him and embraced him closely. Jesus laughed heartily at his enthusiasm.

"Matheno! How good to see you. How are you doing?"

"Fine, thank you. Everyone here is doing fine, actually. Apart from Brother Michael; he died a couple of years ago. But wait - first I'll let the abbot know that you're here!"

He sent a younger brother off, and the leader of the order appeared a short while later.

"How wonderful to see you again!" he said emotionally, "I've wondered so often if I would ever get to see more of you in action."

He took Jesus off to his room. Jesus let his gaze wander around the familiar spaces and he relived everything that had happened to him there. He completely fell silent. The abbot saw his emotions. Giving him some time to recover, he went to the kitchen to fetch something to drink. When he got back, he found Jesus sitting at the table, holding his head in his hands. Carefully, he laid a hand on the younger man's shoulder.

"Are you all right?" he asked in concern.

Jesus gave him a reassuring nod.

"Yes, I'm fine again. I just hadn't expected quite how much this would affect me."

He let his gaze roam around once more. Then he looked up at the abbot with a cautious smile.

"If only I could still be that child," he said, opening his heart. "Everything seemed so clear and straightforward then. How completely different it feels now. I've been on a long journey, and I've been back in Israel for some time now. But I still have no idea what God wants from me. That's why I've come here. Are you able to point me in the right direction, do you think?"

"I'm afraid not," answered the abbot as he filled two cups. "That really is a question for God. But there are lots of things going on in our country. Have you heard that Rome has appointed a new governor? He's called Pilate and he's moved into the fortress

Antonia. He's already getting quite a name as a vicious overlord. Herod gets on with him nicely enough, of course. Although he's the tetrarch of Galilee, he's actually always in Jerusalem, organising huge feasts. And Caiaphas has taken over the role of high priest from Hillel. He's pretty conservative. All in all, it hasn't got any easier for our people."

"Yes, I'd heard that," nodded Jesus, worried. "And I've been thinking about it too. You know - we've been told so often that our people would have a privileged place above the other peoples. But now that I've been to India and Persia, I'm no longer able to believe that God plays favourites. I mean, He is fair and just, and His love surely extends to everyone. Aren't Persians and Romans just as much my Father's children as we Israelites are? Things will only start going better in our country once we recognise that and really take an interest when we look at our fellow humans, I'm sure of that."

"You're right, of course," confirmed the abbot. "But don't expect that you'll find much sympathy for that point of view. We are an occupied country and people won't take kindly to you talking about the occupying forces in that way. But tell me: what was all that about - have you really been to India and Persia?"

"Yes, I have," replied Jesus enthusiastically. "And I've learned so much there! India is dominated above all by fear. People are bound rigidly into their castes, some of them afraid of losing their power and others afraid of the power that they are subject to. Luckily I was able to give many of them hope for a better life. And did you know that Zarathustra's teachings are still very much being kept alive in Persia? Here, have a look at this!"

He ferreted around in his rucksack and let the abbot read the precious text of Zarathustra, which he had brought from Persepolis. The abbot was deeply impressed. Once again, he realised just how special Jesus' destiny must be.

"What's your experience of this text, Jesus?" he asked. "What does it do for you?"

Jesus took the sheet from him and ran his eyes over the now familiar letters.

"The word 'logos' intrigues me," he answered. "It makes me even more convinced that the most important thing is for me to be a medium for God's words and that I have to keep well away from political games. And what I find difficult is the idea of me as Christ. You know, I do still feel that I'm just Jesus of Nazareth and I hope that people aren't going to start looking up at me too much and putting me into the role of king or Messiah. They tended to do that a bit in Persia, and it just doesn't suit me. By the way - that reminds me: I've got something for you!"

He rummaged around in his bag again, this time producing the copy of the Ayur Veda that he had written out in India. Astonished, the abbot took the book.

"What a wonderful gift!" he exclaimed. "Have you carried that around with you all that time, especially for me?"

"My pleasure!" said Jesus with a smile. "I'm well used to trekking around and having to carry all my belongings with me."

Clearly delighted with his present, the abbot carefully placed the book in his cabinet. And to Jesus' surprise, he brought out a package in turn.

"If presents are going to be handed out, I'm not going to be left out," he laughed. "This has been waiting for you for a long time. Various brothers have worked on it. I hope you like it."

Curiously, Jesus unrolled the package to reveal a wonderful robe. The garment was pure white, woven in a single piece with no seams. It had clearly been made with a great deal of love.

"It's wonderful! Thank you very much," he said, visibly touched, letting the soft, supple material run gently through his fingers.

"I hope you will wear it a lot," smiled the abbot. "And I hope it will make you think of us occasionally... Although I know you'd do that even without the gift."

While he poured them another drink, he added earnestly,

"Besides, there's something else I've got to tell you, Jesus. You just said that you don't want to be seen as a king. If so, you definitely have to know that there's something strange going on close to the monastery here. A man called John is getting a great deal of attention, baptising people in the River Jordan. He says that he wants to prepare them for the arrival of the true king. A lot of people are going to him. It seems as if our people are craving more than ever for someone to show them the true path."

Jesus frowned.

"Why is he doing that, the baptising?" he asked. "What's the meaning of that act?"

"It's meant to be some kind of purification," answered the abbot. "He preaches that people have to cleanse their souls, so that they will be pure when the true king comes. Some of them even think that he's the true king. But we know better, don't we?"

He put his hand on Jesus' arm and said on a confidential note,

"Maybe it would be good if you went for a look. It can't just be a coincidence that he's started this now that you're back in Israel. Who knows - maybe he's the one preparing the way, the one prophesied by Isaiah."

His words elicited a small rush of excitement in Jesus. After all this time, was this finally the sign from God that he had been waiting for? The abbot saw his agitation. Smiling, he said,

"I won't be offended if you want to leave again. You've got more important things to do now!"

He accompanied Jesus to the gate where they embraced one last time. Then Jesus mounted his horse, left the monastery behind and rode towards the River Jordan. To his astonishment, he found an increasing number of people on the road with him. The abbot had not been exaggerating: John's activities were indeed drawing large numbers of people. His heart was beating faster than usual by the time he saw the river. Curious as to what he would find there, he hitched his horse to a shrub and followed the others until they came to a ford. A man was standing there, waist-deep in the water. Full of fire, he was addressing the crowd.

"Get ready, people of Israel, get ready to meet your king! You may think that I am just one person crying out in the wilderness. But I say to you: we have to prepare the way for him, smooth his path, for this Prince of Peace will soon be coming, bringing the love of God to you. So wash away your sins in this river. Let yourselves be baptised to show that you are prepared to cleanse your souls. Only then will you be worthy to see this great king."

Jesus saw that some people were cautiously descending to the river bank and letting him baptise them. Someone in the crowd called out,

"Tell us, John, what else can we do to make ourselves worthy of this king?"

John was right in his flow now, replying,

"Show that you really do love your fellow man. Do not keep all your possessions for yourself, but share them with others instead. If you have two cloaks, give one of them to somebody who has none. And share your food with those who need it."

There were also some tax collectors there, people whose job meant that they were not really popular.

"What about us, John?" cried one of them. "What can we do?"

"Do your work honestly," replied John with intense conviction. "Don't raise the taxes that people have to pay merely to improve your own lot. And you lot," he added, turning to a group of soldiers, "Don't be unnecessarily violent to others. No plundering and looting - be content with the salary you receive."

The people were amazed at the honesty of his words, and someone asked,

"Are you the Messiah then, the one we have been promised?"

Jesus held his breath a moment. Of all the people present, he was perhaps the one who was most curious about how John would answer this question. John spoke up firmly,

"Definitely not! For I baptise with water, but the one who follows me will baptise with love."

His words moved Jesus, and with a surge of emotion he pushed through to the front of the crowd. The gratitude rang clear in his voice as he said,

"Good friend, you are a man after God's heart. And you're right - the kingdom is coming soon, so please baptise me, for now I would like to open up and accept the task that God has entrusted me with."

He shrugged off his coat and reached out with one hand. John looked in astonishment at this stranger, a man he did not know, yet who intrigued him in some way. He waded over to Jesus, took his hand and led him into the water. They looked at each other for a moment and both sensed a strange chemistry between them. Then Jesus allowed himself to be submerged.

And from one moment to the next, a violent storm rushed through his body, a purple and violet tempest that blended past, present and future together into a single, unified and perfectly balanced whole. Jesus realised that this was thé moment, the point when the energy of the Holy Spirit had become part of him and he sank down further, deeper and deeper into a purple ocean of pure love until John helped him back to his feet. Overcome, he struggled up out of the water and back onto his feet. And at exactly that moment, the two of them heard a voice, the voice that already was so familiar to Jesus:

"This is My son, Jesus of Nazareth, who shall henceforth bear my Holy Spirit within him. Through him shall My love be revealed!"

John looked at the man opposite him in amazement. He realised that he had been permitted a glimpse of the reality that controlled Jesus' life. Understanding the full significance of those words, he embraced him closely. Then he had to turn his full attention to the people along the shore once again.

Jesus' heart was pounding as he scrambled back up onto the bank. He had never before experienced the presence of his Father as intensely as in that moment. Totally withdrawn into his own world, he picked up his coat and rode off towards the desert, where he would not encounter anyone else. He hitched his horse to a rock and sat down on the hard earth. He closed his eyes and immediately felt the tingling energy of the Holy Spirit throughout his body. He probed at the new sensation cautiously, trying to accustom himself to the idea that this connection would be part of his life from now on. It did not feel comfortably yet - if anything it was rather frightening - and he prayed,

"Lord God, I know that I should be thankful for this splendid gift, but at the moment it scares me. Please help me to bear this enormous power and guard me against making the wrong choices. I'm only human, after all, and the temptations on my path will be severe. I will very much need Your support."

He heard God's reassuring voice in his head immediately.

"Of course I will help you, Jesus: My love is always there for you. You used to feel My love when you were a child, although that memory may perhaps have faded. That is why my Holy Spirit is now part of you. It is the link between you and My love, which you will henceforth always be able to feel and express. Just let yourself be taken up in this flow of love, as Buddha and Zarathustra did before you, and discover the true meaning of life. That current will always carry you in the right direction, have no fear. Trust in this divine power that will lead not only you but each and every person to their natural destiny. So help people to make contact with the divine spark that is present in every one of them. Let them feel that they are one - one with each other and one with Me. Everybody can be swept along on this divine current and finally reach their destination. Teach them this: that is all that I want from you."

His voice faded away, leaving a very confused Jesus behind. The confirmation that God was indeed putting him in the same line as the great spiritual leaders Buddha and Zarathustra was utterly overwhelming and he decided to stay for a while at this lonely spot to let it all sink in.

It took Jesus quite some time to get used to his connection with God's Holy Spirit. His confidence did grow gradually, though, and he began to get a clearer picture of exactly what his assignment was. He realised that this was the second time in his life that he had sought out the desert. The first he had been full of doubts and God had seemed further away than ever - whereas this time, he knew that he could trust God unconditionally. That meant that he was finally ready for his task. He stood up, stretched and packed his bag. He changed his clothes for the splendid robe that the monks had given him and decided that the first thing he would do would be to pay John a visit. It was still early, so he would at least get there before the crowds. He saddled his horse and rode back to the River Jordan.

John's heart jumped up when he saw Jesus coming. He walked over to him and prostrated himself on the ground before him, hugging the other man's legs. His voice was muffled as he said,

"Thank God that you're here before me once again! I was so afraid that I would never see you again in this life, my king!"

Jesus bent over towards him and helped him to his feet.

"What do you mean - saying you were afraid you would never see me again in this life?" he asked with concern. "Do you fear for your life?"

John looked around nervously. Then he led Jesus by the arm to his tent, only answering when they were safely inside.

"Yes, I fear for my life. Herod keeps an eye on me, day and night. He's terrified that the people will acclaim me as their king. To be perfectly honest, I'm half expecting to be arrested any day now."

He held Jesus' hand tightly.

"Listen!" he said conspiratorially. "If you want to have even the slightest chance of succeeding, make sure that you've always got people around you. I'm a loner and that makes me an easy target. Don't let that happen to you. Believe me: you can't do this on your own. So make sure that your work can continue after you've gone. Take pupils who will be able to keep spreading your message if you should meet with some... misfortune."

Jesus stared motionlessly for a moment. Then he put his arms around the man.

"Thank you for being so concerned about me," he whispered, moved by John's misgivings. "I'm afraid I can't stay here to be at your side. I have things I must do in Galilee. But I shall think of you every day, and I shall pray for you."

John extricated himself shyly from his embrace and they both crawled back out of the tent. They saw two men nearby, busy making a simple breakfast. John walked over to them animatedly.

"Peter, Philip - I've absolutely got to introduce you to Jesus of Nazareth," he said, interrupting what they were doing. "This is the person I've been talking about all this time. I may not be the one who has been chosen by God, but he is!"

The two men studied Jesus curiously.

"We're here because we heard that John was supposed to be the Messiah," said Peter with a smile. "But as it would seem we were clearly mistaken, perhaps it's better that we should stay with you. You can probably make good use of our help."

"That's an excellent idea," nodded John in agreement. "I've already told him that he should take on some pupils."

Amazed that Peter was ready to put so much faith in him so quickly, Jesus scrutinised the man opposite and he could sense that this was someone whose offer of friendship would be unconditional.

"What do you do for a living, Peter?" he asked.

"I'm a fisherman, sir," replied Peter, delighted that Jesus seemed at least to be considering his proposal.

Jesus put a hand on his shoulder.

"Then you may help me to become a fisher of men," he laughed.

He said farewell to John, left his horse behind and went on his way on foot in the company of Peter and Philip. He soon noticed that the two men were keen to learn from him.

"Tell us, master, is the kingdom really that close at hand?" they asked him after they had been walking for a while.

"It certainly is," nodded Jesus. "I have come to plant that spark on Earth, and I will cherish it until it flares up!"

"So Israel will soon be free again?" cried Philip enthusiastically. "With you as the king, someone from the House of David on the throne?"

"That's not what I've been saying!" said Jesus, laughing. "I haven't come here to wage a political battle. Instead, I'm going to teach you about inner freedom, which is how I will show you the way to the true kingdom."

Peter and Philip looked at each other, slightly disappointed. Was this what they wanted to hear?

"So where is that true kingdom, then?" asked Peter somewhat scornfully.

"Not in heaven," replied Jesus, "because then the birds would have got there before you. And not in the oceans, because then the fish would have been there before you. No, the true kingdom lies within you. You can find it by understanding that everything you have learned has only served the interests of politics or selfishness, that vanity has been a driving force in your lives, and that you have not lived the lives you could have done. Divorcing yourselves from all that is the only way to see that all you need to do is be a true person, and nothing more than that. And then you will be content, freed of the burdens that have always oppressed you."

"And it's possible to do that, even if when living in an occupied country?" asked Philip hesitantly.

"Exactly!" nodded Jesus. "I mean, true freedom is something you can find in yourself, no matter what circumstances you are living in."

He was pleased to see that his disciples seemed to understand him.

"Come on!" he said cheerfully. "Let's go and find the baker in that village. I'm hungry!"

They wandered through the streets looking for the baker's shop until their attention was drawn to a commotion a little further up. A Roman legionary with a whip was flogging a man who was lying helpless on the ground. When they got closer they could hear the man howling in pain, seeing with disgust that none of the onlookers was doing anything whatsoever to help him. Furiously, Peter ran up to the group and yanked the whip out of the Roman's hand in a single fluid motion. His whole intervention had only taken a few heartbeats and the soldier stood there looking at him, stunned. Then he suddenly tried to run off. However Peter was quick enough to grab him.

"No way, mate, you just stay here a moment!" he snapped at him. "Or do I have to give you a taste of your own medicine?"

He raised the whip menacingly and the legionary cowered away. Jesus was just able to get between them in time

"No Peter, of course that's not the answer!" he said sharply, taking the whip and throwing it to the ground.

Then he knelt by the victim. The poor man was badly shaken by the incident, not to mention the ugly welts on his back. Jesus quickly took a cloth out of his rucksack and carefully dabbed the wounds with a soothing oil that he had made some time ago. The potion soon did its work. The man gave a deep sigh.

"That's already making it a bit more bearable," he whispered, summoning up a cautious smile. "Thank you very much; I think I can manage again from here."

"There's no need for you to thank me," Jesus smiled modestly. "And that Roman won't be bothering you again, I'll make sure of that."

He stood up and turned to the legionary, whom Peter still had in a wrestler's hold. He looked the man up and down critically, noticing that he was actually little more than a boy.

"What is your name, Roman?" he asked in a stern but not unfriendly tone. "And how old are you?"

"Gaius Octavius, sir," answered the boy hurriedly, tripping over his own words. "I'm Gaius Octavius. And I'm seventeen years old."

"Tell me Gaius. Why were you beating this man?"

"He had been stealing, sir! And our rules say that you're not allowed to do that."

"I understand that," nodded Jesus, "but didn't you first ask him what had led him to be stealing?"

Gaius looked at him in surprise.

"No, to be honest, I didn't," he admitted hesitantly. "I was only thinking about our rules, because I've been taught to enforce them no matter what."

"That doesn't seem to be an excuse for not thinking before you act," said Jesus equitably. "What did he actually take? You haven't told me that yet."

Gaius blushed slightly.

"A... loaf of bread, sir," he stuttered.

"A loaf of bread..." repeated Jesus. "And you beat him up so badly just for that?"

Gaius' cheeks flushed a deeper red and he did not know what to say. Jesus gestured to Peter that he should let the lad go and placed his hand on Gaius' shoulder.

"You're still young, Gaius. Why did you enlist?"

"My family isn't very well off," replied Gaius, "my mother can make good use of the wages I earn."

"A good enough reason, I suppose," smiled Jesus. "Better to earn your money honestly than perhaps having to steal a loaf because your mother wouldn't otherwise have anything to eat, wouldn't you say?"

Gaius looked at him in astonishment. Then he shook Jesus' hand off frantically and sprinted away. Jesus watched him go, shaking his head. Then he turned round and saw that quite a number of people had been following the incident.

"Hey, why do you just let him go?" asked someone in the crowd with venom in his voice. "He doesn't deserve to get away with this unpunished!"

Jesus looked at him with grave disappointment.

"And why not?" he asked sharply. "Wouldn't you prefer people to treat you with a bit of understanding, rather than always treating you with contempt? Suppose you'd been that boy - what then? Surely everyone has the right to be treated fairly, no matter whether they're Roman or Jewish. We are all God's children, and - believe me - He treats us all the same!"

And, ignoring the crowd, he stuffed his things back into his bag and gestured to Peter and Philip that they were moving on. They followed him out of the village, without bread, but with plenty of food for thought. They walked in silence for a while, until Philip said,

"To be honest, I can understand that man's reaction. I don't think many people are so forgiving that they can understand what you did back there."

"Nevertheless, it's the only way," answered Jesus with conviction.

"That boy won't be so quick to pick up a whip again next time. Whereas if we'd punished him, he would have been out for revenge. But it does show that we still have a long way to go."

Philip nodded silently. Quiet admiration was taking root in his heart for this man who was so much wiser than he was.

And so they travelled further, with Jesus drawing attention wherever they went. A number of prophets were roaming around the countryside in those days, but Jesus was so clearly on a different level that people wanted to see him wherever he went so that they could be touched by the loving power of God that emanated from him. Every day, Peter and Philip were astounded by what he did. But Jesus made them promise not to speak of him as Christ, because he did not want to draw attention to himself while they were still in Judea.

When Jesus was finally back in Nazareth, Mary could see the change that had come over him. She could barely recognise her son anymore in this confident figure of a man dressed in his spotless white robe, and she talked at length with Peter about everything he had seen of Jesus as they travelled together. She understood just how much the Holy Spirit was affecting his being, and she too was watching him in tense expectancy.

Miriam was absolutely delighted that her brother was back in time for her wedding. It was promising to turn into a huge party. James, who had taken on the role of master of ceremonies, had hired an inn in Canaan, where Reuben had been born, and invited lots of people from both Canaan and Nazareth. The family set off early in Mary's cart, which Jesus and his friends had festooned with ribbons and flowers. Miriam looked an absolute picture in her bridal dress. When they reached the inn, Reuben could hardly keep his emotions in check. He lifted her carefully from the cart and kissed her full on the mouth, in full view of all the guests. Jesus laughed out loud, because Miriam was clearly so embarrassed that she didn't know what to do. Under the canopy, the rabbi pronounced the seven blessings over them. Then the guests sat down at the long tables. The innkeeper was hurrying back and forth and everyone was soon in a good mood. A group of musicians were playing some rousing tunes and people were laughing and dancing. Jesus was enjoying himself thoroughly too.

James took his role as master of ceremonies seriously. He checked the dishes before they were placed on the table and walked back and forth nervously to make sure everything was going smoothly. Jesus was secretly enjoying seeing his brother making such a fuss of all the guests, while scarcely bothering to glance in his direction. If he had disappeared in a puff of smoke that very instant, James would probably not even have noticed. Mary was delighted that the festivities were going without a hitch. That was until James went over to her at one point as the afternoon progressed. Jesus saw that he was agitated as he spoke to her, nervously brushing his hair back with his fingers. He heard Mary saying something indignantly, after which James went away with his tail between his legs. Jesus stood up and went to sit next to his mother.

"Is something up?" he asked, curious about the little tête-à-tête between his mother and brother.

"Just typical of James," sighed Mary. "The wine's all gone already! I knew it. He was determined to be the master of ceremonies, but I knew he'd get something wrong! What can we do? The party's nothing like over!"

She looked around indecisively and saw the water barrels that were standing there, waiting for the ritual washing of the feet. She seemed to tense up a little bit and looked at Jesus, who was sitting next to her. She hesitated for a moment, but then she nudged him and said, pointing at the barrels,

"I'm sure you could solve this problem, Jesus!"

He followed her gaze and understood immediately what she meant. Her suggestion irritated him; today he just wanted to be the brother of the bride and nothing more. But Mary stood up and walked over to one of the servants, saying,

"I heard that the wine is running out. But my son Jesus will solve the problem. Just do whatever he says!"

The servant looked at her in surprise, but nodded to show that he had understood. Mary walked back and saw that Jesus was deep in conversation with his friends. It did not seem as if he was intending to respond to what she had suggested. Disappointed, she mingled with the guests again and so she did not notice Jesus standing up and beckoning the servant to fill the barrels with water. The man did what he was told, remembering Mary's words. The casks were soon full. Jesus focused his senses inward, looking for God. If he was going to have to reveal himself, then now was as good a moment as any other, so that Miriam's wedding could continue without a hitch. He closed his eyes for a moment. Then he looked hard at the servant and spoke to him with great authority.

"Fill a pitcher and take it to the groom!"

The servant hurried to obey the order. He filled a jug from one of the barrels and took it to Reuben, who filled his cup and then looked up in surprise after tasting it.

"Hey, James," he called out enthusiastically. "Smart move - keeping the best wine until last!"

He raised his cup to him with a grin. James looked like he had seen a ghost. He rushed over to the table and saw to his utter astonishment that Reuben had not been making a joke at his expense. Confused, he looked up and saw Jesus standing by the casks. He immediately realised what had happened and what an overwhelming sign his brother had given. Peter saw the look in his eyes and placed a hand confidentially on his arm.

"Has this surprised you?" he asked. "With the power that he possesses, he's capable of much more! You should see just how many people he has already managed to inspire. Personally, I left everything I had to follow him. We believe from the very bottom of our hearts that he is the Messiah and we'll help him by doing anything he asks of us!"

James felt deeply ashamed. For a moment, he did not know what to do. Then he stood up, walked over to Jesus and embraced him.

"I'm the biggest idiot round here, I reckon", he said bashfully. "Please forgive me!"

Jesus was touched by his sincere regret and held him tight. For a short moment he looked at the picture of the dancing and drinking guests. Then he beckoned to his disciples and turned away, leaving his family behind to follow his own destiny.

Mary

Jesus decided to remain in Galilee for the time being as the priests were not nearly as dominant there as in Judea.

"Will we be going back to Nazareth?" asked Philip. "I'd love to see more of the place where you were brought up."

But Jesus shook his head firmly.

"No, that's not a good idea. No prophet is ever accepted in his own village, just as a doctor can never cure someone who is his acquaintance. The people who know me from before won't accept that I am different now. My ideas will seem crazy to them and they'll say I'm mad. No, we'll be going to Capernaum. Peter's family lives near there and he is very keen to introduce me to them."

More and more people were following Jesus. When they reached the banks of the Sea of Galilee, he gathered them around him and spoke,

"Behold, a sower took a handful of seed and sowed it. Some of the seeds fell on the wayside, where the birds came and ate them. Others fell on stony ground and could not take root. And still others fell among thorns that choked them. But there were also seeds that fell on good ground and they brought forth much fruit. Therefore if you want my message to bear fruit, make sure it takes root in good ground. Do not muddy your common sense with laws and rules. Become free thinkers who have the courage to believe that things can be different."

And he continued:

"The Pharisees and scribes have hidden the key to knowledge from you. They do not understand what really matters and yet they call themselves your leaders. But they have turned people from the path of righteousness onto the wrong track. They think they preach the true word, but it is only their interpretation of the true word. Do not be taken in by this! Search for the truth that lies within you. Be cleverer than them; then you will find the key and understand everything."

The people listened spellbound and they pressed around him to hear more. But Jesus felt he had said enough for now and he called to a fisherman next to his moored boat:

"Good sir, could you perhaps take me to the other side? It's quite crowded here!"

The fisherman turned round and Peter cried out in surprise. He looked at Jesus in delight.

"That's my brother, Andrew!" he beamed. "I haven't seen him for a year at least. He'll definitely take us!"

He ran off and hugged his brother so enthusiastically that the two of them almost fell in the water. Jesus and Philip laughed heartily. After Peter had introduced them, they all got in the boat.

"Perhaps we could go fishing," suggested Jesus.

"There's no point," replied Thaddeus, Andrew's assistant. "We've been fishing all night and we haven't caught a thing."

"Well, if I were you I'd give it another go," insisted Jesus.

Peter gestured to his brother that he should do as Jesus said. But Andrew gave him a cross look.

"Didn't Thaddeus just say we'd already tried," he muttered irritably. "I do know how to fish, Peter. And that man there is clearly no fisherman!"

Peter burst out laughing.

"All right, then don't do it!" he said. "But I'm sure you won't mind if I have a try."

And he cast the net before Andrew had a chance to protest. Almost immediately they felt the weight of the net dragging the boat down to one side. Andrew jumped up. He and Thaddeus pulled the net back in with difficulty. It was so full that it was on the point of bursting. Jesus laughed.

"You won't have to go fishing from now on," he spoke. "For you'll help me teach people all about the kingdom!"

More and more people joined Jesus like Andrew and Thaddeus did. Some of them even abandoned their homes to follow him. The group included many women. They were treated by society as second-class citizens but Jesus stood up for them and they seemed to understand his message better than the men who were always making a fuss about everything. While Jesus had initially found it hard to make ends meet with the little money they had, he was soon relieved of his financial worries. Susanna, a rich widow who had joined him, had given him all her wealth and that was more than enough to keep them going for the time being. They were now able to buy tents, basic kitchen implements and the necessary provisions for the regular group that had gathered around him over the past few months.

After consulting with Peter, Jesus decided to take on more disciples. He selected those among his followers whom he thought were best equipped to help spread his message. They included James and his brother John, Bartholomew, Thomas and the tax collector Matthew who had changed his life completely after Jesus had once come to eat at his home, James and Simon the zealot, who saw Jesus as the only true king of Israel. And Judas Iscariot, the administrator, whom Jesus had assigned the task of managing the finances. With John the Baptist's words in mind, Jesus taught them as much as he could and he tried as best he could to answer their questions. And they certainly had enough questions.

"Master, do you want us to fast? And should we be giving alms or not?"

"Fasting is not good for your body; you will be depriving yourself unnecessarily," replied Jesus firmly. "And you can only give alms if you have possessions. Whereas it is better not to have any possessions here on earth but to acquire them in heaven. Few people will be ready to believe that you can only genuinely be happy if you give up everything. Even so, only those who relinquish their position in society will rediscover their true life. You have sacrificed everything to follow me. Your reward will be to get to know the kingdom."

"What's the kingdom like?" they asked next.

"The kingdom is like a mustard seed, the smallest of all seeds. But if it falls on good ground it turns into a large plant, big enough for birds to shelter in it. So don't think you can't start something on your own. It often takes just one person to start a fair society. And if people are open to that person's message, the movement for a more just society can spread like wildfire."

"So will what you are doing make the kingdom come quickly?" asked Simon eagerly.

"Well, that depends," answered Jesus, tempering his enthusiasm. "People don't wake up just like that. They have to fight for it, make their own choice between society and themselves and overcome all kinds of obstacles. Because people have strayed away from their true selves and God's intentions for humanity and it's not so easy to find the way back."

"It's all very well you stating this with so much conviction. But who are you actually if you reckon you know everything?" asked Thomas suspiciously.

"Well, what do you think?" said Jesus, passing the question back. "All of you, who do you think I am?"

"You are the Messiah, come to liberate Israel!" cried Simon passionately.

"No, you are Elijah who has come back to help us," countered Thaddeus.

"I think you're a wise philosopher, like Plato," replied Matthew.

"You are the one who carries the Holy Spirit that has come down to earth to touch people through you," said Peter.

Jesus put a hand on his shoulder.

"Yes, Peter, that's right. I am no different from anyone else. It's God's Spirit that gives me the courage to say: I'm the bread that is the staff of life. It's not the bread you eat but spiritual food that will enrich you. I am the gate to the light, I can teach you how to attain enlightenment. I am the shepherd who will return the lost sheep to the house of the Father. I encourage people to stand up, get moving and start looking for the truth so that they can really live their lives again. And I will teach all this to you too. But remember, never speak of me as Christ, is that clear? I don't want to get caught up in complicated political power games."

His disciples nodded. Then Judas asked quietly:

"Isn't it a burden, Jesus, having to carry the Holy Spirit?"

Jesus looked at him in surprise. Judas was always a little inward-looking, and now he of all people came up with this!

"Yes, I must admit it is," he nodded warmly. "That's why I will occasionally be withdrawing to spend some time alone and recuperate. I'd actually like to do that now, if you don't mind.

Perhaps you could start putting up the tents on the outskirts of Capernaum, then I'll join you later."

He left them behind and took a small path that wound its way between the trees up the mountain. The sun filtered through the canopy of leaves. As he got higher, the trees made way for low-lying bushes. The path grew steeper and he climbed from rock to rock until he reached the summit. He paused a moment to enjoy the splendid views of the Sea of Galilee. Then he descended down the other side.

The scenery here was charming. The leaves on the trees were green and flowers were growing, a sign that there must be water. He savoured nature in all its beauty as he continued along the narrow path, until his attention was suddenly drawn by a sound. He stood still and listened. Somebody was humming a song. He was able to pick up fragments of the melody. It sounded lovely. Curious, he made his way through the shrubs. He soon saw the glint of water - and the source of the melody. A young woman was sitting next to a small pond, in a slightly dip in the ground. She had a pitcher with her and was using it to wash her long hair in the clear water. Jesus heard her continuing quietly with her song and why he could not tell, but he felt a strong desire to talk to her. He walked further down the path, but quietly so as not to frighten her. However he was unable to prevent several pebbles from rolling downhill and the girl heard this. The melody stopped and she turned round. She studied him and apparently she liked what she saw because she gave him a friendly nod and said confidently,

"Hello."

"Hello," he replied. "I hope I didn't frighten you?"

She put his mind at rest.

"No, not at all. Although this is the first time anyone has discovered my spot."

She squeezed the water out of her hair and picked up a cloth to dry it. Jesus smiled.

"It's very beautiful, this spot of yours," he said. "Do you mind if I stop a while here to rest?"

"Of course not," she answered friendly.

Jesus came down the path and looked for a place along the water's edge. He took off his sandals and put his feet in the water. That did feel good. The girl picked up the pitcher, took a cup from her basket and poured some water in.

"Here," she said.

Jesus took the cup gratefully and drank. The water was refreshingly cool and quenched his thirst. While he was drinking, the girl combed her hair and let it dry in the sun.

"Do you come here often?" asked Jesus after he had emptied the cup.

The girl nodded.

"Quite often," she said as she came and sat down next to him. "It's so peaceful here. That always puts me in a good frame of mind."

She smiled at him. He could take a good look at her now she was sat so close. She had a beautiful face, with full lips and a shapely nose. But her most attractive feature were her eyes: brown and with a twinkle here and there, as if the sun itself shone in them.

"And what do you like to do when you're here?" he informed, interested to see what she would say.

"I listen," she replied. "I listen to the silence."

She looked away for a moment. Jesus followed her glance and he saw the green hills surround the pool, he saw the beams of sunlight penetrating between the leaves on the trees and he heard the peaceful chirping of birds in the distance. They looked back at each other and the girl felt a strange connection with this man that she was unable to explain.

"You know," she continued. "If you listen really carefully, you can hear God here. If it's quiet and you're really quiet yourself too, He'll come to you and talk to you here, in your heart."

She put her hand on his chest and laughed, a little bashfully. Then she suddenly realised what she was doing. She quickly withdrew her hand and said timidly,

"I don't really know why I'm telling you all this. I never actually talk about these things to anyone."

Her gentle smile moved him. Cautiously, he put his hand on hers and said quietly,

"Perhaps you're telling me this because you know I understand what you mean."

She looked up at him. Their looks met. And didn't let go anymore. Jesus felt his heart miss at least two beats as he drowned in her eyes. He was overcome by deep emotion. Slowly he raised his hand and stroked her cheek.

"What's your name, actually?" he whispered.

"I'm Mary," she said. "Mary Magdalene. And you?"

"I'm Jesus," he replied. "Jesus of Nazareth."

The girl could not have got more of a shock if lightening had struck at her feet. The special moment evaporated at once. She smothered a cry and covered her face with her hands.

"You're... Jesus," she spluttered. "Jesus ... of Nazareth..."

Jesus, who could not understand her sudden confusion, nodded in confirmation.

"Yes, that's me. But..."

He was unable to finish his question, though, as Mary had jumped up and rushed off towards her basket, which was lying a little further away. She gathered her belongings, throwing them hastily in the basket and ran off in the direction of the path. But Jesus had got up too. He was at her side in a couple of bounds, stopping her from leaving.

"What is it?" he asked urgently. "What did I do or say to frighten you so much?"

Mary shook her head in confusion and the basket fell out of her hands. Then all of a sudden she fell on her knees in front of him and wrapped her arms around his legs. Her voice choked with emotion, she faltered,

"I know who you are. You're the vessel of the Holy Spirit and my Master. And then it was you of all people for whom I thought I felt something..."

She did not finish her sentence. A sob welled up in her. Jesus was dumbfounded. He looked shyly down at this figure kneeling before him. Then he bent down towards her and took her gently by the arm.

"Come," he said tenderly. "Come, please stand up. I think we need to talk."

She let him pull her up. Once again Jesus found it difficult to take his eyes off her. Never before in his life had a woman had such a strong effect on him. In wonder, he asked,

"Why were you so startled? And how do you know who I am?"

"John the Baptist told me about you," replied Mary. "But when he encouraged me to follow you, I had no idea you might be the kindred spirit I've spent so long searching for."

She turned her gaze towards him and continued firmly,

"I know for certain that there's a connection between you and me and that I knew you before I met you. Because I still have clear memories of the spiritual world and I recognise the energy radiating from you."

Only now did Jesus understand why he had felt attracted to her from the very first moment he saw her. After all his wanderings, he had finally found someone who came from such an elevated spiritual place that she would at least be able to understand him. Once again their eyes met, fused together. In a surge of emotion, he put his arms around her and kissed her without further ado on her cheek. His kiss had a deep effect on her. Knowing who he was, she was moved by the way he kissed her just like that. Tears came to her eyes and she started laughing and crying at the same time. And Jesus asked,

"Will you stay with me?"

Mary nodded. Without a moment's hesitation, she answered,

"Yes, I'll stay with you."

It was dusk by the time they finally started climbing back up the path. They carried her basket between them as they walked to the town where his friends were waiting for him.

When they arrived there, Mary saw to her great surprise that a crowd of perhaps a hundred people were waiting in the hope that Jesus would turn up after all. And she saw the tents where his regular band of followers slept. She looked at him in amazement.

"Is it like this everywhere you go?" she asked.

He gave an embarrassed smile and answered almost apologetically,

"I'm afraid so. You'll have to get used to sharing my attention."

His words were confirmed at once for the crowd caught sight of him and laid claim to him so that he was encircled by admirers in no time. Mary stood on the periphery feeling a little lost, her basket next to her. But her presence did not go unnoticed; a woman came up to her and spoke to her in a friendly voice.

"Hello! I saw you two arrive. You're new, aren't you?"

Mary nodded.

"Yes, that's right. We met at the pool and I decided I'd like to stay with him. But I do find all this a bit overwhelming."

"You'll get used to it," laughed the woman. "Everything's out of the ordinary once you decide to follow him."

She put out her hand.

"I'm Susanna. There's quite a group of us women, and that's just as well because nothing would get done if we didn't take care of everything!"

Mary burst out laughing and shook the woman's hand.

"I'm Mary. It looks like you could use an extra pair of hands."

"We certainly could!" nodded Susanna. "Come on, I'll show you around the place."

They walked to the encampment and Susanna showed Mary a tent where several of the women slept.

"Why don't you stay here to start with?" she suggested. "Then you'll get to know everyone a bit. Wait, I'll take your basket."

She went in the tent, arranged a place for Mary to sleep and introduced her to the other women. Mary shook hands with them all, then unpacked her basket. As she laid out her possessions, the bed began to feel a little more as if it was her own space. Then she went back outside. It was nearly dark now and the people were slowly going back home. And finally she saw Jesus again. He was looking round, combing the area, when he suddenly caught sight of her. A warm smile spread over his face.

"Mary!" he called excitedly in a loud voice. "You're still there!"

Susanna and the other women looked up in surprise. They were not used to seeing him so effusive and they understood at once that Mary would have a special place amongst them. Jesus left the others and came towards her. He put his arms around her and whispered privately in her ear,

"I was afraid for a moment that you'd left. But I'm pleased to see that you haven't been put off by all this."

Mary smiled somewhat hesitantly.

"Not yet," she replied. "But I do hope your time won't always be taken up like this."

He looked at her affectionately.

"We'll see," he said with a smile. "Perhaps we'll have to make an effort to have some time alone together when we can talk privately. But I'm sure we'll manage."

His high spirits were infectious and Mary laughed off her

objections.

"Then let's start as we mean to continue," she suggested. "I'll fetch some water to wash your feet with. And have you already eaten?"

He shook his head.

"No, not yet. If you could find something, that would be wonderful."

Mary nodded and went off. Jesus walked to his tent. It was only when he sank down onto his bed that he realised how tired he was. He saw once again in his mind's eye the faces of all those people who were persistently making claims on him. It was difficult to shut out the images and relax. Fortunately, Mary soon returned with a pale of water and she knelt down next to him. She took off his sandals, washed his feet and massaged them with a wonderfully aromatic oil. Jesus felt the tension disappear. He smiled down at her gratefully. Then she went out to fetch some food. They ate together in his tent. He longed to know more about her and asked,

"Tell me about yourself, Mary. Where do you come from and what kind of a family did you grow up in?"

"I grew up in Bethany," she replied. "I have one sister, Martha, and one brother, Lazarus. My father was a baker and when he died, my brother took over the business. I had a lovely childhood. These days I live in Magdala, where I work in my aunt's inn. I make the beds, wash up, cook... I wanted to see more of the world than just my childhood village."

"And, do you enjoy your work?" asked Jesus in between bites.

Mary nodded enthusiastically.

"Oh yes! We get so many different people visiting and I love to watch them. I also like the fact that I'm earning my own keep and can decide for myself what to do. For example, I've been taking lessons in Greek and Latin. I wanted to be able to read the Greek philosophers and get a better understanding of Roman culture."

Jesus looked up in surprise.

"How unusual!" he said in admiration. "So, have you made any progress?"

"Certainly!" replied Mary confidently. "I've read a lot already. You wait, I'll amaze you with all the things I know!"

Jesus gave her a tender look.

"You already have," he said, smiling, and he planted a kiss on her hand.

Bashfully, Mary let him do this. Then she made a move to join the other women. It had been a long, emotional day for her too and she was tired. But Jesus stopped her from leaving. He put his arms around her and laid his cheek against hers. Softly he whispered,

"Thank you for everything. I'm so happy I met you! Even though we may not have much time for each other, it means an awful lot to me just to know you're there!"

He kissed her gently on her cheek just as he had done that afternoon. Only then would he let her go. Mary felt as if she was dancing on air when she walked back to her tent. Her heart was pounding and she could still hear his voice in her head. He had completely swept her off her feet with his irresistible personality. And she knew that whatever might happen in the future, her life would never be the same again.

Mary lived through the next few months as if in a dream. Susanna had been quite right - following Jesus really did mean the start of a new life. During the first few weeks in particular, she was constantly being surprised. Although he had told her about the strength of the Holy Spirit, she was still astonished by the things he did. When he spoke to the masses and boldly demonstrated his authority, she hardly recognised him as the same man who would sit next to her to eat, or sometimes tenderly put his hand on hers and his arm around her shoulders.

It soon became clear to her that she was head over heels in love with him. She had never felt so strongly attracted to a man before. She had often met with disappointment in the search for the special one, who perhaps would come from the same elevated spiritual place as she did. One way or another, she had never been able to find the man with whom she felt that all important spiritual connection. She had more or less accepted that she would probably always remain single, knowing the high demands she made. And now he had come into her life and she could barely grasp what was happening. Often all they needed was one glance, and they felt they understood one another even when they had not exchanged a word.

As time passed, her desire to spend more time with him grew

stronger and stronger. She had asked Susanna for a tent of her own, hoping that he would visit her there. But he had yet to do so. Indeed, it was not clear to her what exactly he felt for her. It was true that he regularly sought her company, and that he would take her in his arms and kiss her lovingly on her cheek or in her hair. But there were also days when he would barely notice her because he was so preoccupied, not just because of the crowds but also by his own thoughts. He could spend hours on end sitting by himself, praying and meditating. At such times, no one dared approach him, knowing these were the moments when he renewed the connection to God, and to the Spirit within him. Then he would enter a place where even she could not follow and she realised this could well be an insuperable obstacle. That his love of God and his loyalty to his mission would always taking precedence over his relationship with her and that this was why he was not making any moves. She understood he had to find his own solution, so she did not force herself on him. She simply made sure she was there when he needed her, hoping that God Himself, who had obviously already seen her love for him, would bring them together.

Jesus' activities in Galilee did not go unnoticed in Judea either. The priests in Jerusalem nervously followed all the rumours that were circulating. What they wanted was to bring an end to the corrupt reign of Herod by replacing him with a king from the house of David. This honest ruler would put a stop to the moral degeneration and set an example by faithfully observing the laws in the Torah.

However, they listened to the stories about Jesus with mixed feelings. They regularly got the impression that he did not always abide by the laws either. For did he not stand up for Romans and heal the sick even on Sabbath? And while he may have been a member of the house of David, he did not seem to show any ambition to usurp Herod's throne. In fact, it was not clear what he did want. For this reason they sent a delegation to John the Baptist, who was still energetically carrying out his work. He was rather surprised to see the scribes approaching him in their splendid robes. They had not honoured him with a visit up to that point, embarrassed as they were by his unconventional appearance and the message he was preaching.

"Greetings, good man," said the priests and they even gave him a small bow. "We would like to ask you some questions if we may."

John nodded and led the way into his tent, where he offered them something to drink. But the priests refused politely, giving a rather disparaging look at his pitiful quarters. They preferred coming straight to the point and asked him,

"You are preaching that Jesus of Nazareth is the Messiah we were promised. But how can you be so sure of that? We hear stories about him that confuse us."

John looked at them somewhat compassionately and replied boldly,

"Don't you recognise Christ when he's here amongst us? Look at the signs he gives: wherever he comes, people feel happier and they have the courage to act independently and freely. And God's message is being preached everywhere. So I don't understand your confusion. Surely you too realise the kingdom is close by now!"

The priests looked at each other in surprise. John's words were not really the answer they had been hoping for.

"We were assuming that because the Messiah comes from the house of David, he would at least demand to be put on the throne," they argued.

John was unable to suppress a smile.

"But he does!" he said, full of conviction. "Only his throne is not of this world. I personally have not a moment's doubt that he will be king for evermore!"

Once again, the priests looked at each other in despair. They had no idea what John was talking about and his rather indulgent smile irritated them. John saw that they were disconcerted. He continued in a sharper tone,

"To be honest, I don't really understand what you are doing here! Why don't you concentrate on the more important things that are going on at the moment? Surely you see that Herod is living in sin now that he has chased his wife out of the house and taken Herodias, his cousin's wife, to be his mistress? Rather than wasting your time here, you would be better off visiting him and taking him to task for his scandalous behaviour!"

The priests felt like small children being reprimanded. Of course he was right. But they did not dare admit that it was fear that had prevented them taking action in protest at Herod's corrupt lifestyle. John, who considered their conversation had finished, stood up.

"If you don't mind, I'll continue with my work," he said curtly. "There are people waiting for me who fortunately do understand me."

He left the disappointed priests behind. This conversation had not brought them one jot further. However, poor John paid a bitter price for their visit because Herod found out what he had said about him. That very same afternoon his soldiers intercepted him as he returned to his tent from the River Jordan. Without even any pretence of a trial, they flung him in a dark gaol, thus effectively silencing him.

Jesus soon found out his friend had been taken prisoner. He was deeply shocked. The next morning, he left his followers in the care of James and set out for Jerusalem with his disciples and Mary. He spurred them on to travel as fast as possible. He knew how capricious Herod could be and he was afraid he would arrive too late.

When they got in the vicinity of Jerusalem some days later, increasing numbers of people gathered round them. The rumour that the one and only Jesus of Nazareth had come from Galilee and was on his way to the city had spread like wildfire and many people wanted to see him for themselves. However, Jesus resisted the temptation to show much about himself. He kept his mind focused on the reason he was there as he entered the city by one of its many gates. When he reached the temple, he strode purposefully towards the building where the Sanhedrin had their quarters.

"You wait here," he said to his friends and he went inside.

In the hall there was a priest sitting at a table, writing. He looked up when Jesus entered.

"Good afternoon, sir," he said in a friendly voice. "Can I help you?"

"I hope so," replied Jesus. "I'm trying to find out how my friend John the Baptist is getting on."

The priest looked at him intently for a moment. Then he stood up.

"Please follow me," he said. "As it happens, the council leaders are gathered together for a meeting and I'm sure they'll be willing to speak to you."

He led the way down a long corridor and opened a door at the end. He gestured to Jesus to enter. Jesus saw a long table, behind which were sat seven priests. When he walked in, one of them stood up.

"Good afternoon, Jesus of Nazareth," he spoke politely. "We were expecting you. My name is Caiaphas. I am the high priest here. Please come further."

Jesus advanced and remained standing a few yards from the table.

"If you were expecting me then you probably know why I've come as well," he said, equally politely. "I would be grateful if you could tell me where my friend John the Baptist is and whether I can visit him."

"We'll certainly tell you that," smiled Caiaphas. "But first we have some questions for you, if you don't mind."

"To be honest, I do mind," replied Jesus coolly. "I've come here for my friend. So if you have news about him, please tell me."

"Tell me, is it true that you are the Messiah?" asked Caiaphas, totally ignoring Jesus' remark. "And why are you undermining our laws with your teachings?"

"I'm not sure you understood me correctly," Jesus, however, said in return. "I'm not here to answer your questions, I've only come to ask about my friend, John the Baptist. I'd appreciate it if you respected this and didn't plague me with questions you already know the answer to."

"We've heard that you are encouraging people to refrain from circumcision and stop giving alms," continued Caiaphas imperturbably. "Is that right?"

Jesus sighed. He realised he would not get out of this so easily.

"No, you're not describing it right," he replied brusquely. "I said that if circumcision was better, men would have been born without foreskins. And alms don't eliminate the inequalities between people. It would be better to give beggars the prospect of a better life by helping them find work or improving their living conditions."

"So, are you the Messiah?" asked Caiaphas again, pleased that Jesus did seem prepared to answer his questions after all.

"If you mean do I have aspirations to become the king of Israel, I'm afraid I'll have to disappoint you," answered Jesus candidly. "I have no such ambition. I am Jesus of Nazareth and I get my inspiration from God's Holy Spirit. I try to reveal God's kingdom to people. And you too could share in this inspiration and let it give you new insights."

"Well, I don't believe we need these new insights," reacted Caiaphas somewhat condescendingly and Jesus heard some of the priests sat behind the table snigger quietly. "But anyway, I'm sure there'll be other occasions for us to discuss matters. What you came for was your friend John the Baptist."

Jesus nodded expectantly.

"Unfortunately I have to tell you that he's no longer with us," continued Caiaphas in a voice devoid of emotion. "Herodias has had him beheaded."

Jesus looked at him in shock.

"Beheaded?" he stammered in bewilderment. "But ... how did that happen?"

"There was a feast where everyone got pretty drunk. Salome, the daughter of Herodias, danced for Herod. The king was so impressed by the girl that he promised he would grant her a wish. Herodias whispered to her that she should ask for the head of John the Baptist. Apparently Herod presented it to her on a golden plate."

Jesus listened to the story in astonishment. Grief-stricken, he was speechless at first from the lump in his throat. Then he asked in a choked voice,

"And what did you do to prevent this? Did any one of you have the guts to go up to Herod and demand his release?"

The priests looked at each other in embarrassment. Then one of them, Nicodemus, stood up. He said softly,

"Even if we had done that Jesus, we probably couldn't have done anything for him. After all, Herod never listens to us."

Jesus looked bitterly at him.

"I understand," he said aloofly. "No really, I understand. Of course you couldn't do anything for that poor man. Of course Herod's the only guilty person here. And of course the fact that it was quite convenient for you to be rid of John the Baptist in this way had nothing to do with it! No, please don't go to any trouble to show me out, I'll find my own way!"

He turned round abruptly and exited the room. When he got outside, his friends were waiting tense to hear the news.

"Well...?" they asked.

But Jesus said nothing. He just looked at them and his eyes told them all they needed to know. Mary felt close to tears. So they had got there too late after all! She put her arms around him to console him and for a moment he turned to her for support. Then he faltered in a hoarse voice,

"Come on. There's nothing else for us here. Let's go back."

But Mary said gently,

"Are you sure you want that? You look tired. Perhaps it would be better to go to my brother in Bethany, rest there and return later."

Jesus hesitated briefly.

"You're right, I am tired," he then conceded. "It would be good if we could spend the night with him."

No sooner said than done. They left the town in silence, each preoccupied with his or her own thoughts, and made their way to Bethany.

They arrived in the village in the early evening. Judas had been sent ahead to announce their arrival and they got a hospitable reception. Martha, Mary's sister, was busy preparing something for them to eat while her brother Lazarus had made room for them in the barn. While the disciples sorted out their sleeping arrangements, Lazarus took Jesus into the house. He poured out two cups of wine.

"I'd hoped we'd get to meet you in more cheerful circumstances," he said sympathetically as he passed Jesus one of the cups. "My sister has been swept off her feet by you, I believe!"

Mary blushed. Why did he have to say that! Jesus pretended not to notice her embarrassment.

"I'm also happy that I met her," he smiled, throwing her a tender look. "We have a very special bond. That's why it's nice now to be able to meet her family."

He quizzed Lazarus about his work and the situation in Judea. The man confirmed what he already knew. Many people had had their fill of Herod, and John the Baptist's death had caused a considerable unrest. The Zealots in particular, a militant splinter group active in Jerusalem, were trying to arouse people to rise up and dethrone Herod. But this strategy was doomed to failure as the king had the Romans on his side.

While Lazarus and Jesus were talking, Martha was rushing back and forth with the snacks she had prepared. She was also taking care of all the people in the barn and every now and then she gave an irritated look at Mary who was sat at Jesus' feet, listening enthralled to the conversation of the two men. Jesus felt that he could trust Lazarus absolutely and he spoke candidly,

"You know, Lazarus, the people think that I've come to bring peace but they don't realise that things will only get more tense because of me. Fathers will quarrel with their sons because the one supports me while the other opposes me. And the priests will try to stay in control, come what may. They know all too well that if the power structures collapse, they will be brought down with the rest. So I need to go about my work carefully. A change can only come once a lot of people have put their trust in me. Freedom can only come from within. You can't use power to destroy power."

"But will enough people be prepared to follow you?" asked Lazarus curiously.

Jesus shrugged.

"That's a good question," he answered hesitantly and he took a sip of wine. "You would imagine that people would choose en masse to finally go back to living a real life. But to do that, first they have to learn about true love. For only love can conquer power - that's an eternal truth. I hope I'll be able to bring them that love - that's my mission. But as to whether I'll succeed..."

"If I look at how frightened our people are, I can imagine you might not be that optimistic," nodded Lazarus pensively. "And the death of John the Baptist is just one more example of how powerful our country's rulers are."

Their conversation was interrupted by Martha, who came to refill the cups. Once again, she gave a spiteful look at her sister, who was still listening enraptured to Jesus' every word.

"Eh Jesus, surely you've seen that Mary's left me to do all the work on my own?" she snapped. "Why don't you tell her to help me?"

Jesus looked up and laughed.

"Oh Martha, are you getting worked up just about that?" he teased. "You're so busy you haven't even got to know me properly and you've heard nothing of what I've been saying. But Mary is wiser.

She chose to do what is truly important."

Once again he threw her a loving look. Martha was indignant and on the point of replying when she became distracted by a knock on the door.

"Now what?" she muttered and left the room sullenly. She soon returned and said curtly:

"Someone for you, Jesus. You'll never guess who!"

Curious, Jesus went to the door and was amazed to see one of the council priests standing in the twilight.

"Please forgive me for disturbing you at such a late hour, rabbi," said the man humbly. "But I just had to see you after what happened this afternoon. My name is Nicodemus. I hope you'll speak to me. I waited until it got dark on purpose so that no one would see me go."

Jesus nodded sympathetically.

"Yes, I remember you. I'm pleased you've come. Wait, I'll fetch my coat, then we can find a quiet spot to talk."

He looked for his bag in the barn and retrieved his coat. Then they sat down on a bench in Lazarus' courtyard.

"When I saw you this afternoon, I knew at once that you must have come as a teacher for God," said Nicodemus fervently. "No one can do what you do unless God is on their side. You put it so wonderfully when you said you are inspired by the Holy Spirit and want to teach people about the kingdom! Those words really moved me. And I feel ashamed of the condescending way Caiaphas reacted."

"I'm pleased that you were able to feel the love of God through me," replied Jesus simply. "And you too can see the kingdom if you want. Because everyone who is born again will enter the kingdom and experience God's love."

Nicodemus looked at him in confusion.

"What do you mean, rabbi," he asked wonderingly. "I'm so old already! How can someone be born again if they are already old? I can hardly crawl back into the womb!"

This made him laugh and Jesus laughed with him. But then he spoke in a serious voice,

"Do you really not know what I mean? You're a high priest of the Pharisees and people come to you with their religious questions. How can you show them the path to light when you haven't found it yourself yet? Of course the rebirth I'm talking about is a spiritual rebirth. Only once your ego has died will there be room for God's spirit in you and then you will feel as if you have been reborn. It's our ego that prevents us from doing God's will. The kingdom will only come in sight once we give Him the room to let His energy do its work through us."

Shamefaced, Nicodemus nodded. Now he understood. And Jesus continued kindly,

"It's not that difficult, Nicodemus. Let go of everything and let yourself be carried by the wind. Don't agonise about where you're heading or what you left behind. God will make sure you get to the destination that is your lot. After all, that's why you're here now."

Nicodemus listened to him reverentially. The wisdom in what he was hearing now was more than he had ever heard in the Council. He said,

"I still remember well the time I first saw you. You were twelve years old and you'd come to pick up your bar mitzvah text. I can even remember the text you read and the explanation you gave. But I didn't realise then that when you were talking about God's messenger you were referring to yourself."

"I think at that point I wasn't yet able to grasp the full extent of that myself either," smiled Jesus. "But now I do know that I came to this world to be a witness to the truth so that whoever finds the truth can be taken up in the light and become a worker for God."

They remained silent for a moment after these words. Then Jesus stood up and said in a slightly tired voice,

"If you don't mind, I'd like to end our conversation now. It was a long day and it's time for me to find my bed."

Nicodemus got up hastily.

"Of course!" he replied apologetically. "Please excuse me for not thinking of that myself. And I haven't even said how sorry I am about the loss of your friend. But perhaps we can discuss further another time."

Jesus gave a friendly nod.

"I know for certain that we'll meet again sometime. And when we do, I'd be delighted to continue our conversation. Goodbye!"

He left the priest and took the path back to the barn. There he found the place enveloped in deep peace. His disciples were already asleep and the only light was from a small camp fire. He sat next to the fire to warm his feet and stared at the flames dancing around the twigs. The wood crackled and hissed as the red and yellow tongues licked at them. As he savoured this scene, he felt the long day's tension slip away. He closed his eyes and saw the sparkling purple pin pricks showing the Holy Spirit's presence. He thanked God that he had been able to reach out to Nicodemus and that the man had had the courage to seek him out. And he decided to sleep next to the fire. He got up to fetch his things from the barn but when he was at the door he bumped into a man who was secretly slipping inside. Jesus got hold of his arm and pulled him to the light of the flames. To his surprise it was his own disciple Simon.

"Simon? Where've you come from, so late in the evening?" he asked in astonishment.

Simon could feel he was blushing.

"I... um, just went back to Jerusalem, Jesus," he confessed. "I made contact with Barabbas, the leader of the Zealots. They've been making preparations for years to drive Herod from the throne. More and more people are willing to help them, especially since the murder of John the Baptist. Barabbas has now gathered together quite an army, all in all."

He put his hand on Jesus' arm and continued earnestly,

"You made a big impression on them because you had the guts to confront the priests and stand up for John. Also, you're from the house of David and a lot of people trust you. That's why this is our chance! If you want, Barabbas will mobilise all his people and let you enter Jerusalem as the new king!"

Jesus looked at him in dismay. Then he roughly shook off Simon's hand. He shook his head disbelievingly. How could he? How could he even suggest this? Had he really understood nothing of what he had been preaching all this time? Without saying a word, he marched off to the barn, grabbed his sleeping mat and blanket and installed himself next to the fire. Simon watched, perplexed. It was clear that his master did not wish to discuss his plans. Disappointed, he slunk off. And Jesus curled up in his blanket. Exhausted from all the day's emotional developments, he soon fell asleep.

After spending a few days in Bethany, they returned to Galilee. Jesus was almost sorry to leave the village behind. He felt he had a friend for life in Lazarus and he would have liked to have spent more time with him to discuss his ideas.

"Your brother's a lovely fellow," he said to Mary. "It's strange that I also feel that inner bond with him. I get the feeling that he too often gets homesick. He must know the feeling of being half in this world and half in the spiritual world."

Mary looked at him in surprise. How striking that he had picked that up!

"Yes, that's right," she agreed. "He sometimes finds it very difficult. Things are going well at the moment but I can still remember a time when he was seriously depressed. I know he even thought about committing suicide, although he never talked to me about that."

"And what about you?" asked Jesus softly. "Have you ever felt like that? I know how strong the desire can be."

Mary hesitated briefly.

"Yes, I know that feeling too," she then replied. "Mainly because I didn't have anyone around me who understood how lonely it can get. But now I've found you and that's all in the past!"

He felt moved by her words. He wrapped his arms around her and whispered in a hoarse voice into her ear,

"Thank you for putting your trust in me. But remember - when I'm no longer there, you must always choose life! The only way to conquer your loneliness is to spread God's love in this world. And by sharing that love, you will get love in return and that way this world will start to look more and more like the other world. Do you promise me you'll do that?"

She nodded silently.

"I promise. Although I can't bear the thought that one day you'll no longer be there."

He stroked her cheek tenderly.

"Well, you're stuck with me for the time being anyway," he smiled.

Capernaum

When they arrived back at their camp, crowds of people were waiting to offer them their condolences. The news of John the Baptist's death had preceded them and everyone wanted to comfort them. After Jesus had shaken hands with everyone, James came up to him.

"There's something you need to know, Jesus," he said in a serious voice. "Yesterday a Roman legionary came along. He insisted on talking to you. When I told him you weren't there, he was very disappointed, so I offered to let him stay here until you got back. I hope I did the right thing."

"I should think so," nodded Jesus. "Where is he now?"

"In his tent, I suppose. Come on, I'll take you to him."

He led Jesus to the edge of the camp, where they found the Roman grooming his horse. When Jesus caught sight of him, he cried out in surprise.

"Gaius! Gaius Octavius!"

He walked up to the youth enthusiastically and shook his hand. Gaius greeted him timidly.

"Good day, Lord Jesus. I'm pleased that you are here! And I'm impressed that you've remembered my name!"

"How could I forget it?" laughed Jesus. "How are you? And tell me, why have you come here?"

"I'm fine," replied Gaius. "I'm still stationed in Judea and I believe my superior officers are pleased with me. The thing is though... that I don't know what I want anymore. I thought I would enjoy being in the army and I am, up to a point. But I'm seeing more and more things I don't agree with."

He stared ahead for a moment in silence. Then all of a sudden he grabbed Jesus' hands and continued intensely,

"There's something I have to tell you. I've never been able to thank you for what you did to me back then. I'll never forget it - never! At the time I felt humiliated. But now I realise it changed the way I look at life. That's why I came here, because now I can finally do something in return. Here, read this."

He retrieved a parchment document from under his leather jacket and handed it to Jesus.

"This is an official decree from Pilate. I thought you should know about it even though it doesn't yet apply in Galilee."

Curious, Jesus unfolded the document and read:

To the citizens of Judea!
On the instructions of the High Council, I hereby announce that all persons who recognise Jesus of Nazareth as the Messiah are forbidden to enter a synagogue with immediate effect. The Roman army shall enforce this measure and violations shall be severely punished! Signed:
Pontius Pilate.

Jesus stared at Gaius in amazement.

"When did this come into effect?" he asked in a shocked voice. "I didn't hear anything about this and I've only just got back from Jerusalem."

"A messenger brought it to us a few days ago," replied Gaius quietly. "So I assume it applies by now. Did your visit to Jerusalem have anything to do with this, by any chance?"

"I can hardly imagine that it could have," said Jesus despondently. "I didn't really show myself in public. But it's a good thing you brought me this. Thank you."

He folded the parchment back up and returned it to Gaius. He laid his hand on the youth's shoulder for a moment and their eyes met.

"Why don't you stay here, Gaius?" he asked softly. "I can feel that you long in your soul for justice. You don't belong in the army. Stay with me, and I'll give you something you have never seen, heard or felt before: the overwhelming feeling of oneness with creation, with everything around you, with God. And once you experience that unison, you'll get a glimpse of what it feels like to be in God's kingdom."

"I'd love that," answered Gaius longingly. "But I signed up for four years and I've only done two. If I left now, it would be seen as desertion. And you know what the punishment is for that!"

He grimaced at the thought.

"It's no accident that Roman soldiers are so loyal. It's a terrible thing to have to die on the cross as an example to your comrades."

"That does sound quite horrific!" agreed Jesus and he felt a shiver run down his spine. "So I won't ask you again."

He embraced the lad and held him tightly.

"I wish you all the best, Gaius. Who knows, perhaps our paths will cross again some time. Thank you again for coming and I hope you have a save journey back to Judea."

Then he turned round and walked back to his tent. Gaius watched him go with a feeling of great respect. How was it possible that such a wonderful person could meet so much opposition? He felt ashamed to be part of the power that was responsible for this. Feeling rather depressed, he saddled his horse and set off back to his camp.

Jesus could not get to sleep that night. John the Baptist's death was on his mind more than he was willing to admit. The good man had probably never hurt a soul and had certainly not deserved this fate. The realisation that the same could easily happen to him weighed heavily on him. Up to now he had felt safe in Galilee. But of course that was only an illusion. After all, if they wanted to take him prisoner there would be nothing stopping them. And now there was this decree that would put the pressure on his supporters in Judea.

When he finally fell asleep, he dreamed. Fragmented images appeared. He saw Mary crying, her face distorted with grief. He saw his mother, pale and haggard. He saw Peter with a look of horror on his face. And then he saw himself, his hands bound to a block, his feet in chains, his back whipped. And he saw even more. How a cross was being lifted up and himself stumbling, falling, struggling to carry the heavy beam on his wounded shoulders. He woke up with a shock, bathed in sweat, sitting bolt upright in terror. Desperately he turned to God.

"Father, please explain: what does this dream mean?"

But what seldom happened, happened now: his heart remained silent. He lurched out of his tent in agitation. Above him stretched the infinite sky, full of stars. God was showing Himself in all His majesty and Jesus sought that majesty he usually felt so close at hand.

"Father, please help me. What did I see? Is this how it will end? Will that be what it comes to? Is that what I've done all this for?"

He felt the affirming answer in his heart. He fell onto his knees in despair and his wail of agony rose up.

"O God, tell me - what have I done wrong? Tell me, where did I let You down? Is it my fault that it's going to end like this? Did I do something wrong after all?"

But now God was there, and He said,

"Don't worry, Jesus. You did not do anything wrong. You are simply wonderful. Believe me, this has nothing to do with you."

Jesus could not understand and shook his head; he called God again, urging Him to answer and justify this terrible end. And God's answer came and Jesus detected an emotion he had not seen before in his Father.

"Perhaps it is my fault, Jesus. Perhaps I have raised your expectations too high. Perhaps you had hoped to achieve more in this life. And I see your loneliness and how heavy the burden is that you have to bear. But you must not think this is the end, for it is just the beginning. Just like the grain of corn that falls onto the ground and dies in order to bear fruit, so you too will bear fruit. With the help of the Holy Spirit, your words will not be lost. Through your death, you will free the Holy Spirit so that it can spread over the whole Earth. Millions of people around the world will recall your words and will grow to understand them. Once that has happened, our kingdom on Earth will be established. And you will see it all because you will be sat here at My side and you shall be the king who will rule for eternity. So you must not give up. If you persevere now, you will live forever in the heart of every single person, as I live in your heart."

His answer astonished Jesus. He stretched out on the hard ground and his body shook as he wept passionately. He understood now that he would need to prepare himself for the sacrifice of his own life in order to free God's Holy Spirit.

The days and weeks afterwards were hard for Jesus. Now that he knew what his ultimate sacrifice would be, he realised that he would need to say goodbye to everyone and everything that was dear to him. Only now did he truly understand what the abbot had meant when he had said he would need to learn to become detached. With the memory of the spiritual world so fresh in his soul, he did not find it difficult to see the world in a different light. The trees, the flowers, the animals... Oh, he could put all that into perspective.

But the people around him were another matter. Peter, who tried so hard. Judas, who perhaps best understood how much effort it cost him to bear the Holy Spirit. Lazarus, with whom he felt such a strong bond. And Mary of course, the only one who could come anywhere near to feeling it the way he did. He never let it show but he cared more for her than he would like to admit. If he had just been Jesus of Nazareth, carpenter, he would undoubtedly have declared his love for her. But now that he knew what was going to happen, this was simply no longer an option. He needed to focus all his attention on completing his mission and she would undoubtedly distract him from that.

He was embroiled in a fierce inner conflict. He felt resistance and that made him rebellious. Until now, he had given himself entirely to his assignment for God, accepting that there would be little room for his own desires. But it weighed heavily on him now that he knew he would have to go one step further.

Mary noticed his struggle. After all, she knew him so well. She was familiar with every detail of his face, the inflections in his voice and the way his body language revealed what he was feeling. And her heart went out to him. He was so special. So far their relationship had been purely platonic. But the longer she spent in his company, the more she desired him physically as well. She longed to stroke him, kiss him, feel his naked skin against hers. But Jesus showed no interest in taking their relationship in that direction. On the contrary; whereas in the early days he had sometimes taken her in his arms to kiss her, such embraces had become less and less frequent of late. And when he did take her aside, it was primarily because she was the only one in his group of followers that he could talk to on an equal spiritual level and because he found her so much more understanding than his disciples. He often told her about his ideas in an inspired and passionate way. But now she could see that he was cast down by a seriousness that was unusual for him.

Therefore one evening, after eating, she went looking for him.

"Let's go for a walk, Jesus," she suggested. "It's such lovely weather and I haven't spoken to you for a while."

Jesus nodded in agreement. He liked the idea of a stroll. They walked a long way, leaving the camp far behind until they came to a fallen tree where they sat down. Mary took his hand, gave him a concerned look and asked,

"Are you all right? To be honest, I'm quite worried about you."

He smiled to take away her concern but she could see it did not come from the heart.

"Yes, I'm all right," he replied. "I just haven't been sleeping so well recently."

Mary had to admit he did indeed seem tired. And he also appeared restless, which was not something she associated with him. Worried, she said,

"It seems to me something is bothering you. Are you sure you're all right?"

He smiled again but it was a sad smile and he said softly,

"I can see I can't fool you. But I really do feel all right. It's just - how should I put it - such a contradictory situation. I feel I'm getting closer to God and that means so much to me. But sometimes it's almost impossible to do what He demands of me. You see, Mary, sometimes I long so much to go back to being just myself, Jesus of Nazareth, carpenter. Because I know I'm becoming more and more distanced from my own self - my calling means I have to step aside more and more often. Tell me, do you think I've changed?"

Mary nodded. With disarming honesty, she replied,

"Yes, you've changed. You're no longer as carefree and eager as when I first got to know you. And sometimes I can't follow you any more, you're too... far away Then I hardly recognise you. At moments like that I'm so afraid I'll lose you."

They looked at one another and Mary recalled the first time their eyes met, long ago by the pool. Jesus admired her honesty. Candidly he said,

"Yes, I too think I'll lose myself soon. One way or another, it's all taking off now and I'll have to do everything I can to stop it from destroying me. And to be perfectly honest, I'm not sure I'm going to make it. I may have a lot of followers, but I've got at least as many enemies who I know hate me because I don't share their ideals. And now God has revealed to me what will happen to me after my death, how my soul will journey towards Him who formed me and who is waiting for me in anticipation. But instead of looking forward to this, the idea fills me with fear because it means that the end is really close by all of a sudden."

He brought her hands to his mouth and gave them a despairing kiss. Mary caught her breath for a moment. Now he was speaking so openly about his demise, she felt a tightness constricting her heart. Of course she knew how vulnerable he was and that his worries were far from unfounded. But she was not ready for this either. Hesitantly she stroked his hair and said,

"Tell me about your journey to God, Jesus. Perhaps that will cheer you up a bit, and me. Because what you're saying is frightening me and I'd like to know what will happen after your death."

Jesus became contemplative. The picture God had painted came to his mind again as clear as anything. Mary heard the passion return to his voice and just for a moment he seemed like the old Jesus again as he spoke,

"Mary, you must not be sad after my death - however terrible it may be - because God will be waiting for me and will guide my soul past all the guards of the heavenly kingdom. The first guard, that of Desire, will ask me, 'Well, I didn't see you when you were on your way to Earth but now I do see you, on your way to Heaven. How is that possible?' And my soul will reply, 'I did see you but you didn't notice me because I left all desire behind.' And then my soul will continue on to the next guard, that of Ignorance. It will ask me, 'Where do you think you are going? Were you not kept prisoner by wickedness? Did you not judge others and should I not therefore detain you?' But my soul will answer, 'I was condemned but I did not judge. I was kept prisoner although I myself brought liberty. I was not acknowledged, although I acknowledged that God is the ruler over Heaven and Earth.' After these words, this guard too will let my soul pass. See, the next guard - Jealousy - is already standing there. Enraged, it asks me, 'Where have you come from? Why did the people kill you? And why will you never be forgotten?' And my soul will reply, 'I had to die in order to free what I held captive. I was murdered but my death will change everything. And because I was prepared to offer up my life, I will be spared oblivion. I have already passed the guards of Desire and Ignorance, and now God is waiting for me and will give me peace. The Holy Spirit has been freed and so my task has been completed." Then this last guard will also let me pass and I'll be reunited with God and live forever in His kingdom where His love will surround me for eternity."

He fell silent, still with the introspective look on his face. Mary's heart was pounding. His words had affected her deeply and she fully understood the message he had given her between the lines. She realised more than ever how much she loved him and that she was definitely not ready to lose him.

She squeezed his hands lovingly, jolting him back out of his thoughts. He was about to say something but she stopped him by putting a hand to his mouth. She caught his eyes, put her hands around his face and caressed him with infinite tenderness. She stroked his cheeks with her thumbs, soothed his forehead and followed the lines of his eyebrows, his nose, his mouth... Jesus let her continue. He felt how every fibre in his body was responding to her touch and this time he did not want to suppress this feeling, as he had done before.

Mary noticed his excitement. Her heart suddenly beat fast and she pulled his face towards her and kissed him ardently on the mouth. He felt her warm, moist lips and the passion in her kiss. And he surrendered, pulling her roughly against him. Mary could no longer contain herself. She had waited so long for this moment! Her tongue sought his and he parted his lips for her. Their breathing became a panting craving for more and they abandoned themselves to their kissing. Now her hands feverishly sought and found the cord that kept his robe closed.

And finally, after waiting and hoping all that time, she felt his naked body and it was delightfully warm and soft. Her hands explored his body to find the most sensitive places and he drowned in this sea of unaccustomed, overwhelming emotion. Mary's desire was still far from satisfied. She undid the ribbon tying her blouse and guided his hands to her breasts. Her eagerness took him by surprise and the sight of her exposed curves brought him back with a jolt. He smothered a cry, pushed her off him and hastily put his robe back on. Mary realised immediately that she had overstepped the mark. She stood up unsteadily and stepped back a couple of paces, away from him. She covered her face with her hands in despair.

"I'm sorry," she whispered as she quickly rearranged her clothes. "Please forgive me!"

Jesus saw tears in her eyes, and her misery cut deeply into his soul. He got up too and wiped the tears away that were flowing down her cheeks.

"No, it's not you who should be apologising," he said vehemently, his voice hoarse from emotion. "It's my fault, I lost control. That should never have happened. For I know what my fate is and that there is no place there for you. Please forgive me."

But she carried on crying and he detested himself and could no longer bear to see her grief. He turned round and disappeared into the night that had now fallen.

Mary remained behind, motionless. She made no effort to stop her tears from flowing. Oh, how she loved that man! But she knew it would never turn out the way she so badly wanted it to. He had slipped from her grasp. She thought back to everything he had told her. And whereas she had initially thought they were equals, she now realised he was far ahead of her and that the spirit that inspired him and was taking possession of him was higher than what she had ever encountered, higher than what she thought possible.

"Oh Lord God," she prayed. "Please take good care of him, because now there's nothing more I can do for him."

Then she too turned round and sought her way back to the camp in the dark.

After a restless night, Mary was woken up the next morning by the sound of voices arguing. Still half asleep, she crawled out of her tent and saw a group of men talking vehemently to Jesus. She walked over to Susanna, who was watching the scene from a distance.

"What's going on?" she asked.

"Oh, it's Simon again," sighed Susanna. "That man is always so hot-headed! What he'd really like is for Jesus to start chasing the Romans out of the country today, and Herod with them!"

Mary raised her eyebrows quizzically.

"But he's got no intention of doing that at all," she said, in a tone of wonder. "At least, I've never heard him saying anything along those lines!"

"Yes, I know," nodded Susanna. "It's simply their own ambitions that they are projecting onto him. They've been waiting so long for a charismatic leader. And now there is Jesus who comes from the house of David and is standing up to the priests, so they reckon he could be that leader."

The argument among the group of men was getting more heated now and the two women heard Jesus talking loudly and saw him gesturing wildly as he tried to get his message across. It looked as if he had managed to persuade them for the time being. At any rate, the men left him in peace and went their own way. Only Simon and Judas remained behind, whispering to each other somewhat conspiratorially.

"Good, peace has returned," sighed Susanna. "I'll get started on breakfast. Could you ask Jesus what he'd like?"

Mary hesitated. She did not like the thought of having to speak to him after what had happened the previous evening. On the other hand, she did want to look him straight in the eye to see whether they would still be able to be friends, even if on a somewhat different footing.

She put her reservations to one side and walked up to Jesus, who had sat down at the table. She thought he looked tired, despite the early hour. She sat down next to him and asked,

"What was that all about just now?"

He shook his head.

"I don't know," he replied despondently. "I thought my message was clear. But somehow or other I'm not able to put an end to these false expectations. Simon thinks I'm the ideal leader for his movement. But that is really not my goal. I'm hardly going to get involved in an armed struggle where no-one knows how it could end up, am I? No, that's not the role I'm supposed to play. But all this does put me in danger."

He was quiet for a moment. Then he continued, in a voice that was as confidential as ever,

"Do you remember what we were talking about yesterday, Mary? That events were moving so fast that they would destroy me? Well, that end is coming really close now. Because a lot of people won't be at all happy if I keep refusing to take on that political role."

He looked at her and she had never seen so much grief in his eyes. And bitterly he said,

"I'm certain now, Mary, that I won't have much longer. Soon I'll have to pay for all this with my life, just like John."

Mary winced. The idea that she could lose him soon roused a feeling of fear and panic in her. Jesus saw how dejected she was.

"Come on, girl," he smiled affectionately in an attempt to cheer her up. "After all, I told you what will happen afterwards. I may die, but thanks to me the Holy Spirit will be able to remain on Earth and that spirit will help you establish God's kingdom after all."

He squeezed her hands and in a tone of encouragement he continued,

"Don't be misled by what seems, but is not. God Himself promised me that I would sit next to Him in His kingdom for ever more and that my message may not be accepted now, but will in the future. And I trust Him completely."

Mary looked at him and experienced a strange feeling. She heard his words, she saw the familiar face but yet it felt as if she was sitting next to a stranger. She realised that he was becoming more and more engulfed by the Holy Spirit and that she really would have to let go of the Jesus she loved so much. She stared ahead for a moment in silence. Then she asked earnestly,

"What'll happen now, Jesus? What'll you do?"

"I'll go to Jerusalem for Passover at any rate," he replied. "And then we'll see what happens. All the pieces are in play now and that's where the dénouement will take place."

Mary could not help asking,

"Isn't it possible to do anything about that... dénouement, Jesus? Or is it definite that things will happen as you described?"

Her question moved him.

"It's all in God's hands now, Mary," he replied tenderly. "We'll just have to wait and see how it'll finish."

He caressed her hands a moment, then signalled to Susanna, who had been waiting patiently with his breakfast all that time. But Mary was not hungry. She stood up and went off to clear up her tent.

Meanwhile, Judas and Simon were still huddled up talking. They appeared to be in disagreement as their words flew backwards and forth.

"Just give up, Simon," said Judas fiercely. "He won't do it. Surely you see that."

"But we've never had such a good opportunity!" countered Simon. "Look at all the people following him! If we give them all weapons, Herod won't have a chance. And the inhabitants of Jerusalem support us too. I'm still in contact with Barabbas and he told me that people are actually becoming more prepared to fight. He's willing to pronounce Jesus the rightful king. Our biggest problem is how to persuade Jesus himself!"

And he continued eagerly,

"How much money have we got now? How many weapons could we buy?"

Judas retrieved the bag containing the money he looked after for Jesus and let the coins pass between his fingers.

"That's a good start!" cried Simon enthusiastically.

He grabbed Judas by the arm and whispered conspiratorially,

"Don't let me down, Judas. We've never been so close to our goal. Let's keep trying. One day he's got to realise that he'll never be able to achieve his own dream either with Herod on the throne and the Romans here."

Judas hesitated and then nodded.

"Well, all right then, I'll see what I can do. At least now he knows our views on the matter. And I'll talk to Mary. She has some influence over him."

"Mary!" laughed Simon sarcastically. "Oh, shut up about her. That whore spends all her time fawning over him. Can't she see he's not interested?"

"Now, now. There's no need to be like that!" said Judas soothingly. "Mary's an intelligent woman and she definitely can help us. And why do you call her a whore? That's how rumours get started!"

"Well," insinuated Simon, "as far as I'm concerned, there's only one way a woman can earn her own money. I'd sure like to see that so-called inn her aunt is supposed to have. I'm willing to bet it's just a vulgar brothel!"

"Simon, how could you!" cried out Judas indignantly. "Stop that! You're just jealous because Jesus spends more time with her than he does with us. But that doesn't give you the right to talk about her like that! You should be ashamed of yourself! But all right, I'll try to speak to Jesus himself then."

Judas got his opportunity that very same evening. It was chilly and Jesus had gone a little way off on his own. Judas saw him busy collecting sticks and trying to light a fire with a tinderbox. But it was quite windy and he could not get the fire to catch. Judas went up to him and offered,

"Shall I help you? You'll never manage on your own with this wind."

Jesus looked up.

"Oh, yes please!" he said gratefully. "It blows harder than I thought."

With Judas helping, they soon got the fire going and the two men sat watching the ever-mesmerising weaving of the flames. Then Jesus broke the silence, asking,

"So tell me, Judas, what did you want to speak to me about?"

Judas looked up in astonishment. How did he know?

"Um, well... I actually wanted to apologise for my behaviour this morning," he said to his own surprise. "Simon and I shouldn't have kept on at you like that. I know you don't have any political ambitions and we mustn't bother you with that any more. But you'll understand we'd rather see you took a different view."

"Of course I realise that," replied Jesus. "And it's not easy to understand my ambitions either. To be honest, I didn't have that clear an idea myself when I started out. But as time progresses, I've been getting a better picture of God's intentions for me. The only thing He wants me to do is to bring love. Only love has the power to let people feel that they have a dual nature: a human one and a divine one. Fortunately I don't have to do this all on my own, for the Holy Spirit has merged with me. This spirit is unbelievably powerful and it comes from God Himself. Together we want to show people that they too are part of God."

"That's a pretty tough task!" said Judas with respect.

Jesus nodded and stared out ahead for a moment in silence.

"I don't think I'll be able to cope with bearing this huge power for much longer," he then confessed frankly. "I notice I'm finding it harder and harder going physically. That's why it's good that the

Holy Spirit will soon be freed."

"Freed?" asked Judas, intrigued. "How?"

Jesus smiled sadly.

"I've already explained how a few times," he replied gently. "You can only reach your destination by dying."

Judas looked at him in surprise. Then, slowly grasping what he was saying, he faltered,

"You mean...?"

He left his sentence unfinished. Jesus nodded.

"Yes, you've understood correctly. And I hope I'll be able to do it. I must admit I'm more attached to this life than I thought. Perhaps I'll need some help... when the time comes... to make the right choices."

He smiled at Judas and continued with affection,

"Of all my disciples, you're the one who best senses what it's like for me. Thank you for that."

Embarrassed, Judas shrugged his shoulders. He did not know what to say. They went back to staring in silence at the flames until the wind fanned them to dangerous heights.

"We'd be better off putting it out," said Judas in a concerned voice.

Quickly they threw some sand over the fire. They were only just in time. The wind was becoming even more ferocious and turning into a genuine storm.

"Let's go," called Jesus. "We'll need to check the tents or else they'll take off!"

They hurried back to the camp where the others were already busy weighting down the guy ropes with stones. Jesus gave a worried look at the tempest brewing and said in a loud voice to Peter,

"I hope there's no-one still out there on the lake!"

Peter nodded. Being a fisherman, he knew as well as anyone how rough it could get on the water. They all nervously went to their beds.

The next day they saw the damage the storm had caused. Branches had been torn off trees and some tents had been damaged. And early in the morning, some people turned up at the camp. What Jesus had feared had indeed happened. Various boats had been shipwrecked and a total of fourteen fishermen had drowned. One man could barely contain his grief. With tears in his eyes, he took Jesus' hand and begged him,

"Jesus, sir, please, help me. I've lost two brothers. Both had a wife and children. What am I to do? We are completely dependent on the fish we catch to survive and now we've lost everything: our boats, our nets..."

Jesus put a comforting arm around his shoulders.

"Come now," he said encouragingly. "I know it'll all work out in the end. I myself am a carpenter by trade and I can help you make a new boat. And we have some money to buy things."

He turned to Simon and instructed in a tone of voice that would not brook any objections,

"Simon, fetch the money bag from Judas and give it to this man."

Simon looked at him in utter astonishment. Did Jesus want to give their money away?

"But Jesus ..." he stammered. "Shouldn't we at least keep a little for ourselves? We could give them some, of course, but all..."

Jesus' jaw dropped in amazement.

"How can you say such a thing, Simon!" he said, exasperated. "Have you really understood so little of the truth to which I have been witness all this time? After all, God Himself will make sure we don't go short of anything! Have you ever lacked anything while you've been with me?"

Simon realised he was not going to be able to avoid this. Completely perplexed, he walked leaden-footed to Judas' tent, came back with the purse and gave it to the fisherman with visible reluctance. Jesus gave a satisfied nod. He patted Simon on the shoulder and laughed,

"Now, that wasn't so difficult, was it? Just think of what they'll be able to do with that!"

But Simon testily shook off his hand and strode away. Jesus looked at him in wonder. But he did not spend long pondering this incident as his hands were itching to get to work. He gathered some young men and taught them how to saw planks while Andrew and Peter took out their tools and started making new nets. Their labours drew a great deal of attention. Many people had not realised that Jesus was a carpenter and they were surprised to see him roll up his sleeves and get down to work. The spectators included a Pharisee priest. After having watched all the activity for a while, he said to Jesus,

"Tell me, Jesus: if God rules the world, then surely it is He who is responsible for the death of these fishermen. Why did He not do anything to prevent this storm?"

And he turned to the crowds standing around and continued, in a tone designed to incite them,

"Listen! You've undoubtedly heard how our brothers went from Galilee to Jerusalem and were then executed by Pilate on the basis of some crazy decree. Why did God allow that?"

A wave of unrest rippled through the crowd. That was a good question - where was God when this happened?! The priest listened to the murmuring with evident satisfaction. He was convinced that now he had confronted Jesus with a problem to which he would not have an answer for once. Jesus was dumbfounded. He looked at the priest in shock and exclaimed in what was for him an unusually aggressive voice,

"How dare you! How dare you even think such a thing! God is pure love. Even the tiniest sparrow that falls to earth can reckon on His compassion! Do you really think someone like Pilate can remain unpunished for what he has done? If that was the case, then you would be right to feel your sense of justice affronted and to cry out, 'There is no God, or if there is a God then He is an unjust ruler and we would be better off without Him!' But there is cause and effect and where there is a cause in the one life, the effect may only be seen in the next life. It may seem that someone appears to escape his rightful punishment in this life, but you should know that his deeds will always have consequences. And is it not humans themselves who do wrong to others without reason? Well, humans can also make that wrong right again by focusing not on revenge but on forgiveness. And God, who is justice itself, has given us the perfect example. In His everlasting love, He does nothing other than allow us to make good our errors time and time again. So never blame God for the suffering in the world, because it is man himself who is responsible for this!"

After saying this, he turned brusquely and strode off. He was so upset by their lack of trust in God that he did not even want to listen to their response. And as for the priest who was only interested in setting a trap for him - well, he never wanted to see that man again.

He walked to the lake, took a rowing boat moored there and rowed grimly along the shore, only stopping after he had travelled a long distance.

The crowd was left behind in confusion about his sudden departure. His words had clearly made an impression.

"He's right," someone called out. "It doesn't get us anywhere, blaming God for everything. We should examine our own consciences first!"

Some people turned to the priest.

"What are you lot actually doing over there in Jerusalem?" they asked angrily. "Why do we have to pay so much temple tax and why aren't you giving Jesus support in his work? You should follow his example instead of lining your pockets so shamelessly!"

The priest realised his plan to damage Jesus' reputation had backfired and Simon saw an opportunity waiting to be seized.

"So you too think Jesus should be our king?" he called out with gusto.

A cry of 'yes' went up.

"Then follow us to Jerusalem!" continued Simon enthusiastically. "We're in contact with the Zealots there. They'll help us to get rid of that entire clique of priests - and Herod as well. So who's with us? Who wants to fight for our new king?"

This too was followed by loud cheers of agreement. Mary, Peter and the others looked in astonishment. On the one hand, they were pleased that Jesus' words had had so much effect. On the other hand, they were worried by how little was needed to sway such a crowd.

"We need to talk to Jesus," said Peter in a concerned voice. "If we go to Jerusalem now, who knows what will happen."

"I can have a word with him," offered Mary. "Although I won't be able to tell him anything he isn't already aware of. He knows all too well what forces have been set in motion. I don't think anyone will be able to stop him from going there, not even me."

"Well, in that case there's not much point in you talking to him, is there," reacted Andrew angrily. "Why would he discuss such important matters with you anyway? Or do you think we can't come up with a solution on our own?"

Tears welled up in Mary's eyes. She turned miserably to Peter.

"Is that how you see it too?" she asked sadly. "Do you think I'm trying to get all the attention and that I'm just making it up when I say Jesus sometimes discusses important things with me?"

"That's right, ask Peter of all people!" laughed Thaddeus sarcasmtically. "That hothead always agrees with his brother anyway! But I'm telling you, we shouldn't put Mary down just because Jesus gives her so much of his attention. I know you mightn't want to hear this, but she really does understand Jesus better than the rest of us put together. And we can get worked up about this but that won't get us anywhere. We should really be ashamed of ourselves for not keeping to his example better. When are we going to stop this political rubbish and start really living his message?"

The rest looked at each other in shame. He was right, of course. Peter sighed. Resignedly, he said,

"All right then, I'll keep everything in order here. Mary, you go and find Jesus and talk to him please. And come back quickly - it looks as though we're going to have a lot of extra mouths to feed this evening!"

He left her behind and rushed off to make sure everyone who now wanted to join them on the journey to Jerusalem would have enough to eat and a place to sleep.

Mary set off nervously. The increasing tensions were wearing her down. She felt the web of misunderstanding tightening around them. She was deeply worried and wondered whether it was ever going to be possible to manoeuvre events in the right direction. Probably only Jesus himself would be able to do that. And she realised very well that he would not buckle under the pressure but would continue to follow his own course.

She had now reached the lake, where she followed the well-used path that ran along the shoreline. She had to walk a long way because Jesus had rowed quite a distance. She was starting to have serious doubts as to whether she had gone in the right direction when she spotted him. He was sitting at the water's edge, immersed deep in thought. He did not hear her approach. She studied him closely and decided he did not look well. It was clear that everything he was doing and the reactions that it aroused were draining him. She went up to him quietly and put her hand on his shoulder, making him jump.

"Mary...? Oh, you startled me."

She smiled apologetically.

"I'm sorry. I didn't mean to, of course, but you were a long way off with your thoughts. Do you mind if I sit with you?"

He shook his head.

"Not at all. I never do with you, you know that."

She sat down next to him.

"What were you thinking about?" she asked.

He shrugged.

"Nothing, really. I was actually trying to empty my mind to let God in."

"I'm very impressed with what you said just now," said Mary and a silent look came into her eyes. "When I hear you talk like that, I see God so clearly at work in you. And it's not just me. A lot of people have joined us who want to follow you to Jerusalem, although I've got my doubts as to whether it's for the right reasons."

"So you should," replied Jesus laconically. "Most of them are not doing it for the right reasons. But you can hardly blame them for that."

He looked at her and continued affectionately,

"It really helps me, Mary, having you understand me so well. Unfortunately I see so few people who come from the same spiritual sphere as you. Most of them still have a long way to go."

Mary nodded. She recognised the feeling he was talking about and sometimes it made her despair. After all, she herself had spent so long searching for a soul mate.

"So wouldn't it be better not to go to Jerusalem after all?" she asked. "Perhaps it's too early?"

He hesitated briefly. Then he confessed,

"Perhaps I did come too early. But God is convinced that my message will find its way, perhaps only to one or two people now but eventually to a lot of people. That gives me the motivation to keep going. So I'll simply go to Jerusalem to celebrate Passover as I have done every year."

And with a roguish smile he added,

"But you knew that anyway, Mary!"

Mary gave a somewhat bewildered laugh. Of course she had

known that. For a moment she did not know what to say; shyly, she twisted the ribbon of her blouse around her finger. Then she looked back up at him and said,

"It always amazes me, Jesus, the way you talk about God. How can you be so sure about what He thinks? How do you hear Him and experience His presence to let you talk about Him so naturally? Please try to explain it to me."

He looked at her familiar face tenderly. Her request touched him and he wanted so much to comply, because if anyone was capable of understanding, it was her. He became meditative and immediately felt God's presence in his heart. She had sensed it correctly: God was a real presence in his life. This was not a question of belief for him anymore, it was a certainty he could not avoid. But how could he ever make that clear to her?

"I don't know how to explain my experience of God to you, Mary," he replied. "You're asking me to do the impossible. Any words I'd choose wouldn't be up to the job. Can anyone ever convey at all - truly convey - to someone else what they are feeling? How am I supposed to tell you what I perceive in my soul, what I experience in my spirit? After all, you can't see things through my eyes, nor I through yours."

Mary felt a lump in her throat. For some reason his answer made her sad. She had hoped that he would have been able to reveal some of the mystery to her, precisely because they had this special bond. But she realised he was right. How could he do that, when she herself was absolutely unable to put into words what she felt for him? Apparently people in general were incapable of genuinely communicating with one another and so doomed to eternal solitariness. And how tough had to be his solitude. How difficult it had to be for him being unable to share with others his special bond with God.

"That must be very lonely for you," she said softly, "not being able to talk to anyone about the thing that most affects and drives you."

She saw him remain quiet a moment. It was clear she had touched a nerve. But he recovered quickly and replied,

"Perhaps it seems that way, but God fills my soul and surrounds me wherever I go. So I never feel really lonely."

However, his answer did not sound too convincing and his body language gave a very different message. Mary was overwhelmed by a desire, stronger than she had felt in a long while, to put her arms around him and comfort him. But she controlled herself and simply said,

"I wouldn't think that's quite the same. But of course I can't speak for you."

He remained silent. She saw him struggling hard with his emotions. And only after a long pause, he spoke to her again, saying softly,

"Perhaps that's simply the tragic side to my life, Mary. I couldn't live without God and I chose to be His instrument of my own free will. But it's not easy. It's still a constant battle between what I'd like to do and what He demands of me. But despite that, it's all worth it. I'd never have become what I am now or be able to do what I can do now without that battle. And I'm convinced that if I succeed in doing His will in every respect, I'll achieve the ultimate fulfilment of my life."

He gave her an honest smile and continued in a voice filled with love,

"God is my Abba. What else can I do other than surrender myself entirely to Him?"

Once again, Mary felt a lump in her throat. This was another reminder that she would never play the part in his life that she wanted to play so dearly. How could he ever make room for her alongside the Holy Spirit that inspired him so? She knew that she should really renounce such wishes as he had made himself perfectly clear on the subject. And rightly so. For could she ever be satisfied with the sparse scattering of crumbs of time and attention that would be left over for her?

Besides, soon she would be losing him anyway. Losing him to God who was claiming him, losing him to the Holy Spirit that he had let into his soul. And even, although she hardly dared think of it, losing him to the death he had spoken of. Carefully concealing her grief, she stood up and said,

"I'll see whether I can help Susanna prepare the meal. There's plenty of work now with all those extra people and I've left her on her own with it for too long."

With pain in her heart, she left him by the water's edge. He stayed there praying at least another hour, which merely underlined the distance that had grown between them.

Judea

It was getting closer to Passover and as this was probably going to be the last time he would celebrate it, Jesus gathered his disciples around him in a field to tell them what was going to happen. They could tell he was in a strange mood and watched him expectantly. Jesus surveyed the twelve men who had become so familiar over the past couple of years.

"My dear brothers," he said softly. "I probably won't be with you for much longer. God will soon call me to join Him and then you will need to carry on the work of spreading my message."

His friends looked at each other aghast. Jesus could see they were bursting to ply him with questions, but he raised up his hand to stop them, saying,

"I will be rejected by the priests and I will be killed, but my message will live on. And that will be your task."

He walked amongst them as he spoke.

"Although you have all learned a lot in the past few years, there is still much to do. For you too will come up against opposition and you'll need to learn how to deal with that. So never forget: blessed are those who are poor and bereft. Don't let yourselves be guided by all those thoughts going through your head - trust blindly that everything will come to pass as it should. And blessed are those who mourn, because in the darkness there will be light. You too will learn that this life is not the true life but only its semblance, a façade. And you will feel pain because you have to lead this illusory life. But you will also feel the loving touch of God and that will give you the strength to continue."

He sat down and continued,

"Blessed are the meek because they will be the saviours of the earth. Have the courage to take off the mask you wear and break down the walls you have built around you. Only when you are prepared to show your true self will others put their trust in you. Of course this is daunting: you'll be tormented and you'll run a very real risk of being killed. But there too you will be helped by the power from the spiritual world. And blessed be those who hunger for righteousness because there will come a time when their wishes shall be fulfilled. Whoever hungers for righteousness suffers from what they see in this life and what people do to one another. You might prefer to live in true love, in line with the love you know from the spiritual world. That very hunger will help you to keep going."

He could see his words were having an effect and he smiled.

"Perhaps you are thinking that you'll never be able to do all this. But believe me, you will get so much in return. For blessed are those who are merciful, for others shall show them mercy in return. After all, you reap what you have sown. And when you have done that, you will be pure of heart. And blessed are those who are pure of heart as they will see the divine world. When you receive that gift, you will see that all your efforts, all that inner struggle, all the lack of understanding from those around you - it will all have been more than worth it. For you will be living in confidence, freed from the burden of the past. You will be blessed because you will exude peace and love, and people will see that God abides in your heart."

He turned to Judas and asked,

"Tell me, Judas, did you ever feel an outsider as a child - with feelings, views that were different to the rest of your family?"

Judas nodded, somewhat embarrassed.

"Yes, Jesus, that's familiar enough. Sometimes I would feel as if I was looking at them from a distance, like a stranger."

"But that too was ordained," explained Jesus. "Because it taught you even at that young age to remain true to your own instincts as to what was right, even if that meant contradicting the views of your parents. So you must not be afraid to be the black sheep, because you will open up the path to the future."

He gave the man a warm smile and then addressed the entire group.

"Blessed are those who are rejected and condemned for what they know deep down to be true. It is thus that you will make the Holy Spirit be felt on earth. Unfortunately as messengers of God, we cannot avoid being condemned and rejected. But don't let this stop you! Stay true to yourself, follow your own path and remember that you will always be kept safe in the heart of our Father."

He fell silent and his disciples realised that he had finished his discourse. Without speaking, they stood and walked back to the camp, their heads full of what he had said.

The next day they took down their tents, packed their belongings, loaded up some donkeys and carried what was left over themselves. Jesus felt relief they were now finally on their way. Although he had found it difficult to accept this final phase of his assignment, he was now filled with tense expectation and he felt renewed energy charging through his body. His enthusiasm was contagious as he mingled with his followers.

Only Mary felt downcast. She could not understand how he could be so unconcerned when he knew exactly what end was awaiting him. How could he laugh like that and be so cheerful? Had he forgotten her, her grief and the emptiness that he would leave behind when he had gone? Tears welled up in her eyes and she walked gloomily with the rest of the group, knowing that each step was one step closer to the end. Jesus had noticed her sombre mood. He came and walked next to her.

"Hey there! Why haven't I heard you singing lately?" he said in an attempt to cheer her up. "I hope you're not worrying about things?"

Mary shrugged a little testily and gave no answer, as she was afraid he would hear the emotion in her voice. Jesus could see her struggle.

"Come, come, girl," he said tenderly and he took her hand. "Don't be like this. I've changed the way I look at it and so should you. It's really quite wonderful that soon everyone can be touched by the Holy Spirit, and you know better than anyone that this life is a mere façade and that there is nothing terrible about losing it."

"Yes, of course I know that," replied Mary softly. "But what my head says and what my heart feels are two different things."

"That's not the case for me," said Jesus convincingly. "I really have accepted it! And of course you know we'll see each other again anyway!"

This made Mary laugh, despite everything, for he had a point there. Their bond did indeed transcend death – hadn't they felt that right from the start?

"You're right," she admitted. "Please forgive me. I promise I won't mope any longer."

"Good, I'm glad to hear that," laughed Jesus and he gave her an encouraging pat on the cheek.

Then he walked on to the head of the procession to discuss the route they should take with Peter. They decided to spend the first night in the vicinity of Nain, then to proceed to Sichar and to continue to Bethany via Ephraim. Jesus wanted to set up camp at Bethany as it was walking distance from Jerusalem and he looked forward to seeing Lazarus again. The journey went without a hitch. Although Jesus noticed they were being spied on from a distance, no-one tried to stop them. When they reached Bethany after travelling for several days, Martha came running out to meet them. They could immediately tell something was wrong as she had tears in her eyes. Mary rushed over to her sister.

"What is it?" she asked worriedly.

"Oh, Mary, I'm so pleased you're here," sobbed Martha. "It's Lazarus. He's been so depressed lately. And now he's gone and shut himself up in a grave. He's been there for three days without anything to eat or drink. I've no idea if he's even still alive."

"He's alive!" said Mary adamantly. "We have such a strong bond! I would know if he wasn't."

"So there is still hope," comforted Jesus her. "Come, take us to him."

Martha led the way to the grave. Several villagers had gathered there to pray Kaddish. Jesus was moved by this and overcome by the fear that they might have arrived too late after all. With the help of some of the villagers, he rolled away the stone at the entrance of the grave and went inside. It took him a moment to get used to the gloom but then he saw Lazarus lying there, wrapped in a simple white shroud. He knelt next to him and took his hand. It felt icy, like the rest of his body. Jesus was shocked. It upset him terribly to see his friend as unmoving as if he were dead. He cried out desperately,

"Lazarus, come back! I know it's difficult sometimes but this life is worth living. You too have a place in this life. You are such a wonderful, unique person. Think what that is worth. Don't let go of life!"

Full of emotion, he took Lazarus' hands in his, called up all his forces of concentration and tried to make contact with his friend whose soul was now so far away. And miraculously Lazarus's hands gradually started to warm up and after a while he opened his eyes. He looked around in confusion, but then he saw Jesus. He sat up, put his arms around his friend and burst into tears. Jesus patted his back. Shaking his head, he said tenderly,

"Why did you have to go and do that? You can't turn your back on life like that."

"I felt so abandoned," replied Lazarus in a choked voice. "I could tell things weren't going well with Mary, and you had your own troubles with that decree and so on. And I got so crestfallen that I couldn't see the point any more. I had such a strong longing to go back to where I came from. I wondered what I was doing in this world, when even someone like you doesn't get the recognition he deserves. From that moment on, I could only think of one thing: going back to the spiritual world. And I almost did!"

Jesus looked at him intensely.

"Tell me," he asked in a tense voice. "What did you see?"

Lazarus closed his eyes for a moment. He seemed to be in a rapture as he said,

"Oh Jesus, it was so wonderful! I went through a dark tunnel but I didn't feel afraid at all because at the end of it I could see the divine light. And then I was in that light. All I felt there was love, respect and affection, surrounding me on all sides. I'd never experienced anything so sublime before and I realised I never wanted to go back. Until you called me."

Jesus was deeply touched by his ecstatic words. His voice hoarse, he stammered,

"I understand so well what you mean! My soul too longs to return. But we still have a task to carry out here."

He helped his friend stand up, then continued in a serious tone,

"Lazarus, you must look after Mary when I'm no longer around. You're right that things aren't going so well for her at the moment. She finds it really difficult to deal with the fact that I'll soon be gone. Will you do that for me?"

Lazarus squeezed Jesus' hands and replied in an emotional

voice,

"Of course I'll do that, Jesus! I love her so much! But I hope it won't be needed any time soon - I hope you'll be with us for a while yet!"

Jesus smiled reticently.

"Unfortunately that's not something I can control, Lazarus."

He embraced his friend and with their arms around each other's shoulders, they walked to the grave entrance. A large crowd had now gathered there. Many people had heard that Jesus had come to Bethany to call his friend Lazarus back from the dead. When they saw the two men appear together in the entrance to the cave, a huge buzz went through the crowd. The people whispered to each other in amazement, saying,

"Look! He's raised him from the dead!"

The rumour spread like wildfire throughout the town and its surrounding area. Soon everyone was talking about Jesus of Nazareth who had awakened his friend Lazarus from the dead!

Mary heard the news too and she was confused by the utter conviction with which people told the story. She went looking for Jesus and asked,

"Tell me: was he really already dead?"

Jesus looked at her, astonished that she of all people was asking him this question.

"No, of course not," he replied curtly. "You should know that! I have to obey God's laws of nature as well."

He strode off, shaking his head. But it was not so easy to stop the rumours and the news reached the priests in the temple too. They wondered desperately how on earth they would ever be able to make a stand against him.

There was a week to go before Passover and Jesus was preparing to enter Jerusalem. As he did not want to give anyone the opportunity to accuse them of not observing the Sabbath peace, they left on the Friday. They stopped on the hillside close to the city walls and pitched their tents. Jesus arranged for small fires to be lit in a circle around the camp so that no unwelcome guests could sneak in unseen. That evening, the inhabitants of Jerusalem could see the flames and many of them harboured the hope that this Jesus had come to put an end to Herod's corrupt rule.

There was rising excitement among the Zealots too. Many of the supporters of Barabbas had obtained weapons, despite the fact that Simon had not been able to do much for them. Herod was painfully aware that he was not particularly popular and he had watched the explosive growth in Jesus' support in the past year with misgivings. However, everything seemed quiet as yet. Jesus' followers had taken his command not to disturb the Sabbath peace to heart and the day passed without incident. Jesus was quite unconcerned about having to face up to the priests the next day and he calmly started preparing to go to bed. But all of a sudden he heard some commotion and Peter broke into his tent.

"Please excuse me, Jesus," he said nervously, "but there's someone here for you. I don't trust this at all so please be careful!"

Curious, Jesus stepped outside his tent. He was surprised to see a guard from the court of Pilate standing there. The man bowed politely.

"Good evening, lord Jesus. Our honoured prefect Pilate wishes to speak to you."

He pulled his cloak to one side, letting Jesus see that he was heavily armed. Peter grabbed Jesus' arm.

"Don't go with him, Jesus!" he whispered insistently. "They'll kill you!"

"No, I don't think they will," replied Jesus in a calm voice. "I'm destined for a different fate."

He wrapped his cloak around him, pulled the hood down low and followed his guide to the citadel of Antonia where he was received by Pilate in one of his private rooms. Pilate was without a doubt an awe-inspiring man, with broad shoulders and muscular legs. He exuded authority, with the air of someone who is used to being obeyed. But Jesus was unimpressed. He stood expectant in the luxuriously furnished room while Pilate walked round him and surveyed him from all sides. So this was that Jesus of Nazareth, known as the Christ, who was threatening to bring his province on the verge of a civil war, if Herod was to be believed. He had to admit that this man did have a certain something although he was unable to put his finger on it exactly. He started speaking in a confidential tone.

"Good evening, lord Jesus. I've asked for you to be brought here in order to warn you. The leaders of the Jews are planning to have you arrested and executed. King Herod has mobilised all his troops. I can see serious unrest developing if you decide to enter the city with all those people following you for whatever reason. So I will arrange for you to be taken to a safe place. I've already got a team of fast horses and a bodyguard standing by for you."

If he had been expecting Jesus to hug him in gratitude, he must have been sorely disappointed, for Jesus was unable to suppress a smile as he said in a firm voice,

"You clearly don't know me, sir. How could you imagine for one moment that I would scarper like a coward! I've come to bring God's message of love and I would rather sacrifice my life than renounce my mission by fleeing."

Pilate felt that he had been told off like a small child.

"Listen here, young man," he replied with irritation. "I'm not going to let this province slide into civil war just because you have some kind of mission to carry out that might endanger Roman rule!"

Jesus realised what he really meant.

"Oh, I understand!" he reacted in a sharp voice. "You're afraid I'll undermine your power! But that power of yours doesn't mean anything anyway. God doesn't care about earthly status. The people you look down on with contempt will enter into His kingdom and the powerful, who have never shown any genuine concern for another human being, will be send back. Only those who accept this truth will be King."

Pilate was dumbfounded. No-one had ever spoken to him so insolently before. He burst out angrily,

"Take care what you say, Jesus of Nazareth! I can call up a hundred men in no time and get you flung in jail. And then you won't be king of this country, that's for sure!"

Jesus shook his head. The Roman had clearly not understood him.

"You have been misled by the stories doing the rounds about me," he said candidly. "It's not my ambition to become king. The kingdom I'm talking about is not on this earth; it is in the soul of every individual. If you open up your soul to God and put aside your earthly desires then you will be a king and God will grant you eternal life. But I realise you'd rather not hear this, because when that time comes, it will mean an end to Roman rule. The only power that will rule then will be the love of my Father and He will rule for eternity. If you want to arrest me for what I just said, please go ahead. But your actions will anger some of my followers and they will undoubtedly try to free me. And that decree you signed will not change that at all."

For the first time in his life Pilate felt an incredible powerlessness. It was clear he had no hold over this man who was susceptible to neither his flattery nor his threats. And there was nothing he could accuse him of as he was not guilty of any displays of power whatsoever. The only threat he presented was the fact that he was probably the only person able to control his followers, at least to some extent. This meant arresting him was simply not an option. Furiously he strode up to Jesus and snapped at him fiercely,

"You just wait - one day you'll learn something about yourself! For the time being, I've got more power around here than that God of yours! And I hope for your sake that your followers remain faithful to you because if not, I'll be coming for you!"

And out of frustration, he spat right in Jesus' face. Jesus looked at him in deep shock, a look that showed not only his feelings of personal pride, but also of sympathy for Pilate, for this man had clearly a long way to go. Pilate could not take his look for long and soon averted his eyes, before marching off to the door and calling to the envoy waiting in the hall,

"Take him back. We're done!"

Then he sank into a chair, exhausted. He was so fed up with this province! He had had more than enough by now of the continual intrigues about religious matters. It was so much easier in Rome: you just freed up some space in the temple for the latest god to be added to the list. But here... He sat deep in thought for a moment. Then he picked up the bell on his table and rang it. A servant appeared almost immediately to receive his orders.

"Listen!" Pilate snarled curtly. "Go at once to our army camp at Jericho and tell the commander to mobilise a cohort of soldiers. I expect them to be here by dawn tomorrow, all right?"

The servant nodded. And when the sun rose over Jerusalem the next morning, it was not just the heat that made the air tremble but also a thrilling tension.

Despite Pilate's threats, Jesus had slept well and he woke up refreshed. After they had breakfasted, Peter rounded up everyone. Jesus spoke earnestly to his followers, explaining that all he wanted to do that day was to persuade the priests to give the people free access to the house of prayer on this Passover and to refrain from burnt offerings. He also pointed out to them that they might be in danger. Some returned to their tents, but most remained. They could sense something was in the air and they were full of hope in their hearts.

Mary and Susanna remained with the group too - how could they have abandoned him on this day of all days? Jesus surveyed his people one last time and then started the descent into Jerusalem. Just as he was about to enter one of the narrow gates to the city, a man emerged from the shadows and approached him. Jesus felt a hand on his shoulder and the man, a stranger to him, said pressing,

"Jesus, do as our prophet Zachariah predicted. Sit on this donkey so that the people recognise you as their king!"

Jesus looked at him in consternation.

"My good man, I'm afraid you have the wrong idea about what I've come to do here," he replied with conviction. "I have never said I wanted to be the king of Israel and I certainly don't want to give that impression today! So please take away that donkey and let me through!"

Simon, who had recognised the man as Barabbas, pushed his way through to Jesus.

"You won't be able to do anything, even in the temple, without the support of the people, Jesus!" he said forcefully. "You must take advantage of anything that can help you achieve your goal."

But Jesus shook his head emphatically. He had worked so hard for so long to make sure his message was untainted and he had no intention of sending out the wrong signals now. But he had not reckoned on some of his followers taking things into their own hands and before he was fully aware of what was happening, they lifted him up and put him on the donkey. The animal set off at once.

Large numbers of the city's inhabitants had now gathered along the streets and a great cheer went up when they saw him riding into their town. Many people took off their cloaks and spread them on the road in front of him to show their respect while others waved brightly coloured cloths and palm branches. An euphoric atmosphere developed in no time.

Jesus could barely grasp what was happening. On the one hand he was annoyed that he had let this happen but on the other he found it overwhelming to be the centre of all this attention and his heart pounded in tense expectation. Perhaps he would be able to achieve what he had dreamed of for so long after all! He decided to let everything take its course for the time being and assumed God would take care of things. He really did not have much choice because now people were thronging around him from all sides. They held out their hands in an attempt to touch him, if only for a moment, so that they could feel God's love he radiated. He pressed the hands that reached out to him, touched by their enthusiasm and then deliberately choose the route to the temple. When he got there, his followers lifted him off the donkey, hoisted him onto their shoulders and carried him into the temple grounds, singing at the top of their voices,

"Hosanna, son of David, who comes in the name of the Lord!"

Jesus raised his arm and called out,

"Please put me down. You mustn't raise me up as if I'm someone people ought to look up to. Are we not in the temple where the only being worthy of respect is God Himself?"

The priests, who had been watching his glorious entrance anxiously, saw Jesus' followers put him down as requested and breathed a sigh of relief. It looked as if he was still in control of the situation. But now Jesus turned to them and spoke in a sharp voice,

"Why are you looking at these people with such fear in your eyes? Why are you wondering how all this could happen? Do you still not realise that this is the result of your own behaviour? You preach the law of Moses and order the people to keep to that law but you yourselves don't obey it. And you do nothing to help prophets who preach the true message of God, like my good friend John the Baptist. Yes, I too am in danger because I preach that people can find God in their hearts and don't need you with your unjust tax system and pointless offerings. Yet you still refuse to believe that God Himself revealed these truths to me because you want to be honoured as gods yourselves. But you forget that we are all brothers and that there is only one Father, only one Counsellor, and that is God who has put these words in my mouth. I'm telling you: if you carry on this way, you'll bring disaster on Jerusalem and there won't be two stones left on top of another to show this temple ever existed. But it is not too late yet. Open up your hearts. Embrace the truth that I am bringing you. Then you too will find God and enter into His kingdom."

A great cheer reverberated when he had finished speaking and the priests, fearful of what the crowd might do, fled inside and stayed there out of sight. Jesus let his gaze wander over the square. As always, it was bustling with activity. More people than ever had come to the city to celebrate the approaching Passover and his entry on the donkey had also attracted people, eager to see this new sensation. The outer courtyard was seething with merchants selling sacrificial animals. Despite the extortionate prices, there were still large numbers of people queuing to buy them. Jesus watched the trading going on and felt pain in his heart. He had rebuked the priests, an enormous crowd of people were following him but it still looked as if business was simply continuing as usual. He was determined to restore some dignity to the temple. He strode across the square, speaking indignantly to various merchants in an attempt to persuade them to change their ways.

"Good people, surely you too are law-abiding Jews from the house of Israel who want to serve their God? So help me turn this building into a place of prayer and meditation. Sacrificing animals is no way to please God. We should be renouncing that practice and looking for God in our hearts instead. It is God Himself who has instructed me to tell you this. He wants the temple to be a place of calm and meditation, but you have turned it into a den of thieves. With the extortionate prices you are charging, you are stealing from the people. So I ask you to take your trash away from this holy place so that it can receive the honour and glory it deserves."

But the merchants laughed in his face, saying,

"We don't have anything to do with you. The priests have given us permission to trade here. Besides, we had to pay a hefty fee to be able to have a stall here. So if you don't agree with it, you should be talking to them. Not us."

Jesus found it difficult to hide his disappointment at their response and he spoke to them even more heatedly,

"I beg you! Is it too much to ask? There are plenty of squares outside the temple where you can sell your trade. Just don't do it here. Make space so that those who want can pray here - and give those poor animals you are selling their freedom."

His words caused considerable commotion and his followers called out,

"That's right, Jesus, you tell them the truth!"

But the people standing in the queues muttered,

"What does it matter if these merchants are here? We want to make a sacrifice and buy a sacrificial animal from them. What's wrong with that?"

The priests heard the commotion and came back outside out of curiosity. They saw Jesus embroiled in a heated debate with the merchants, with more and more people gathering round them, interested to see how it would end.

Jesus was close to desperation as he saw that his words were not having any effect. And on an impulse he marched over to the tables laden with merchandise and tipped one over. All the goods that had been so carefully laid out for display rolled onto the ground. His act looked like it had been a signal to start off a decisive protest because his supporters followed his example en masse. It did not take long before not a single stall was left standing and the square was littered with broken jugs, coins and foodstuffs.

The unaccustomed noises made the sacrificial animals panicky, adding to the cacophony themselves. Jesus rushed over to free the doves from their cages first. He was no more able to bear their suffering now than he had been when he was a child. They cooed in pleasure at being liberated from their cramped coops as they made for the skies. Then he cut through the ropes tying the lambs with a swift jerk of his knife. And with a whip he had picked up, he drove the merchants from the temple.

The square had now turned into a shambles. The priests looked on in shock but did not dare call Jesus to order. Not only were they afraid that his supporters might resort to violence to defend him, but they had also seen a large number of Zealots in the crowd, which terrified them. The crowds who had until now been standing around the edge now thronged onto the square too and there was a strange feeling of tension in the air. The people who had been queuing to buy sacrificial animals turned on the followers of Jesus to express their displeasure, which resulted in one or two blows being exchanged. But Jesus' supporters were deeply impressed by his action and they had no intention of abandoning him now, the man who had given them the hope of a better life. They converged around him to form an unyielding block. Some of them called out,

"Jesus, you are our rightful king! Claim your throne now and we'll fight for you and take you to the palace!"

Others joined in:

"Hosanna! Long live the son of David!"

In an attempt to calm things down, Jesus raised his arms and spoke vehemently,

"Good people, please stop this. You know that's not what I came for. I beg you, don't turn this into a political protest!"

But his words had little effect for the Zealots saw they had an opportunity at long last to start an uprising and Barabbas began to egg the crowd on. Some people started fighting and the situation was threatening to get badly out of hand. Peter grabbed Jesus by the arm, saying forcefully,

"We'd better go, Jesus. They aren't listening to you anymore. Surely you don't want to get caught up with that bunch of trouble-makers?"

Jesus hesitated. He felt responsible for the turmoil that had arisen; even though he had never intended to have things turn out like this, it was of course the result of his impetuous decision to drive out the merchants. He looked around him to see whether he could spot Mary and the other women. But Peter showed a more realistic grasp of the situation by making a quick getaway, dragging his friend with him.

They had only just left the square when Herod's troops arrived. Fearful that the uprising would spread throughout the city, he had given them orders to restore the peace. But their arrival was like a red rag to a bull. Barabbas realised it was now or never. He ordered his comrades in arms to surround Herod's troops and they managed to grab hold of many of the soldiers' weapons. A great cheer went up. The people forgot their mutual quarrels and closed ranks to turn on the hated king's troops, driving the soldiers into a corner with their own weapons. But they had not counted on Pilate. The cohort he had ordered to be mobilised suddenly swarmed all over the square, and the legionaries hacked mercilessly at the mass of people with their swords. Horrific screams were heard. In panic, everyone fled towards the square's few exits with a huge throng pushing and shoving in front of the narrow gates as a result. Now it was easy for the Romans to gain control of the situation as they callously lashed out at the crowd. Many innocent people lost their lives and the blood from the wounded stained the marble floor of the temple courtyard red. Only a few came away from the savage attack without a scratch.

But the Romans themselves did not come out of the encounter unscathed either as Barabbas put up a fierce fight. He charged at his enemies with his sword and exhorted the crowd not to give up. As a result, there were violent skirmishes all around him. Simon, Judas and other followers of Jesus also joined in the fighting with grim determination, all the while looking around to see if they could spot their leader. The centurion, who was watching his soldiers carry out his orders from the steps, noticed Barabbas. He turned to one of the priests, who were standing there watching as if struck dumb, and asked,

"Tell me, is that Jesus of Nazareth?"

The man shook his head.

"No, that's Barabbas, the leader of the Zealots. I can't see Jesus any longer."

The military leader swore under his breath. Then he ordered his men with a gesture of his hand to take Barabbas prisoner. Judas saw the man was being attacked and tried to come to his aid but ended up being caught himself. The priest, who had been following everything nervously, called out,

"That man there, he's one of Jesus' people! I'm sure I've seen him in his company!"

Relieved to hear this, the centurion signalled to have Judas brought to him. They dragged him roughly up the steps and threw him on his knees on the ground in front of the commander. The man looked down at him contemptuously.

"I hear you can help us find Jesus," he snapped sharply. "As responsible for this bloodbath, he's not going to get away with it unpunished!"

Judas' jaw dropped in amazement. Had he hearing that correctly? Did that Roman want to put the blame on Jesus for all of this? He scrambled up and realising that he had nothing to lose, he said indignantly,

"I'm sorry but I refuse to cooperate. Jesus isn't responsible for this, it's you who chased all these poor people to their deaths!"

The centurion saw his determination and realised he would have to change tack.

"Nice leader, that Jesus of yours," he said, trying to win Judas over. "It looks like he shamelessly abandoned you lot to your fate."

"And I understand he hasn't been making particularly good use of your money either," added the priest. "Didn't he force your best friend to give away all your savings? So I can imagine you could probably use some."

He pulled out a purse of coins and let it swing back and forth temptingly in front of Judas' eyes.

"I don't need your money," replied Judas however abruptly. "God makes sure we never are short of anything and Jesus doesn't depend on you for his destiny. He will decide for himself what path he will take."

And at that time he suddenly recalled as clear as anything the words Jesus had said when they had been sitting together by the camp fire: 'Perhaps I'll need some help... when the time comes.' And he also remembered how he had said specifically to him, 'You must not be afraid to be the black sheep, because you will open up the path to the future.' And it became crystal clear to him what Jesus had meant with his words. He closed his eyes and let out a big sigh. Then he put his emotions to one side, looked up at the priest and said in a flat voice,

"Well, all right then, I'll help you out. I know for certain that Jesus will be returning to celebrate Passover here. When he's in the city, I'll take you to him. But you can keep your filthy bribe! I'm only doing what Jesus wants me to do."

The centurion laughed disdainfully and signalled that Judas was free to go. Then they turned their back on him to focus again on the events in the square.

The revolt was slowly losing steam now that Barabbas had been carted off and it was possible to assess the unhappy results of this failed uprising. There were dozens of dead and hundreds of wounded on the side of the people, but many Romans and soldiers of Herod had fallen too.

Those among the crowd who were fortunate enough to have escaped slowly trickled back to the camp and told Jesus about the bloodbath. He was aghast. Although he knew that he was not to blame, the affair still made him deeply unhappy. He looked around restlessly to see who had returned and who had not, and was dismayed to see that many faces were still missing, including Mary.

More stories reached the camp later on in the day. The Romans had occupied all the gates leading to the city and it was impossible to enter or leave without passing through their checkpoints. Jesus wept in his heart, for it now looked as if his plan to celebrate Passover in Jerusalem had come to nothing. He ensconced himself in his tent and his heart cried out to God:

"Father, please tell me, how could this happen? Didn't I make myself sufficiently clear to them? I thought everything I was doing was to fulfil Your expectations. Or was I wrong?"

But God put his mind at rest.

"You were not wrong, Jesus. And you have more than fulfilled My expectations. But you must try not to judge yourself by the human criteria others use to judge you. Keep persevering, remain true to our message, even now - especially now! After all, you are My light bearer, My bringer of love. Follow your heart because I will guide you through your heart and show you the right path."

God's words helped Jesus and he felt somewhat more at ease. He sat up, rested his head on his hands and thought about what he should do now. It would not be advisable to go back to the city any time soon at any rate, even if that had been possible, but he did not yet want to renounce his plan to celebrate Passover in Jerusalem. It was now Sunday and the Passover Seder would be on Thursday, so there was still time. His first responsibility now was for the welfare of his followers. He realised that their camp must rile the Romans and that it would be better to break it up. He crept out of his tent and saw that many had come to the same conclusion. At least half his people had already gone or were about to depart. It made him sad to see how few were prepared to follow him purely on the basis of his message. He looked round and caught sight of Peter talking to Simon and Judas. He was pleased they had survived the attack although they had inevitably sustained wounds. Then suddenly he spotted Mary with them: she looked pale but apart from that seemed all right and his heart jumped for joy. He hurried over to them. When Simon saw him, he came up to him and called excitedly,

"Good news, Jesus! Some of our supporters have managed to capture the gate of Siloam! So we can get inside the city if we want!"

Jesus studied him carefully and then said sharply,

"You mean your supporters have captured that gate, because my supporters will have nothing to do with hatred and violence. Your path is not the path I want to take and you know that all too well."

He put his hand on Simon's shoulder and continued,

"Listen: come back with me to Bethany. Don't go to the city - what do you think you can achieve there? Hasn't there been enough suffering today?"

Then he addressed all the people who had not yet left.

"Who among you is still prepared to follow me because of who I am?" he said loudly. "Who is genuinely loyal and pre-pared to renounce political gains? Who truly believes that I am the way, the truth and the life and that I will lead you to the kingdom of my Father? Tell me, who has the courage to say 'yes' with all their heart?"

Peter jumped up.

"I believe in you, Jesus!" he called out passionately, "and I will follow you wherever you go, master, because you are the Christ, the only true messenger of the Lord our God!"

His words met with approval and now many people crowded round Jesus to assure him they still believed in him. Mary came up to encourage him too, putting her hands around his face and resting her forehead against his. They stood there, eternally grateful that they had both survived that day. And Jesus whispered,

"I'm so happy to see you! If only you knew how worried I was when you hadn't returned!"

He felt her trembling and heard her whispered reply:

"I felt just the same. I had no idea where you were. But I see you took the right path and I'll follow you to the end, whatever happens."

He swallowed hard and looked at her. He felt comforted by her unwavering faith in him and once again he drew strength from the thought that even if he left behind only a handful of people who understood the true nature of his message, he would not have lived in vain. He gave her a grateful look and for a moment they felt that old familiar bond between them once again. When they set off towards Bethany, there was still a substantial crowd following him.

When they arrived in Bethany, large numbers of people were waiting for them because the news of the bloodbath had reached them. Lazarus was the first to greet Jesus and they held each other close.

"Are you all right?" asked Lazarus with concern in his voice. "What an awful situation! But it's a good thing you've come back. At least you'll be able to rest a little here."

Jesus nodded silently and followed his friend back to his house. They talked together for a long time and as they talked it became ever clearer to Jesus that what he wanted in the depth of his heart was to celebrate Passover in his beloved Jerusalem. Lazarus shook his head when he heard this.

"Make sure you know what you're doing, Jesus," he said in a serious tone. "The priests will stop at nothing to find you and you certainly won't be able to count on protection from the Romans after what happened today."

"I know," nodded Jesus. "But this is still something I must do. I too came back from Egypt after I'd been kept in hiding there. That's why Passover means something special to me. But I will need help. Do you happen to know someone who can arrange a room for us where we can hold the Passover meal? It has to be someone who knows the city like the back of their hand and can take us quickly to the spot from the gate of Siloam."

"I know some Essenes in Jerusalem," replied Lazarus. "They know your background well enough; I'm sure they'll help you."

Jesus smiled gratefully. Touched, he said,

"Thank you, Lazarus. I'm aware what a risk I'm running and this may be the last time we meet here. But if I didn't go I'd be betraying myself – you do understand that, don't you?"

Lazarus nodded sadly.

"Yes, I've got a pretty good idea by now of what you're like, I think. Where anyone else would think twice because their life is in danger, you simply refuse to give up. You're just ... a fantastic idiot... amazing and... crazy and that's precisely why I love you!"

And he gave his friend an emotional hug.

The next day, Lazarus set off early to find his Essene friends in Jerusalem. Jesus joined up with his followers while he waited for him to return. He helped Susanna and Mary share round the bread, and he spoke,

"You all know I won't be with you for much longer, but you're well equipped now to continue without me. I've really only told you what you already know, but you have been looking without actually seeing and hearing without listening. I have listened to myself, to the voice of my own conscience and to the voice of God within me. And you can do that too. Perhaps it is actually better that I won't be around soon, as you don't have to listen to yourselves when you can listen to me. Maybe that makes you lazy."

He walked amongst them and continued,

"Do not be dependent on me. Each individual has his own inner master and each of you has the potential to become wise. It is your choice whether to be a wise man or a fool. There is no middle way. Whether you are one fathom under water or one hundred fathoms, you still drown either way. So make sure that you conquer your limitations and find inner peace!"

He gave a look full of encouragement at the expectant faces staring up at him and his attention was particularly drawn to a young man who was sitting at the back rather quietly. Although his hood was up, he seemed familiar to Jesus even though he was almost sure the man was not one of his permanent band of followers. He went up to the lad and said in a friendly voice,

"Hello. Haven't I seen you somewhere before?"

The youth stood up timidly and drew back his hood. Now Jesus could see it was Gaius. His long cloak was covering his legionary's uniform.

"Good day, Jesus, sir," he said softly. "It may be a little late but I would still like to take up your offer of joining you."

And he continued with a look of horror in his eyes,

"I was at the temple as well yesterday. It was awful! I heard what you said and I agreed with you so much! But I was forced to fight against you, although that wasn't what I wanted to do at all! Then I realised I couldn't keep on being a soldier any longer, I wanted to be with you. Please forgive me - I even used my sword against your people. But I had no choice, surely you understand that?"

And he started to sob. Jesus wiped the tears from his cheeks almost tenderly.

"Of course I understand that, Gaius," he said to put the young man's mind at rest. "And you are forgiven for everything. Come on, I'll give you some different clothes to wear. And it would be a good idea not to shave anymore; then you'll be less likely to be recognised."

He took the youth with him and gave him some of his own clothes, while he himself put on the splendid robe the abbot had given him. Gaius saw an aura of light encircling him. They looked at each other like a couple of conspirators.

"I feel like it's my birthday and soon everyone will be coming along to congratulate me!" cried Gaius excitedly, "Please, Jesus, sir, will you let me organise a party so that I can celebrate the fact that I'm starting a new life today?"

Jesus was not really in the mood for a party but he did not want to let the lad down.

"Well, all right then," he said, good-hearted.

When Lazarus returned on the Wednesday, he found his house had become a hive of activity. Gaius had invited not just Jesus and his disciples but also various followers, while Susanna was there too helping Martha and Mary serve the guests.

Despite the festive atmosphere, Mary could not find her way. The shocking events in the temple courtyard had been haunting her all week and a feeling of impending doom weighed heavily on her. She recalled how Jesus had said the events in Jerusalem would eventually cost him his life. She watched the laughing guests and listened to the banter flying backwards and forth; she found it hard to imagine that she was the only one who was so dispirited. She looked at Jesus and saw that he too was letting everything pass by. Although Gaius probably had not noticed, she could see he was having difficulty keeping himself under control. And it was true, there was no way of bridging the chasm between the bloodbath in the square and this party that had been hastily cobbled together.

She sighed, wishing the evening could be over so that she could put this charade behind her. She looked over to Jesus again and this time their eyes met. He smiled at her but it was a sad smile and they both sensed perfectly what the other was feeling. For a moment they remained caught in each other's gaze and Mary could see his despair. Then Gaius spoke to him and the moment was gone. She saw him talking to the youth in a friendly manner but his look of despair had only made her feel more despondent. Terrible images passed before her mind's eye. She saw the temple square before her, as she had done all week, with the dead prostrate on the ground and she heard once more the groans of the wounded soaked in their own blood. And suddenly she saw Jesus himself lying there and he was motionless because he too had been robbed of his life in this sea of violence. A shiver ran down her spine. She was beset by the awful thought that this could easily happen and that the Romans would just hurl his body into a mass grave with no respect for their Jewish traditions. Surely that was not the end that was in store for him?

She walked over to the kitchen but could not rid herself of this image. With her mind unable to focus, she filled her bowl with the snacks Martha had prepared. Then, just as she was about to return to the room, she spotted an elegantly shaped jar of perfume. On an impulse, she put down her bowl, took the jar and lifted up the lid. The heady, heavy scent of myrrh wafted up, a scent she knew all too well from those many occasions on which she had embalmed the dead. And suddenly she knew what she wanted to do. She abandoned the snacks, took the jar with her to the main room and walked with a look of determination over to Jesus. Without any hesitation, she poured the myrrh over his head and feet. The room was filled with the strong odour and the chatter of the guests stopped. They all looked at her in utter astonishment, not comprehending what she was doing. Ignoring them, Mary knelt before Jesus and proceeded to dry his feet with her long hair. She heard the guests beginning to whisper to each other. Judas too was unable to contain his indignation.

"Mary, why are you wasting this expensive myrrh?" he reproached her. "That jar must have been worth... maybe up to three hundred pence! That money would have been enough to buy us food for several days and have something left over to give to the poor!"

But Jesus came to her defence. Tenderly placing his hand on her head, he said in a voice full of emotion,

"Be silent Judas, and the rest of you, for you don't know what you are talking about. The poor will always be there for you but I will not be here much longer and Mary is the only person who is so concerned for me that she has taken my sad destiny to heart. That is why she has done this. She has poured this embalming ointment over me in anticipation of my burial. And when the story of my life is passed later from one person to another and is recorded in writing, her loving act will be recalled... but will the same be said about the rest of you?"

His words caused quite a stir and most of the guests made no secret of their displeasure. But Jesus said nothing more, all his attention focused on Mary who was still on her knees before him. He took her hands and squeezed them affectionately. They looked at one another and Mary smiled, grateful that he had understood her intentions so well. Lazarus saw the way they looked at each other and the deep love it revealed. It surprised him that they had never found each other, for he had never seen such a strong attraction between two people. The other guests had also fallen silent again and were watching them in fascination. Mary felt their prying eyes. Suddenly she had had enough and she stood up, tearing herself away from Jesus' gaze with difficulty. Silently she left the house and made her way back to the encampment. The festivities had ended for her at any rate. The other guests soon followed her example, unable to recover the celebratory mood.

Jesus remained behind on his own in the empty room. He sat there motionless, his thoughts swirling through his head. Tomorrow was the big day. Despite the huge risk he would be running, he would go to Jerusalem. And he was sure now that what God had predicted would take place there. How sensitive Mary had been to feel that! A shiver ran down his spine. He wished from the bottom of his heart that God had not shown him what an awful end was awaiting him and his destiny weighed heavily on him. At the same time he felt an irresistible longing, a strong desire to return to his Father and finally leave behind this life that was no longer a real life to him.

Lazarus had been seeing the guests off and now came quietly back into the room. He sat down next to his friend and put an arm around his shoulders. They sat there in silence until Lazarus said,

"Why don't you go to her, Jesus? To Mary, I mean. Everyone could see it: you love one another. Why else do you think she did this? And why are you so resisting?"

Jesus shook his head.

"I will never be able to give her what she wants," he replied softly. "My relationship with God will always come first for me. And she deserves better than to have to take second place and be forced to remain loyal. She's simply too good for that."

"As if that matters now, Jesus," reacted Lazarus with disarming honesty. "Be realistic. This may be your last chance to show her what you feel for her, your last chance to give her at long last what she pines for so much. You do love her, don't you?"

Jesus nodded without hesitation and Lazarus heard deep affection in his voice as he replied,

"Oh yes, I love her. But I didn't want to get involved as it'll only make the end more difficult."

His voice caught and he turned his head away, not wanting Lazarus to see his fear and doubt. Lazarus was quiet for a moment. This was the first time that Jesus had spoken to him so candidly about his end and he felt a lump in his throat. He took his friend's hand and said in an emotional voice,

"I'm afraid I can't really give you any advice, Jesus, but if you follow your heart, as you always have done, then I'm sure you'll make the right decision."

Then, after giving Jesus a hug, he left the room with tears in his eyes to go to bed. Once again Jesus sat there alone and he let what Lazarus had said sink into his heart. He could still smell the scent of the myrrh Mary had poured over him and he realised that in doing so, she had let him see that she accepted his fate. She knew that he was going to die in Jerusalem, just as he himself knew this, and yet she had shown him all her love. He intertwined his fingers and searched for God. And his Father showed complete understanding.

"Follow your heart, My son. After all, you know what is right."

Jesus stood up. Even now he hesitated. Should he go back to his room here in the house of Lazarus? Or should he... He was not going to be able to sleep, there was no doubt about that. And finally he knew what he had to do. He left the house carefully and made his way to the camp in the dark. The flickering flames of the campfires his people had started here and there guided him in the right direction. It was quiet in the camp. Apparently everyone was asleep. Taking great care to make sure he did not disturb anyone, he searched for Mary's little tent and soon found it. His heart beat faster than usual as he opened the flap and looked inside. He saw she had not yet gone to sleep. She had lit a small oil lamp and was sitting on her bed, sunk deep in thought. Her face was illuminated by the flame. He lovingly drank in the sight of her and was overcome by a powerful emotion.

Mary only realised she was no longer alone when the scent of myrrh reached her nose. She turned her head towards him. For some reason she was not surprised to see him and she surveyed his familiar face with a serious look. Jesus was unsure for a moment what to do.

"Hello," he said softly and somewhat timidly.

"Hello," she replied and looked at him expectantly.

He bent down and crept inside the tent. He carefully put the flap back down, then turned to her.

"Mary..." he began, but his voice broke down with emotion and he was unable to speak for a moment.

Mary saw tears in his eyes. Her heart missed several beats but even so, she waited for him to take the initiative. And he recovered, although his voice was still trembling as he said,

"Mary, can you forgive me for leaving you in doubt for so long? I do love you, in fact I love you with all my heart and soul and have done ever since I met you. But I couldn't tell you. I didn't want to make you unhappy. I didn't want to have you always having to feel you were only the second most important for me, after God, or for my death to cause you more pain than it will already. But now you know everything and have accepted it, I don't want to keep my secret any longer. You deserve to hear this while I'm still around to tell you."

He flung his arms around her, embraced her ardently and kissed her mouth desperately. Mary saw in his eyes his fear for everything that would come to pass, as well as his determination to see his task through right to the bitter end. But above all she saw his love for her, which he was finally able to reveal. Full of emotion, she whispered,

"I love you too, Jesus, more than anything else in this life. And God, You know so long already how much I love him!"

She returned his kiss and all trace of awkwardness between them was gone. They undressed each other slowly with a naturalness that showed they were destined for one another, kissing each area of bare skin as it was revealed. They stroked each other's naked bodies and their flaming desire soon transformed into a blind passion.

And Jesus spent the whole night with her. By the light of her small lamp, she taught him everything he did not yet know and they made passionate love in a vehement attempt to banish all thought of what awaited them, gratefully availing themselves of this one night that they had been granted.

Passover

The air was already shimmering in the heat soon after the sun came up. Jesus woke in Mary's arms and saw that she was no longer asleep. They both felt the oppressive weight of the realisation that this new day everything would come to a head. They looked each other in the eye, serious and worried and he gave her a long and passionate kiss, holding her body tightly to his own, until he finally stood up and dressed without saying a word. Then he bent over her to kiss her once again, before turning round abruptly and leaving her tent. Mary heard him washing quickly using one of the tubs of water that were standing between the tents for the purpose. His footfall then faded into the distance.

She stayed behind in her bed forlornly, and a strange sensation came over her. It seemed as if she had dreamed everything that had happened that night, as though he had not really been there to make love to her with his hands feverishly seeking out the most sensual places on her body, his sweaty torso on top of her own, his lips hungrily on her nipples and her mouth, and finally their passionate union. She found herself gasping for breath, because the very thought of what they had finally dared to do excited her. She stood up abruptly and, in a determined effort to come to her senses again, she crept outside and poured a pitcher of cold water over her head. She spluttered as the water got into her nose and mouth, but it did cool her down and she quickly went back into her tent to find a clean dress.

The camp was now bustling with activity. They were going to divide into small groups and try to get into the city through the Siloam gate. It ought to be possible to sneak inside in small groups of two or three, from the groves on the Mount of Olives. Jesus himself would be the last to set off, with his disciples. Mary watched the hive of activity, seeing Jesus speaking words of encouragement to everyone. For her part, she went looking for Susanna and Simon, the two people she would be making the attempt to enter the city with. She found Susanna by the breakfast table. When her friend saw her coming, she could not suppress an amused smile.

"According to me, you didn't get much sleep last night," she teased her.

Mary blushed, realising that the thin canvas of her tent was not remotely soundproof and that many might have been able to hear their passionate lovemaking. But Susanna waved her embarrassment aside.

"Don't worry, Mary, I think it's great for both of you," she said, with genuine honesty. "You've been working up to it for so long!"

Mary laughed her embarrassment off and helped Susanna share out the breakfast. Jesus came to get something to eat as well. He gave her a tender smile, but did not touch her. The day passed by in a haze. Small groups of people kept leaving and the camp grew emptier and emptier. Mary was ready to leave now as well. She went to find Jesus to tell him she was going. For a moment, neither of them knew quite what to do, but then they embraced each other. A great sense of turmoil overtook Mary.

"I will see you again, Jesus, won't I?" she whispered anxiously.

"Of course," he reassured her, holding her tightly. "In the hall of the Essenes, remember? As long as you follow their instructions, it will all be all right."

Mary nodded silently. They stood there together, not really ready to say farewell. Finally Jesus extricated himself carefully from her embrace.

"Come on, my dearest, you really do have to go now."

He gave her into the trusted hands of Simon and Susanna. Once she was gone, he was unable to settle and he was glad when it was finally his turn to make a move. He called his disciples together and said,

"You know what we have to look out for, don't you? A boy with a pitcher of water will show us the way. So no dawdling - the earlier we get to where we have to be, the better."

They nodded, understanding just how serious the situation was.

Then they set off. To Jesus' surprise, Lazarus and Gaius joined them.

"There's got to be someone here to keep an eye on you," grinned Lazarus.

His words sounded light-hearted, but Jesus could hear the worried subtext. He clasped his friend's hand, touched by his concern. They reached the Mount of Olives as twilight began to fall. They could see the Siloam gate before them. A figure clad in white came forward out of the shadows, carrying a water jug. He gave them a penetrating stare and then led them through the gate without saying a word. They hurried after him. He went so quickly that they had difficulty keeping up with him through the tangled maze of alleys and streets. They rushed after him until they noticed that the street was climbing upwards and they were coming to the highest point in the city.

Lights in the houses could be seen here and there, and they realised what a good spot this was from a strategic point of view. The whole surrounding area could be seen from this point. If any kind of attack were to be launched, the lookout would see it a long way in advance and they would have plenty of time to get away. The boy with the pitcher gave a pre-arranged pattern of knocks on a door. It was opened immediately and they went inside.

They were in a large room, where most of Jesus' followers had already found spaces to sit. Jesus glanced around the hall and saw that Mary was there too, talking animatedly to an older woman next to her. His heart skipped a beat when their eyes met and he recognised who it was.

"Mother?" he cried in disbelief, his voice betraying a blend of delight and astonishment.

Just a few large strides took him over to her and he gave her a big hug. Utterly amazed, he whispered,

"Mother, what are you doing here? I'm absolutely delighted to see you, but this is surely much too dangerous!"

Mary smiled.

"I just had to see you," she said simply. "I knew that you were supposed to be going to Jerusalem for Passover, and it seemed very likely that I could meet you here. But that it would all turn out like this... it wasn't exactly what I'd expected, of course. Anyway, are you all right?"

Jesus nodded, full of emotion.

"Yes, everything's fine," he replied tenderly. "You'd never believe just how good seeing you makes me feel!"

Gratefully, he met Mary's gaze, as he realised that she must have been looking after his mother all afternoon.

"Mother," he said softly as he took Mary's hand. "I'm pleased to be able to introduce you to the woman I love. This is Mary. She will undoubtedly look after you very well."

And in front of everyone, he kissed Mary passionately on the mouth. His mother laughed delightedly. So finally there was some-one else in his life! Mary gave a friendly nod and when Jesus took his place at the head of the table, the two women were talking quietly together.

Jesus saw that the traditional four cups of wine were ready and waiting. His hands were trembling slightly as he picked up the first of them, but his voice was steady as he said,

"Let us remember what God said: I will bring you out from under the burdens of the Egyptians!"

He took a swallow of wine from the cup and everyone followed his example. Then he took the second cup and said,

"I will save you from their bondage!"

He drank, picked up the third cup and continued,

"I will redeem you!"

Yet again he drank, and then picked up the final cup.

"I will take you unto Me as My people and bring you to the promised land."

He drank. Then he took away the cloth that was covering the Seder plate, took some bread and gathered his disciples around.

"Come," he said. "I want to break the bread with you. Let's go to the upstairs room."

They nodded. Only Judas hesitated. Jesus saw his reluctance.

"Aren't you coming too, Judas?" he asked.

Judas shrugged rather awkwardly and stammered, his voice full of emotion,

"I'm sorry Jesus! Please forgive me! But you know... why I have to do this."

He turned around and ran from the room. Rooted to the spot, Jesus watched him go. So this was it: the beginning of the end. Peter also saw immediately what Judas was intending to do. He gesticulated vigorously to their Essene guide to go and follow him. The boy sprinted off at once. The others looked at each other in shock. But Jesus said calmly,

"Come, don't let this stop us from celebrating Passover properly. Let's go upstairs."

He led them up the stairs to another room where the Essenes had also laid out the table in the traditional way. Jesus put the loaf down respectfully. Knowing that Judas was on his way to warn his enemies cast him into a strange mood. His life seemed to be going past in a flash. He saw himself sitting on the lane to the well, the place where he had first heard God's voice. He saw himself mounted on Bianco, trying to escape his destiny. He saw himself with John the Baptist in the River Jordan, where he had become one with the Holy Spirit. And it was this Spirit that came over him now and spoke to them,

"Remember Jesus the man. Remember the man who was prepared to open himself up, offer his body as a temple in which I could reside. Think of him in a little while when they are breaking his body."

He broke open the loaf and shared the bread out. Then he said,

"By eating this bread, you will be taking a small part of me into yourselves and you will feel the strength that he felt."

In awe, his disciples took the bread and ate it respectfully. Then Jesus took a pitcher of wine that was on the table and once again it was the Holy Spirit that spoke,

"Remember Jesus the man. Remember the man whose blood will flow because he unhesitatingly spoke of me, risking his own life, all so that the people could be brought into the light."

He poured out the wine and handed the cups round. Then he said,

"By drinking this wine, you will be able to feel me in your blood just as he felt me in his blood. It will give you the courage that will be needed to bear witness to me freely, so that his message will continue to live on after his death."

His friends picked up the cups and drank, some of them with tears on their cheeks. Jesus saw their sorrow and he said comfortingly,

"Please don't be sad. My Father is waiting for me and I know that

I shall sit next to Him for all time. So even though you will no longer be able to see me here, I shall still be with you. And the Holy Spirit will remain with you to help you all spread my message further."

He stood up, walked around them and embraced them all in turn. Peter was the one he stayed with for longest.

"Peter, you have always been a rock for me to rely on. Thank you for everything that you have done. Show that you are worthy of that faith. Be brave! Don't let your fear stop you from doing what has to be done. Bear witness to me, and your reward shall be great!"

He embraced his friend tightly and Peter was crying like a child in his arms. They all sat down again and Jesus got ready to read the traditional psalms that signified the end of the Passover meal. But suddenly there was a loud knock on the door. Their Essene guide rushed in with a shrill cry.

"Jesus! They're coming! He really has shown them the way here. But there's still time - get out while you still can!"

The disciples jumped to their feet in panic; only Jesus stayed calm. Patiently, he spoke,

"Why should I flee? I can't escape my fate."

But Peter grabbed him roughly by the shoulders and shook him hard.

"You're not going to let yourself be led like a lamb to the slaughter!" he shouted. "We're following that lad, now!"

He dragged him off and their guide led them without a false step back to the Siloam gate. They left the city unobserved and fled to the Mount of Olives where they could hide away amidst all the greenery in the garden of Gethsemane. However, Jesus realised that it would not be long before they were found here too. A feeling of great unease came over him. In a serious voice, he said to his friends,

"Stay here and keep alert. I'm going a bit further up, to pray."

He walked on in the garden and then fell to his knees. Full of doubt, he hid his face in his hands and begged,

"My God, please, Father, please have pity on me. Is there really no other way to fulfil my task?"

It was a question that needed no answer; he knew that there was no other way. An extreme fear overtook him. And he prayed,

"O Lord, my soul is strong. Your Spirit knows no fear. But I, Jesus, am still here too. And I'm grateful for all the good things You have given me, of course. There can be no greater gift for a person than to be able to receive Your Holy Spirit. It has brought me so much wisdom and depth of insight. But You have chosen a human body to plant the seed of Your wisdom in, and You do not know the pain that such a body feels. But I do. I have seen those poor souls nailed to the crosses, as will shortly happen to me. I've seen their gruesome death throes. And, my Lord God, I'm so scared of that struggle and the intolerable suffering. Father, I ask You - how can You do this to me, Your son?"

And he wept. He thought of his dear friends who had been expecting so much of him. Lamaas from India, Caspar his guide in Persia, and Matheno - his good old friend Matheno who had always been there with advice and help for him in Qumran. Would they ever be able to understand the significance of his death? Seeing his anguish, God felt pity for him and He sent an angel to him to give him courage. But Jesus was horrified when he saw the angel and he called out,

"God my Father, what is this? You are surely not coming to fetch me already! Father, please. How will people ever understand the magnitude of my sacrifice if You take me up to be with You already? If they find my dead body here, they will think that I have acted as a coward and taken my own life. Lord God, I beg you, let me make this final sacrifice - otherwise it has all been for nothing and the truth will be lost forever."

The angel looked down on him compassionately. It laid its hand on his shoulder tenderly and said,

"See? You have just conquered your fears. Go, and the blessings of mankind will be with you."

This loving care helped Jesus calm himself. And he realised that his words did indeed mean that he had accepted the final part of his task. He took a couple of deep breaths. Then he bowed down, closed his eyes and wordlessly asked God whether He would lead him through everything that was about to come to pass. He felt God's promise in his heart, saying that he would not be alone, no matter what happened. Fortified by that promise, he stood up and walked back to the spot where he had left his disciples. To his astonishment, he saw that they had fallen asleep. He poked them awake and said, deeply disappointed,

"Were you really not able to stay awake? Look - there they are coming to get me."

Startled, his disciples jumped to their feet. Seeing the much greater force that was on its way there, they realised they would never be able to stand up to these soldiers and they fled away in panic. Only Peter remained, drawing his sword.

"I'll defend you with my life if I have to, Jesus!" he shouted fervently, taking up a protective position in front of his friend.

But Jesus shook his head.

"Oh Peter, these boys are only doing what they were sent to do. No: I shall not resist and simply go with them."

The legionaries were now walking up to them. To Peter's disgust, he saw how Judas showed them the way. Deliberately he walked up to Jesus and kissed him on the cheek. Jesus felt unsteady. He knew that he had more or less urged Judas to do this, but now that it had actually reached that point, it felt very awkward. They looked at each other intensely, and even Peter was able to feel the chemistry between them. Then the soldiers grabbed Jesus and shackled him none too gently. Judas shook his head in confusion, watching with tears in his eyes as his friend allowed himself to be led away without offering any form of resistance. Peter was oblivious to Judas' emotions.

"So, are you proud now of what you've done, you rotten traitor?" he spat angrily. "How could you do this? How could you!"

Judas opened his mouth to defend himself, but then turned round sharply and ran off. He had absolutely no desire to explain that Jesus himself had asked him for help in taking this final, difficult step. Peter watched him for a moment. Then he hurried after Jesus to see what would happen next.

The soldiers took the road to the temple and led Jesus into the High Council's hall. The entire Council had been present in the palace that night to pass judgement on this important question, and Caiaphas was unable to repress a certain feeling of triumph when Jesus was led in. With no further ado, he spoke,

"So, Jesus, you are surely not going to deny that you are responsible for the bloodbath that took place here and all the wounded and dead who have fallen? Or did you think that you would simply be able to avoid your punishment for that?"

Jesus looked at the man confidently.

"I most certainly do deny any responsibility," he replied decisively. "I abhor violence and I have never presented myself as a claimant to the throne. And I have never wished to harm you either - to point out the error of your ways, perhaps, but no more than that. It is your conduct that has driven the people to desperation and that is why this rebellion should be on your conscience. You know very well who I am and why I came here. I have never made any secret of that."

Caiaphas gave a condescending smile.

"Oh, you mean your claim to be Christ," he said laughingly. "Well, if that's really true, just say so openly!"

But Jesus replied,

"I don't know what you mean. I have always spoken freely, both here in the temple and elsewhere. So what's the point of your question? You know perfectly well what I've proclaimed!"

One of the temple officials, who was standing guard next to him, was irritated by his response and slapped him hard in the face.

"Keep a civil tongue in your head!" he hissed at him. "That's not how we address the high priest, understood?"

Jesus felt that his lip had split and he could taste blood in his mouth. He turned to the man indignantly and asked sharply,

"Why did you hit me? If I've said anything wrong, just tell me what was wrong. And if I didn't - well, why did you hit me for no reason then?"

His bold words sent a wave of indignation through the room and the temple officials swarmed furiously around him. But Caiaphas raised his hand and called out,

"Wait! Control yourselves. He hasn't answered my question yet."

And he repeated,

"Tell me Jesus, are you the Messiah?"

"If I were to say I was, you still wouldn't believe me," replied Jesus bitterly. "But let me tell you this: God has taken me under His wing, and His promise that I shall sit next to Him in His kingdom is the eternal truth, and everyone who embraces this truth shall live forever."

Caiaphas jumped up, enraged. He turned to address the members of the Council and cried out,

"Do we need any more? He is now claiming that he is God's equal! It's a scandal!"

The excitable throng could no longer restrain themselves. They grabbed Jesus and started beating him. Somebody even put a piece of cloth over his head so that he could no longer see and his tormentors called out mockingly,

"Right, son of God - if you're so powerful, why don't you tell us which of us is hitting you now?"

Jesus raised his arms in an effort to ward off the blows. But someone kicked his legs out from under him so that he fell down hard, and they kicked and trampled him. He curled up, groaning with pain. Then one of the priests stood up. He cried out in a loud voice that could be heard above the tumult.

"Shame upon you! That's not the way to treat someone who can't defend himself. Help him to his feet!"

For a moment, nothing happened. Then he was hauled upright and someone yanked the cloth roughly from his head. Jesus looked around to find the priest who had stood up for him and saw that it was the reliable figure of Nicodemus. Their eyes met and Nicodemus asked softly,

"So Jesus, would you now perhaps tell us the truth? Are you the son of God?"

Jesus hesitated for a moment. Then he answered in a firm voice,

"That's what you say," and would not add anything more.

Nicodemus shook his head sadly, realising that uttering these words meant that Jesus had signed his own death warrant. Nobody had ever come before making a claim like that, threatening everything they had achieved. And Caiaphas called,

"Take him to Pilate so that he can be sentenced!"

The news that Jesus had been captured ran through the city like wildfire, and everyone who was on his side came and crowded around Pilate's palace. They were unable to get close, however, because a cordon of soldiers had completely sealed off the entrances to the square. Large numbers of Zealots, as well as the priests and other agitators had already gathered there earlier. The square was full to bursting and the Romans closed the gate to prevent people from being crushed underfoot. The shouts of support from Jesus' followers were drowned out by the clamour of the mob inside.

Mary and Jesus' mother were among those left outside the gate. They did manage to worm their way forwards through the crowd, but then they came up against the soldiers too.

"Please sir, have pity," Jesus' mother implored one of them. "My son's been arrested, completely unfairly. I beg you: let me through so that I can speak in his defence."

But the soldier pushed her roughly aside. In tears, the women looked to one another for support. Then Mary felt a hand on her shoulder and a woman whispered in her ear,

"Come. Follow me."

Mary turned round in surprise. She did not know this person, but she felt that she could trust her. The woman led them around the square to a staircase that was closed off by a high iron gate and produced a key from her pocket. She led them upstairs and they came out in a kind of colonnade from where they could look down on the square below. They saw Jesus standing in chains, with the mob behind and Pilate's immense palace before him. The woman said,

"There's nothing else I can do for you now. But you can see the trial from here. I'll be somewhere around; maybe I'll be able to do something else for you later."

Mary thanked her gratefully and focused on the scene that was being played out down below. They saw Pilate emerge and walk over to Jesus. He looked at his bloodied face and the bruises on his arms and legs.

"Is it really worth all that?" he asked, shaking his head. "Do you really want to go that far?"

In resignation, Jesus replied,

"It was my fate from the very first. Those who bear witness to the truth shall always suffer in this world."

Pilate gave him a derogatory stare.

"Ah. Well, what is truth?" he responded cynically. "I have my truth, and you have yours. Aren't you simply laying down your own laws, clashing with ours?"

But Jesus stated,

"I'm not making any laws. On the contrary! All I wanted to do was relieve people of some of the restrictive rules. Laws should serve the people, not make slaves of them. The law has led people away from the light of God that is in their hearts. And you too have lost the memory of that light and are blocking people from finding the way to the truth."

He looked at the man boldly. The Roman felt uneasy under his gaze and sighed,

"I am standing here with empty hands. I have no understanding of the religious intriguing here. And on top of that, you have spoiled a perfectly good night's sleep. Not only was that priest Nicodemus here until late pleading your case, but even one of my own people - one Gaius Octavius - came to claim you were innocent as well. He swore to me that you had nothing to do with the rioting last week. According to him, Barabbas the Zealot was the guilty party. I have to admit that I'm minded to believe him. But I do wonder if that's what the people think too. So I'm going to fetch him, and then we'll see."

He called a squad of ten soldiers over and ordered them to make a defensive wall to shield Jesus. Then he went inside to fetch Barabbas.

His absence gave Jesus time to consider his situation. His gaze wandered around and he saw the bastion of power - Pilate's colossal palace - opposite him and the enormous wall surrounding it. And suddenly he spotted the two women up on that wall. He recognised them instantly and his heart quickened. Mary saw how much he appreciated the fact that they had followed him into the lion's den and her heart wept and shouted for joy at the same time. Jesus' gaze moved on and he saw the anger and powerlessness of the crowd in the square. But he also noticed the large number of people outside the gates who had gathered there in silent protest, and a spark of hope was rekindled in his heart. He remembered God's promise, the one He had made some time ago:

"Millions will recall your words and understand their significance. And you shall know it, for you shall be sitting here next to Me, a king for all time."

He shut his eyes for a moment, thanking God that he had managed not to forget his purpose in this pandemonium. Strengthened by that thought, he saw Pilate come outside again and the tension in his body flared up. Pilate turned to the crowd and stated clearly,

"I have made my decision. You may decide for yourselves who in your eyes is guilty for everything that has happened here and who therefore deserves death by crucifixion!"

He waved a hand and a number of soldiers brought Barabbas forward. Jesus saw to his shock that the Zealot had been severely beaten. But it had not broken his resistance. Far from it! Proudly, he raised his shackled arms into the air and began goading the mob. His followers cheered him on ecstatically. They realised that Barabbas might be a far more useful figure-head for them than Jesus if they were ever to make another attempt to drive Herod out.

The priests watched the situation develop with no small satisfaction. It seemed as if they would not have to make any effort to achieve the outcome they desired. Jesus heard all the cheers acclaiming Barabbas. Resigned to what would happen, he lowered his head and tried to prepare mentally as well as possible for everything that was now going to happen to him. Pilate watched the events unfold in surprise. This was not what he had anticipated! Shocked, he said,

"I see no guilt in this man, Jesus of Nazareth. But very well: you have made your choice. Prior to his punishment, and in accordance with your laws, I sentence him to the maximum of thirty-nine strokes of the lash."

With a curt gesture, he ordered his soldiers to carry out the lashing. The legionaries grinned broadly, happy to have this extra divertissement. They grabbed Jesus, tied his hands to a block of stone and roughly ripped his clothes off his back. Jesus tensed himself, straining every fibre in his body so that he could take the lashes as well as possible. When the blows began to land, he bit deeply into his lip but did not give in.

Mary and his mother had an all too clear view of the disproportionate torture being meted out to Jesus and Pilate's voice rang through their heads as he counted out the lashes. After thirty strokes, there were rivulets of blood running from Jesus' back and he collapsed. Pilate raised his hand sharply and the soldiers stopped. One of them threw a bucket of water over Jesus' head to bring him round again and with a monstrous effort, he rose to his feet. He looked Pilate straight in the eye, challenging him to keep going. Pilate could only admire his victim and his attitude. He nodded to the soldiers and kept counting.

By the time it was over, Jesus' back had been laid completely open. But he was as immovable as ever and Pilate wondered where this man got his strength from. He had never before seen anyone who was able to maintain their dignity even in these circumstances. Although he could undoubtedly break Jesus' body, he realised that he would never shatter the inconceivable spiritual strength of this impressive man. Ashamed, he turned away abruptly, leaving his soldiers to complete what was by now a routine job for them.

The legionaries laughed mockingly. They walked round Jesus, looking him up and down and weighing up what they saw. Belittling him, they said,

"So, King of the Jews, how are you doing now, huh?"

Jesus pursed his lips; determined not to respond to their provocations and bullying in any way. However, his lack of reaction only goaded the soldiers further and one of them put a wreath of thorny twigs on his head. The sharp spines pierced his scalp and grated mercilessly against his skull. Jesus was unsteady on his feet, feeling trickles of blood running down his forehead and cheeks. The soldiers laughed again.

"That crown suits you perfectly, your Majesty," they taunted him, throwing a tattered red cloak around his shoulders.

Astounded, the two Marys were clinging tightly to each other. Then suddenly the woman was there before them again. The emotion was clear to see on her face as she said in a choked voice,

"Believe me, this is not what we wanted either! But my husband had no choice - he has to keep the peace here. And you saw how those Zealots were ranting and raving!"

She led them back down the staircase and opened the gate. Completely benumbed, the two women found themselves a moment later amongst the crowd that was still there. Unlike the Zealots, who had cheered Barabbas as they took him away on their shoulders, the people here had been left speechless by the events. Mary looked around forlornly. She had an arm firmly around Jesus' mother, but she did not know what to do next. Then to her great relief she saw Peter and Lazarus coming over. They held each other and wept.

"Didn't he see this coming?" stammered Peter hoarsely. "We could have fled. Really - we could have fled!"

Mary shook her head.

"Of course he saw this coming," she said softly. "And it's the path that he chose to follow. If he had run there'd have been nothing left. But this way, he has kept his dignity and made sure that his message will be heard all the more clearly for it. So let's try to support him now in every way we possibly can!"

Peter looked at her in admiration. He began to see why Jesus had so often sought out her company in preference to that of his disciples. The crowd began to move suddenly. The gates around the square swung open and Mary saw how Jesus, surrounded by numerous guards, was being pushed forwards to the execution site, which was on a low hill outside the city walls. They had bound the heavy crossbeam of the crucifix to his back and the soldiers were driving him on at such a merciless pace that he could hardly keep up.

"Come on, come on," they were saying impatiently. "We don't have all day!"

They struck him across the legs with a whip in an attempt to get him moving more quickly. Instead, though, it made him stumble and fall. Irritated, one of the soldiers was about to give him a kick, but another one held him back and cut the ropes that tied the crossbeam to Jesus' back. He dragged a man roughly out of the crowd and snarled brusquely at him,

"Right. You're carrying that cross now. We don't want him to give up the ghost right here, do we?"

Then he bent over Jesus and hauled him upright. He put his arm round him firmly and growled,

"And you get walking. Understand?"

Jesus leaned heavily on him and looked at him through his puffed-up eyelids. He could hardly believe what he saw.

"Gaius?" he stammered.

The boy, now dressed in his full legionary's uniform, nodded briefly and whispered in a quiet voice so that nobody else would hear,

"This was the only way to get to you. Listen, there's something I have to tell you. Judas was found this morning, dead. He hanged himself. You were such close friends... I thought you ought to know."

For a moment, he could feel Jesus leaning on him more heavily than before. Then he heard an almost inaudible whisper in return,

"Don't... worry. Today I shall be... meeting him in ... my Father's paradise."

And he even managed to force a small smile. Peter and Mary, who were following the procession and trying to find their way through all the people lining the route, had also recognised Gaius and thanked God that Jesus would at least no longer have to carry that heavy beam on his wounded back.

They had now reached the small hill and, with tears in his eyes, Gaius handed his friend over to some of his fellow soldiers. They did not give Jesus even a moment's respite, pulling his robe off roughly over his head so that the fabric that had stuck to the wounds on his back was ripped off and started them bleeding again.

The legionaries, who were used to their victims struggling violently in a desperate attempt to avoid their impending fate, were about to grab him and force him to lie down on the cross, but Jesus shook their hands off him. He looked around and saw that Mary, Lazarus, Peter and his mother had followed him all the way and that a huge crowd of people had gathered around the hill. Thankfully, he realised that his efforts had apparently indeed put wheels in motion and so it had not all been for nothing. Then he knelt voluntarily and lay down with his arms stretched along the crossbeam. Lying there, he could see God's infinite heavens above him, seemingly bluer than ever on this particular day, like a promise that would last for ever.

The soldiers bound his arms and feet with rope. They were astounded by the man before them: his attitude demanded respect and they asked him whether he wanted a painkilling draught of sour wine and myrrh. But Jesus shook his head emphatically. He had not given an inch of ground so far - not when they were whipping him, not when they had pressed the crown of thorns onto his head, nor when they had lashed the heavy cross onto his flayed back. And they were not going to see him falter now. He clamped his teeth tight and gathered all his mental strength. Surely the pain could not be worse than everything they had done to him already. But he was wrong. It was worse than he could ever have imagined. When the thick point of the nail sliced mercilessly through the nerve to his hand, he cried out. His scream merged with the raw wail from his mother, who collapsed as all the emotions got the better of her. And his cries reached new heights as the second nail pieced his other wrist and the third his feet.

God in His highest heaven shrank back at the sound. Dark clouds massed, smothering the sun's light. God was grieving, veiling his radiance. An ill-omened silence descended and Jesus whispered urgently,

"Father..."

At once he felt God's presence in his heart, invigorating and comforting him.

"Father, forgive them, for they know not what they do."

And God did not desert him, instead staying with him and filling him with His vibrancy.

The cross was now hauled upright. Jesus suddenly felt his full weight suspended from his wrists and a horrendous pain shot through his arms and chest, making it almost impossible for him to breathe. Cautiously he tried to see if he could push with his feet in any way to relieve the pressure on his wrists a fraction, but that too produced a hellish jolt of pain. He began sweating, with the perspiration streaming down his face. Only the vibrant presence of his Father stopped him from crying out once again. Restlessly, he let his gaze wander. His mother - where was his mother? Had she been able to bear all this? To his relief, he saw that Lazarus was taking care of her. Thankfully, Jesus met his friend's stare and - despite how difficult he found it to speak at all - he said,

"Look after her, please."

Lazarus nodded, deeply impressed that he was capable of worrying about others, even at a moment like this. And Jesus' gaze roamed further. He saw the huge crowd who had gathered around, silent in their distress. Some of them had fetched lanterns so that they could stay with him despite the oppressive darkness. And then he looked for Mary. The desire burned through him to see her once again for a moment, here and now where it was all going to end.

Mary saw his questioning look and, keeping her emotions as tightly reined as she could, she looked straight at him, determined to support him with every last ounce of her strength. Their eyes met and she could tell that her presence was good for him. And she drank in his image, letting it burn onto her retinas so that she could be sure she would never ever forget how he had looked like, the man she loved so very dearly. She saw how he was gasping and his lips were slowly going blue because his chest was being distorted so much he could hardly breathe. Indeed, the severe breathlessness was affecting Jesus badly. He braced himself for the searing pain that would run through his feet when he pushed up against them so that he could breathe again for a moment. He straightened his knees and sucked a few burbling breaths into his lungs. Despite the terrible pain in his feet, it gave him a moment's respite and he sought out Mary's face before whispering almost inaudibly,

"I'm ... thirsty."

Mary understood immediately what he had said. The soldiers beneath the cross had heard nothing, however, because they were fully absorbed in a game of dice with Jesus' precious robe as the stakes. Incandescent with indignation, she went up to them.

"He's thirsty," she said sharply. "Give him something to drink, now!"

Startled, one of the soldiers jumped to his feet. He stuck a sponge onto a twig and dunked it into a tub of sour wine. Then he pressed the sponge against Jesus' lips. Jesus eagerly slurped down some of the liquid, but then was unable to take the agonising pain in his feet any longer. His knees buckled again, but that only made the pain in his wrists intolerable once more. His eyes glazed over. How long would he be able to keep this up? He felt his heart absolutely racing in a desperate effort to pump round the little oxygen that was getting inside. But despite that, the shortness of breath was weighing ever more heavily upon him.

Mary could see how dreadfully he was suffering and despite her resolution that she would stay strong, she wavered and her mouth voicelessly shaped the words,

"Go, my darling. Just go. I'll see you there again after all."

She did not know whether or not he had understood her. But she did feel that he had now finally said farewell to her, because his struggles were now taking all his strength. She found herself hoping fervently that it would soon all be over.

But the hours passed and it seemed as if there would be no end to the cruel torture. A sorry cycle developed in which he kept pushing against the nail through his feet for a while in order at least to give himself a moment to breathe freely, until the pain in his feet made it impossible to stay standing and he had to lower himself again. The effort cost him more and more every time, and the falling darkness weighed upon him too. He had always loved the sun and enjoyed feeling its warmth upon his face. With a final, ultimate feat of strength, he raised his voice and cried out,

"Helion, helion, lama sabachthani!" - "O sun, o sun, why have you forsaken me?"

His wail rose up into the heavens and God could no longer bear his anguish. Everyone who had gathered around the cross saw how a golden ray of light suddenly pierced the banks of clouds. The light shone directly on Jesus' head and Jesus heard the loving voice of his Father in his heart. That voice had never previously sounded so tender as when He said,

"That is enough, My child, it is done. Come, I am ready for you now."

God's loving words touched Jesus deeply. A final shudder ran through his body. Then he submitted. He gave himself over into God's arms and with his final words he showed that he had not doubted for a moment and that he knew where he would be going: to this Father, who had never deserted him and who had always been the reliable foundation of his strength. He whispered,

"Father, into Your hands I commend my spirit."

And he lowered his head and died.

An oppressive silence fell. Everyone held their breath, shocked. But then a breathtaking show began unfolding around the cross. A radiant fountain of purple light burst apart high above Jesus' head, bathing the hill and the skies above it in an intense purple glow. A magnificent wave of energy washed over every single one of the onlookers, and all felt a surge of inspiration and a remarkable new force.

And the Holy Spirit enveloped him, carrying him up past all the guardians of heaven, carefully protecting his soul and taking him directly to God before immediately turning round and returning. For there was a task to be performed.

Now that God knew Jesus was safely with Him, He turned His fury on those who had the death of His son on their conscience. The forces of nature broke loose violently. The earth trembled, the city of Jerusalem quivered back and forth, trees broke and fell. The temple too shook on its foundations and the veil in front of the Holy of Holies was torn in two. The priests were filled with dread. They fled the temple building and sought refuge in their houses, fearful of God's vengeance. And they understood how they had failed Jesus and they were deeply ashamed.

Mary, Gaius, Lazarus, Peter and Jesus' mother stood there in the midst of all this violence of nature. They looked at each other with a mixture of astonishment and relief. All of them had tears running down their cheeks and when Mary finally spoke, her voice was hoarse with emotion.

"He was right. God did not desert him, not then and not now. He is up there now, I am certain of it. And with the help of the Holy Spirit, his words will strike home. If he believed that so strongly, we must surely do the same!"

The soldiers who had been on guard heard her words. They looked around in confusion at everything that was happening. Then one of them remarked,

"Now we can finally be certain: this really was the son of God!"

And they sent a messenger to Pilate to inform him that Jesus had died.

LITERATURE

DOWLING, Levi, *The Aquarian Gospel*, Uitgeverij Schors, Amsterdam

SMALHOUT, Prof. Dr. Bob, *Bijbelse tijdgenoten*, 2005 Uitgeverij het Spectrum

STOLP, Hans, *Jezus van Nazareth, Esoterisch Bijbellezen*, Uitgeverij Ankh Hermes bv - Deventer

STOLP, Hans, *De Zaligsprekingen als inwijdingsweg*, Uitgeverij Ankh-Hermes bv - Deventer

LOMMEL VAN, Pim, *Consciousness Beyond Life*, Uitgeverij Ten Have

FREDRIKSSON, Marianne, *According to Mary Magdalene*, Uitgeverij Maarten Muntinga bv, Amsterdam

GNOSTIC WRITINGS
The gospel of Mary Magdalene
The gospel of Judas
The gospel of Thomas

THE BIBLE *Isaiah, Matthew, Mark, Luke, John, Zechariah*, 1951 Nederlands Bijbelgenootschap, Haarlem

EVERS, Lou, *Jodendom voor beginners*, Forum - Amsterdam

BLOCK, Emil, *Tussen Bethlehem en de Jordaan*, 1989 Uitgeverij Christofoor

VERGEER, Charles, *Een nameloze, Jezus de Nazarener*, 1997 Uitgeverij SUN, Nijmegen/Amsterdam

VRIES DE, Sjoerd, *Hindoeïsme voor beginners*, 2003 - Forum - , Amsterdam

MARE VAN, Peter (opgetekend door), *Ooggetuigeverslag van het leven van Jezus*, Uitgeverij Ankh-Hermes bv - Deventer

Other titles by Gerjo van der Horst:

Craving
In this booklet Gerjo describes what effect writing "Jesus, the untold story" had on her life and on her image of Jesus. You can regard "Craving" as the-making-of "Jesus, the untold story". It is a valuable addition when you enjoyed reading this book.

What happened next
After the death of Jesus both Mary Magdalene and the disciples are left behind in confusion. What should they do now? Did you enjoy reading "Jesus, the untold story"? Then this fascinating sequel is a must-have for you!

Are you interested in one of these books?
Then send an email to info@fiola.nl. Please state clearly which title you are interested in. If enough people show interest, these books might be translated in English too.